BLEEDING BORDERS

Conflicting Worlds

New Dimensions of the American Civil War

T. Michael Parrish, Series Editor

BLEEDING BORDERS

RACE, GENDER, AND VIOLENCE IN PRE–CIVIL WAR KANSAS

KRISTEN TEGTMEIER OERTEL

LOUISIANA STATE UNIVERSITY PRESS

BATON ROUGE

Published by Louisiana State University Press
Copyright © 2009 by Louisiana State University Press
All rights reserved
Manufactured in the United States of America
First printing

Designer: Laura Roubique Gleason
Typeface: Whitman
Printer and binder: Thomson-Shore, Inc.

Library of Congress Cataloging-in-Publication Data
Oertel, Kristen Tegtmeier, 1969–
   Bleeding borders : race, gender, and violence in pre–Civil War Kansas / Kristen Tegtmeier
Oertel.
      p. cm. — (Conflicting worlds)
   Includes bibliographical references and index.
   ISBN 978-0-8071-3390-3 (cloth : alk. paper) 1. Kansas—History—1854–1861. 2. Kan-
sas—Social conditions—19th century. 3. Social conflict—Kansas—History—19th century.
4. Slavery—Political aspects—Kansas—History—19th century. 5. Kansas—Race relations—
History—19th century. 6. Sex role—Kansas—History—19th century. 7. Violence—Kansas—
History—19th century. 8. Indians of North America—Kansas—History—19th century. 9.
African Americans—Kansas—History—19th century. 10. Women, White—Kansas—His-
tory—19th century. I. Title.
   F685.O44 2009
   973.7'113—dc22

                                    2008027354

For my parents and grandparents

CONTENTS

CONTENTS

5
"DON'T YOU SEE OLD BUCK COMING?"
MISCEGENATION, WHITENESS, AND THE CRISIS OF
RACIAL IDENTITY
109

Illustrations follow page 84

ACKNOWLEDGMENTS

Many people have guided me on my path from Kansas to Iowa, New York, Texas, and, finally, Millsaps College in Jackson, Mississippi. I must first thank Kathryn Kish Sklar and Tom Dublin for their initial encouragement of my foray into Kansas women's history as a master's student at Binghamton University. Graduate seminars at the University of Texas at Austin with Neil Foley, Gunther Peck, Shelley Fisher Fishkin, and Robin Kilson helped refine the ideas formulated at Binghamton into a doctoral dissertation enriched by their expertise in the history of race and gender relations in the nineteenth century. My graduate student colleagues in Austin, particularly Saheed Adejumobi, Luis Alvarez, William Barnett, Matt Childs, Leilah Danielson, Eric Meeks, Steve Salm, Joanna Swanger, Patrick Walsh, and Jackie Woodfork, helped foster a learning environment that encouraged a healthy and selfless exchange of ideas and nurtured an ideal of scholarship that reminded me that without political commitment, scholarship means nothing.

Antonia Castañeda and Daniel Usner read significant portions of this study and provided constructive criticism that refined my thinking about race in the United States and Native Americans' place in that analysis. I must also thank John R. McKivigan and Stanley Harrold, coeditors of the anthology *Antislavery Violence,* for critiquing an article that would begin to explore some of the gendered themes of Bleeding Kansas that I expand on in chapters 3 and 4 of this work. I also received valuable criticism from Michael Morrison and from the anonymous readers for Louisiana State University Press; their suggestions surely improved the book. Elizabeth Leonard graciously and carefully reviewed the manuscript, and her ideas helped me fill some important holes. My deepest thanks goes to my advisor and friend, James Sidbury, who willingly and tirelessly supported me as I jumped through the numerous hoops necessary to achieve the doctoral degree, revise a dissertation, and acquire a book contract. Without his acute analytical eye and brilliant writing ability, this project and its author would have suffered greatly. Finally, I owe a debt of gratitude to the series editor, Michael Parrish, who offered unflagging support and provided vital (and often obscure) citations for my consideration, and Rand Dotson, who saw promise in this project from the beginning and never lost faith in it or me.

Several archivists at the Kansas State Historical Society in Topeka also deserve recognition. Jason Wesco, Linda Lichter, and Marian Bond all went out of their way to find sources that enriched my research, and they continued to find relevant materials after I returned to Texas and Mississippi. Virgil Dean, editor of *Kansas History*, directed me to some important sources and commented on several versions of chapters 2 and 4. The reference librarians and archivists at the Snyder Special Collections at the Miller Nichols Library, University of Missouri–Kansas City, and the Kansas City and Washington, D.C., branches of the National Archives and Records Administration readily shared their talents with me and uncovered several rare manuscripts. The librarians at Millsaps College cheerfully granted numerous interlibrary loan requests that enabled me to minimize my travel to the above archives. I must also thank the Graduate School at the University of Texas at Austin for granting me a University Fellowship during my final year of dissertation research; the Hearin Foundation for providing financial support during the summer months, which enabled me to revise the dissertation into a book; and the dean's office at Millsaps College for granting me a teaching sabbatical and faculty development money to complete the project.

Finally, I want to convey a profound sense of gratitude for my friends and family, who provided the love and encouragement that helped me complete this project. Susanna Holm, Robin Meyerhoff, Carol Faulkner, and Michelle Kuhl in Binghamton and Scott Perry, Jennifer Thornburrow, and Doug Wootten in Austin shared laughs, tears, and beers with me as I moved from coast to "coast" and chapter to chapter. My Cornell College friends sustained me with their love and encouragement from the beginning of my academic career: Brent Boyd, David Knutson, and, especially, Currie Augustine Gasche, Debbie Sieck, Stacey Fishell Evans, and Jillian Ranney Knutson. Friends in Kansas City and Jackson have consistently provided support throughout each stage of this project. Mark Brentano, Beth Jennings McNeill, Marty Wall, Starr Terrell, Tamlah Williams, and Mark, Diana, and Michaela Tarwater welcomed me back to Kansas each time I returned to consult the archives, and my Millsaps colleagues, especially my fellow historians—David Davis, Amy Forbes, Louise Hetrick, Bob McElvaine, Bill Storey, and Sandy Zale—and Kristen Brown, Raymond Clothier, Mike Galaty, Kathi and Eric Griffin, Patrick Hopkins, Sandra and Julian Murchison, Tanya Newkirk, Darby Ray, and Susan and Stuart Rockoff have kept me sane as we shared ideas, meals, and childcare. Perhaps it is an error of semantics to say that I have *two* best friends, but I must thank both of the most important friends of my adult life, Bela Roongta Eitel and Kelley Durbin. For the past two decades they have rescued me with timely phone calls, letters, and cross-country visits. Their dedication to me and to our friendship means the world to me.

My ability to move throughout the country to pursue my academic goals is due wholly to the emotional and financial support of my family. My mother, Diane, father, Gary, brother, Walt, sister-in-law, Stephanie, and my grandmothers, Marion Tegtmeier and Ann Ogrizovich, deserve my sincerest thanks for always encouraging me to do my best and, most importantly, for loving and supporting me when I fell short of that goal. It is with humble thanks that I dedicate this work to my parents and to their parents.

My nuclear family formed after this project began but sustained me in it for years. My husband, Bob, tolerated my intense work schedule and read numerous portions of the book, providing a critical nonhistorian's perspective on my writing. My son, Owen, and daughter, Lily, spent more hours at daycare than I would have liked to allow me to complete the book. Bob, Owen, and Lily deserve my heartfelt thanks, for they, more than anyone, remind this historian that living in the present is much more rewarding than living in the past.

BLEEDING BORDERS

INTRODUCTION

On the morning of January 12, 1830, several Shawnee Indians and local white traders gathered to attend a birth at the Shawnee Methodist Mission, located just west of a Missouri River trading post called Kawsmouth (later named Kansas City). That afternoon a baby girl named Susannah Adams Yoacham was born to her white parents, who traded goods with the very Indians who helped bring their daughter into the world. Yoacham's birth, the first recorded Anglo birth in the Kansas Territory, signaled the permanent presence of white settlers in the region west of the Missouri border. Susanna Yoacham's marriage a mere sixteen years later marked another significant turn in Kansas territorial history; her uncle, a Missouri slaveholder, presented Susanna with a slave woman named Eliza as a wedding gift. Yoacham and her husband, William Dillon, accepted the gift, as was the custom for southern newlyweds of their privileged class. Thus the first white child in Kansas Territory, born at an Indian mission, would become one of the region's few slaveholders. Red, white, and black merged in the Yoacham family, as they and other settlers ushered slavery into the land soon to be known as Bleeding Kansas.[1]

Susanna Yoacham married Dillon and received her slave Eliza in 1846, eight years before the Kansas-Nebraska Act gave Yoacham the legal right to own slaves in the Kansas Territory. Passed by Congress in May 1854, the act essentially repealed the Missouri Compromise, which for more than three decades had prohibited slaves from being carried north of latitude 36° 30′. The act ignited a fireball of controversy across the country as Free-Soil advocates and proslavery defendants argued over the fate of slavery north and west of Missouri's southern border. Historian Michael Fellman has referred to Kansas in the 1850s as "both the central symbol and actual battleground of the fundamental American conflict between North and

South."[2] Bleeding Kansas, the conflict that ensued between proslavery and antislavery settlers, would involve people such as Susanna Yoacham, her slave Eliza, and the Indians who attended Susanna's birth.

Yet the historiography on Bleeding Kansas has often ignored people like the Yoachams and the related social and cultural history of this important sectional conflict. Instead, scholars have focused more narrowly on the white, male politicians and settlers who battled for control of the Kansas territorial legislature. Thanks to major works by historians William Freehling, Nicole Etcheson, and Michael Morrison, we are well aware of the congressional debates over the Kansas-Nebraska Act and the subsequent political and military conflicts generated by the ineffective application of popular sovereignty in Kansas.[3] These studies leave little doubt that politicians affected the events in Kansas in myriad and profound ways, but one wonders if other actors played significant roles in the drama of Bleeding Kansas. Did Indians like the Shawnee, whose mission was used as the first headquarters for the territorial legislature, shape the conflict in any way? How did slaves who involuntarily emigrated to Kansas from Missouri and other southern states react to the debates over slavery that swirled around them? And finally, did the white women who moved to the region involve themselves in the heated sectional politics and guerrilla warfare that embroiled so many of their husbands, fathers, and brothers?

Bleeding Borders argues that Indians, African Americans, and white women played crucial roles in the literal and rhetorical pre–Civil War battle between proslavery and antislavery settlers.[4] For example, some local Indians fed and housed antislavery settlers, whereas others supported their slave-owning neighbors and helped capture fugitive slaves who fled across Missouri's border into Kansas. Slaveholders may have found some allies among the Indian residents, but southerners struggled to establish their peculiar institution across the border, as many African Americans refused to remain enslaved after migrating to Kansas and absconded from their masters. To further complicate the transplantation of slavery in Kansas, a small network of abolitionists harbored these runaways and encouraged their rebellion by circulating abolitionist literature, and white women comprised a central component of this network. In addition, antislavery women's military and political assaults against proslavery men helped foster an environment that made it difficult for many southerners to support slavery in the territory. Ultimately, I find that Indians, blacks, and women shaped the political and cultural terrain in ways that discouraged the extension of slavery but failed to challenge a racial hierarchy that relegated all people of color to inferior social status.

In addition to recovering "lost voices" in the narrative of Bleeding Kansas, this book also reveals how race and gender ideologies were reshaped as North, South, and West converged. The players in Kansas used weapons other than their Sharps rifles and bowie knives to wage war over the extension of slavery. Kansas settlers attacked one another's cultural values and raised a number of questions about how the expanding nation should be organized: Where do blacks and Indians fit into a nation founded on equality but nurtured with slavery? How did "true" and proper white women and men behave in the context of protracted political conflict and sporadic guerrilla warfare? Proslavery and antislavery settlers answered these questions differently, but the vast majority of them shared complementary ideas about white supremacy that guided a common vision of race relations.

The effort to sustain white racial superiority was at times complicated by the debate over competing gender ideologies in the 1850s. Southerners' embrace of white supremacy was intimately connected to their conception of patriarchy and the social hierarchy that both ideologies secured. White men ruled over all women and black men, and any challenges to slavery or patriarchy upset the carefully ordered society that white southerners cherished.[5] Few proslavery settlers questioned this ideology in Kansas, and they fashioned a traditional patriarchy that preserved notions of southern honor and valued violence as a proper means of defending that honor.[6] Many northerners, however, chipped away at patriarchal ideals by expanding the definition of true womanhood to include certain types of political activism and a modicum of independence; they also promoted a type of manhood that touted pacifism and self-control.[7] So although we may view Bleeding Kansas as a battle over slavery's extension, we can also view it as a debate between opposing gender ideologies. Bleeding Borders examines how Kansas settlers' beliefs about race and gender shaped antislavery and proslavery ideologies and posits that Bleeding Kansas was as much a culture war as a border war.

The preface to Bleeding Kansas traditionally begins in 1854, when Congress debated the Kansas-Nebraska Act and argued over which labor system would extend beyond Missouri's western borders—would the territory be slave or free?[8] Congress left the answer to that important question to the white, male voters who moved to Kansas by instituting the vaguely defined doctrine of popular sovereignty. According to this statute, permanent, "bona fide" settlers who moved to the territory would hold elections to install a local government; the local legislature would then develop a code of laws for the territory and write a state constitution. In the fall of 1854 "Border Ruffians" crossed the Missouri River into Kansas Territory, voted into power a "bogus" proslavery territorial legislature, and violently clashed with the free-state emigrants from the North. Thus, as defined by the current historiography, Bleeding Kansas began when proslavery and antislavery settlers collided over the right to determine whether or not slavery would exist in Kansas.[9]

But conflict in Kansas commenced long before Missourians and free-staters came to blows over slavery's expansion. The strife between proslavery and antislavery settlers during the 1850s echoed the discord that had already characterized relations between different peoples and cultures during the 1820s, 1830s, and 1840s as white missionaries, fur traders, government agents, and Indian emigrant groups arrived in the territory. Chapter 1 of Bleeding Borders examines how these first Kansas settlers brought competing economies, cultures, and ideologies with them and through cooperation and conflict forged a coexistence that was at times filled with violence and at other times characterized by peace.[10] Through economic, religious, and sexual interaction, Kansas Indians and white settlers connected their multiple worlds in uneven and incomplete ways, thus setting the proverbial stage for acute sectional conflict in the 1850s.[11]

As these varied cultures merged, northern and southern whites transcended their sectional differences and united on the ground of white supremacy in their relations with Indians and African Americans. Other scholars have noted that white racism provided a bridge that sometimes connected Kansans from opposing political camps, but none of them have included Indians in this analysis, nor have they examined the racialized and gendered dimensions of the rhetoric generated by Bleeding Kansans. Historian Gunja SenGupta claims that "underlying commercial interests" and a "common commitment to white supremacy" led proslavery and antislavery Kansans to quiet their political rancor, but her study emphasizes the economic and evangelical strains of the conflict.[12] In her recent book Bleeding Kansas, historian Nicole Etcheson skillfully retells the political history of the region and introduces an important and innovative thesis, arguing that both proslavery and antislavery whites were fighting to preserve white liberty in Kansas. Etcheson's work reveals how whites' conceptions of liberty depended on their understanding of popular sovereignty and finds that the flawed political process in Kansas compromised the revolutionary values that both proslavery and antislavery settlers honored and defended. Although I agree with Etcheson that "each side feared the loss of political liberties," I argue that settlers were also profoundly worried about losing their racial purity—their whiteness—the justification for their superiority and power.[13]

This tragic and unfortunate point of unity between proslavery and antislavery settlers provides scholars with an opportunity to examine how the discourse on social and sexual relations with Indians and blacks at once complicated the formation of white racial identity and facilitated whites' assertion of racial superiority. In chapters 1 and 5 I interrogate how "redness" shaped whiteness, thus heeding historian David Roediger's recent call for scholars to revisit the influence of Indians on whiteness and expand "the racial terrain far beyond a Black-white binary." In addition, Roediger suggests that scholars must examine "white racial formation in the context of a settler colonial nation, as well as a slaveholding one," and pre–Civil War Kansas provides a perfect arena in which to engage in such an analysis.[14] The presence of both blacks and Indians in the region presented whites with literal references to their rhetorical discussions about slavery, freedom, and racial hierarchy.

The rhetoric and policies generated by early Kansas settlers indicate that the preservation of white supremacy motivated their approach to organizing their social and political lives. Settlers from both sides of the political spectrum agreed that regardless of the outcome of the slavery question, Indians would be either expelled from the territory or "civilized" through missionizing tactics and/or intermarriage with whites. Of course, proslavery and antislavery settlers presented widely divergent ideas about how best to maintain white supremacy in relation to African Americans: Antislavery ideologues argued for the halt of slavery's expansion, thus preserving the West for white Free-Soil farmers, whereas proslavery politicians advocated carrying black slaves into the West and therefore ensuring the superiority of all whites over blacks. But their opposing ideas about slavery's extension did not preclude their common struggle to refashion their racial identities on a frontier that challenged their whiteness in a number of ways. In the context of life on a bleeding border—living among Indians, battling over questions of slavery and the status of free blacks, and confronting variant gender ideologies—white Kansans fought not only about slavery and liberty but also about whiteness.

The discourse on miscegenation often punctuated this mutual effort to construct whiteness. In chapter 5 I show how white settlers challenged the purity of one another's racial identities, arguing that one group was "more white" than the other.[15] Both camps raised the specter of miscegenation, the very negation of pure whiteness, thus implicating northern and southern fears about interracial sex and marriage in the sectional conflict. Within these discourses, southerners charged that antislavery women bedded down with "uppity Negroes" and northerners claimed that drunken southern "animals" raped slave women. Many white settlers worried that if the boundary between North and South was challenged, the borders between the white "self" and the racial "other" would be jeopardized as well. Thus although proslavery and antislavery settlers may have come to literal and metaphorical blows over the issue of slavery's extension, they revealed their shared belief in the efficacy of white supremacy in the process.

The embrace of white supremacy was not universal, however, as I demonstrate in chapter 2. A number of groups—some Indians, African Americans, and white abolitionists—resisted white hegemony. In doing so, they helped prevent slavery from expanding west and questioned the merits of establishing a racially homogenous society on the Kansas plains. Like many of her peers, Sara Robinson moved to Kansas "with a mission to the dark-browed race . . . to stay the surging tide of slavery," and white abolitionists together with black slaves resisted the implantation of slavery in Kansas using political and military tactics.[16] In addition, Kansas abolitionists opposed their antislavery neighbors, who wanted to exclude free blacks from the state, and affirmed an egalitarian vision for a multiracial society. Furthermore, many Kansas Indians resisted white encroachment and some integrated their families and cultures with white settlers, thus forming mixed-race families that defied absolute whiteness. So although many Kansas settlers embraced a common racial hierarchy that maintained the boundaries among white, black, and red, a good number of them worked to bridge these racial divides and flatten the hierarchy.

The struggle to define race relations at times intersected with a concurrent challenge to delineate ideological borders about gender. As Amy Greenberg, Michael Pierson, and Melanie Gustafson have recently shown, gender shaped politics in significant ways during the antebellum era. Greenberg argues that political and social debates about Manifest Destiny and American expansionism, primarily in Latin America, "were also debates over the meaning of American manhood and womanhood." She finds that pro-expansionists embraced one vision of manhood, a more aggressive, "martial manhood," whereas anti-expansionists were wedded to a different, more "restrained manhood." Similarly, Gustafson and Pierson find that Free-Soilers and Republicans understood gender and family relations in ways that challenged the more traditional patriarchal values championed by the Democratic Party.[17]

As chapters 3 and 4 demonstrate, settlers in Kansas also developed disparate ideas about gender, and whereas Pierson's subjects advocated a moderate break with patriarchy, many free-state families reshaped gender roles in ways that made for a dramatic departure from traditional values. An overwhelmingly male population, precarious Indian relations, and guerrilla warfare sometimes necessitated a radical shift in gender relations in Kansas, challenging the resilience of both northern and southern notions of true womanhood and manhood. For example, some abolitionist women from Boston, arriving in the territory with lace tablecloths and their reputations as "true" women, wielded weapons and threatened proslavery men with foul language. In a related process, antislavery men who professed an aversion to violence before arriving in Kansas found themselves taking up arms and redefining their gender identities to include preemptive and aggressive violence. Proslavery men, however, readily embraced violence as a proper means of defending southern honor. These southern men and the few women who accompanied them to Kansas appear to have entrenched themselves in more traditional gender roles, and they used the antislavery settlers' radical behavior as proof that abolitionism would also upset the patriarchal structure that slavery helped maintain. Thus gender was used by both sides as a rhetorical weapon to attack the diverse social visions articulated by the proslavery and antislavery camps.

Southerners and northerners disagreed on the proper balance of power between men and women and on the legality, economy, and morality of bringing slaves to the West, but the vast majority of all settlers came together on the question of white supremacy. Indians and African Americans would be relegated to second-class citizenship with its accompanying disfranchisement and disrespect. Perhaps the recognition of a common whiteness helped stop the bleeding in Kansas, but it also perpetuated the racism that abolitionists had hoped a free Kansas might discourage.

Bleeding Borders explores the multifaceted levels of pre–Civil War conflict in Kansas in five thematic and roughly chronological chapters. Chapter 1, "The *two* were soon pronounced *one*," details the settlement of eastern Kansas by emigrant Indian tribes and explores their interaction with the growing number of white settlers in the region, considering how whiteness formed in relation to redness. Chapter 2, "Runaways, Negro Stealers and Border Ruffians," examines the attempts by southerners to plant slavery in Kansas and the ultimately successful efforts of slaves and abolitionists to resist the establishment of slave-based agriculture. Chapter 3, "All Women are called bad," analyzes the redefinition of "true womanhood" and illustrates how these new definitions influenced the local and national discourse on Bleeding Kansas; it also explores how these women participated in the political and physical conflicts between pro and antislavery settlers. Chapter 4, "'Free Sons' and 'Myrmidons,'" examines northern and southern definitions of "true manhood" and looks at how competing arguments about masculinity infused political and sectional tensions. Chapter 5, "Don't you see old Buck coming?" concludes the book with an examination of miscegenation—not only how racial mixing among Indians, slaves, and whites influenced the events in territorial Kansas, but more important, how the fear of and discourse on miscegenation fueled both pro- and antislavery arguments about the need for civil war.

1

"THE *TWO* WERE SOON PRONOUNCED *ONE*"

RELIGIOUS, ECONOMIC, AND
SEXUAL EXCHANGE IN INDIAN KANSAS

Clara Gowing, a Baptist missionary in Kansas Territory from 1859 to 1864, attended the marriage of an Indian woman and a white soldier one Saturday afternoon during the Civil War. The couple wedded in haste because the new recruit for the Union army was scheduled to depart Kansas for the battlefield the following day. Though haphazardly assembled, the wedding spectacle impressed Gowing, and she recorded her observations of the ceremony in detail:

> Here was a scene for a painter. . . . The motley group which gathered around the piazza, some dozen or more whites, including one or two military officers; the civilized Indian dressed in neat white costume like the whites; the wilder Indian decked with ribbons and beads of gaudy color, with his leather leggins and moccasins, the shirt collar open, exposing the brown breast; and yellow, black, or dirty white crape shawl tied around the head. . . . The trio of minister, with groom and bride standing on the piazza, the latter dressed with neatness and taste in white muslin . . . the whole lighted up a gorgeous September sunset sky, formed a scene not viewed every day.[1]

The publicly celebrated union of an Indian woman and a white man was not a "scene viewed every day" in mid-nineteenth-century America, but red-white sexual and marital exchanges were far from rare in Kansas. White missionaries and fur traders had lived among the Kansas Indians for decades, and the scarcity of white women in the area inevitably led to cross-racial sexual ties. Though some of these ties were undoubtedly forced and unsolicited, it is clear that consensual sexual relations between the two races existed and often facilitated the convergence of two vastly different cultural worlds.[2]

Gowing closed her report of the wedding ceremony by proclaiming, "The *two* were soon pronounced *one*." As her narrative suggests, the once-separate Indian and Anglo worlds were moving closer, in proximity if not in culture. But Gowing's story illustrates only one locus of exchange between native peoples and Anglos as white settlers infiltrated the valleys of the Missouri River and Kansas River after 1820. Indians and whites also forged religious and economic ties and fashioned an uneven and unstable middle ground that was neither wholly Indian nor purely Anglo. Whether by choice or by force, red and white boundaries merged in Indian Territory long before any cries of Bleeding Kansas were made; by examining Anglo-Indian contact in the region, one can conclude that the wound of Bleeding Kansas had several entry points.[3]

The physical and cultural middle ground created by Anglos and Indians in Kansas carried an important racial component that needs to be explored in order to fully understand race relations in antebellum Kansas. Gowing remarked that the "civilized Indian" was dressed in white, whereas the "wilder Indian" looked "gaudy" in ribbons and beads, complete with a "yellow, black or dirty white" shawl tied on his head. Gowing equated civilization with whiteness, a distinction made all the easier by the presence of "brown breasts" and "wild" Indians. Her diary illustrates that race relations sustained a less dichotomous tone than has previously been assumed, even in a nation obsessed with differences between whites and blacks and in a region fixated on sectional differences. Events in Kansas suggest that although settlers may have battled over the status of African Americans, they simultaneously united on the ground of white supremacy over Indians. Furthermore, white settlers' perceptions of and interactions with Kansas Indians played a crucial role in developing white racial identity at midcentury. To ignore the influence of redness on the construction of whiteness and the maintenance of white supremacy and slavery is to overlook a key factor of racial formation in the United States.[4]

THE BLEEDING BEGINS

Before red and white intersected in Kansas, dozens of Indian tribes, each with its own unique language and culture, came into contact in the Old Northwest and plantation South, as white settlers pushed west of the Appalachians during the decades following the Revolutionary War. Conflict and coordination among tribes and with white settlers ensued, resulting in the social and economic reorganization of several Indian nations. Tribal consolidation and alliances formed new cultural hybrids among Indian groups, and increasing interaction with white settlers augmented this hybridization. The Algonquin-speaking people who traversed this "middle ground" in the upper Great Lakes region would be one of the many consolidated groups of disparate tribes who arrived in Kansas during the three decades preceding the Civil War.[5]

Tens of thousands of Indians moved to what in 1854 became Kansas Territory. In an action less infamous than the Jacksonian era's violent removal of Indians from their native lands in the Southeast to reservations in Indian Territory, the U.S. government "forcefully encouraged" thousands of Indians from Ohio, Indiana, Illinois, Michigan, Wisconsin, and Missouri to move to eastern Kansas between 1820 and 1860.[6] Even before this exodus, several tribes from the East, such as the Iowa, Shawnee, and Delaware, had already infiltrated the region and jockeyed with the resident Kaw, Osage, and Pawnee tribes for land and resources. Citing pressure from settlers in the plantation South and the Old Northwest, Superintendent of Indian Affairs William Clark (of Louis and Clark fame) negotiated several treaties with the Kaws and Osages in 1825. In exchange for financial annuities and agricultural implements, the resident Kansas Indians ceded thousands of acres of their land—not for white settlement but for Indians who had been displaced by violence and white encroachment in the East.[7]

The Indians who moved to Kansas before the passage of the Kansas-Nebraska Act arrived in the region after decades of encountering white settlers and their cultures and economies back in their home territories. One historian writes, "These intruders . . . brought with them syncretic cultures that often included the English language, Christianity or Christian-like religions, modern farming techniques, and sophisticated tools and weapons."[8] Their familiarity with the white world often created tension between these "immigrant Indians" and the resident Osages and Kaws, who had experienced less contact with Anglos. The first blood spilled in the territory was thus Indian, as "old" and "new" Kansas Indians battled with each other for farming and hunting lands.

Emigrant tribes such as the Delaware and Shawnee enjoyed a strategic advantage over their resident counterparts, such as the Kaw, when dealing with the federal government. The Delaware and Shawnee arrived in Kansas Territory equipped with more than a century of experience negotiating treaties with the federal government and trade agreements with white settlers.[9] The reports taken by federal Indian agents on the Delaware reservation reflect the tribe's familiarity with white ways and note their history of making peaceable treaties with the government. Alfred Cumming, superintendent of Indian affairs for the central region, proudly reported that the Delaware maintained faith in the government's ability to protect Indian rights: "Notwithstanding the lawless intrusions upon their lands by citizens and others, the confidence of the Delawares in the integrity of the Government remains entirely unshaken; far accustomed to an implicit conformity on their part to treaty stipulations, they cannot realize the possibility that the Government will tolerate their violation by others."[10] According to Cumming, the Delaware, "a brave, honorable, and generous race," had fulfilled their obligations to the government, and they expected reciprocity on the part of the "Great Father." These shared expectations arose out of decades of negotiations between the two parties, treaty agreements that had become part and parcel of Delaware life since their initial removal from the coastal regions of the Northeast in the eighteenth century.[11]

Though the Shawnee began their negotiations with the federal government later than the Delaware, they too benefited from previous interactions with white settlers, missionaries, and officials. In an 1855 letter to George Manypenny, commissioner of Indian affairs, Superintendent Cumming reported that the "Shawnees are every where advancing towards a perfect civilization; the sound of the hammer, the saw, and the axe are now . . . familiar."[12] In his 1857 annual report to the commissioner, Cumming surveyed the status of each of the various tribes residing in Kansas and concluded his report with a generally positive account of the Shawnee Indian Mission and Manual Labor School. "The Shawnee Methodist Mission was . . . the largest and best conducted institution of that description in the Indian country," he wrote.[13] The Reverend Thomas Johnson, founder of the mission, reported from the school that the "Shawnees, and portions of other tribes, are becoming a working people, and are making considerable progress in the arts of civilized life."[14] Those tribes such as the Shawnee and Delaware who were familiar with the trappings of white society were then more likely to function effectively in treaty negotiations and trade deals.[15]

The Kaw, Sac and Fox, Kickapoo, and Osage Indians, on the other hand, received the brunt of white criticism, as they vehemently resisted white attempts to encroach upon their lands and challenge their cultural values. Cumming wrote in his 1857 annual report that the Sac and Fox tribe risked extinction if they failed to change their Indian ways: "This tribe is as barbarous in all their habits as they were twenty-five years ago. . . . They continue a courageous and intractable peoples, delighting in the chase, and addicted to war,—firmly opposed to every endeavor to inculcate upon them habits of civilization. They are rapidly diminishing in numbers. . . . Indeed, if they should die in the same ratio that they have done for some years past, this still brave, and once renowned tribe will soon be exterminated."[16] The Sac and Fox initially refused to allow whites in Kansas to transform their culture and relocate them to reservations. In the process, however, they engaged the white world militarily and lost many of their number to war and disease.

Like the Sac and Fox, the Kansas Kickapoo were known for their warlike stance with whites. Cumming met with Kickapoo chief Machina during his January 1857 visit and found the tribe to be in relatively good condition. However, he mentioned that the Pottawatomies who lived among the Kickapoo were "sober and industrious" and "furnish[ed] an excellent example to the Kickapoos," implying that the Kickapoo needed such examples.[17] Both the Kickapoo and the Pottawatomie tribes, however, repeatedly found themselves embroiled in conflict with their white neighbors and earned a reputation with white missionaries and settlers as being particularly stubborn.[18]

The Osage, too, persisted in their military and cultural antagonism toward white settlers. During the late 1840s the Comanche and Kiowas joined the Osage in attacks on U.S. Army troops who served as military escorts for government wagon trains on the Santa Fe Trail.[19] In addition to defending their territorial claims in the region, the Osage protected their cultural sovereignty as well. Pioneer Charles M. Chase described the Osage men in Kansas as "the fiercest looking fellows I have ever seen." He described their authentic dress in detail: "The blanket and the breech cloth is their only dress. Their noses and ears are loaded with twinkling trinkets, the heads shaved, leaving a narrow strip of stiff hair a half inch long from the forehead to the crown. Their faces are painted with bright yellow and red."[20] Agent John Whitfield complained about the Kaw and their habit of removing older boys from mission schools, that "instead of cultivating and improving the education they have received, you see them return with shaved heads, painted faces, and dressed in full Indian costume."[21] These observations were undoubtedly shaped by white prejudices about how "savages" dressed, but many of the Kaw and Osage clearly resisted attempts to impose the visible trappings of white "civilization" on their tribes.

While the resident and emigrant tribes differed in their levels of acceptance and/or rejection of white culture, both groups experienced a significant degree of intermixing with each other, before and after their arrival in Kansas Territory. Thus the boundaries among once-disparate tribes blurred as fragmented and dying tribes joined those bands that exhibited more strength and resilience. As early as 1830, the government recognized that "half-breed" mixes of various Indian ethnic groups would have to be acknowledged in order to apportion land properly for reservations in Kansas. In a July 16, 1830, treaty between the Sac and Fox, the Sioux, and the United States, the "half-breed" band of the Omahas, Ioways, and Otoes received entitlement to a tract of land in northeast Kansas. Twenty-five years later, Commissioner Manypenny suggested that a census be taken of the "half-breeds and mixed bloods properly entitled to share in the said reservation," perhaps implying that the degree to which these tribes intermixed necessitated a frequent review of their members.[22]

Some tribes, like the Winnebagoes and Sacs, gained notoriety for their willingness to intermarry and combine tribal resources. Superintendent Cumming reported from the Nemaha Agency that "certain Winnebagoes. . . have lived for several years and intermarried with that [Sac] band. The agent informs me that these Winnebagoes were invited by the Sac Council to participate in the payment of their annuity." Cumming strongly recommended that the close interconnections between the two tribes be maintained. "Many marriages connect the Winnebagoes with the Sacs, so that their tribes can only be separated by force," he claimed, "and if that were used to separate them they would become vagabonds and a burdensome pest to their white neighbors."[23] Apparently, past experience proved that even if the government attempted to force separation of two commingling tribes, the fragmented tribes would loiter and wander throughout the region until reunited with their adopted tribal band.

Like the Winnebagoes and Sacs, the Kickapoos and Pottawatomies shared their resources and land in Kansas. Cumming reported seeing mostly Pottawatomie children at the Kickapoo mission school, and noted that he was not surprised by the tribes' interconnectedness. He claimed that the Pottawatomies "hold the same relation to the Kickapoos as the Winnebagoes to the Sacs, and in both cases I believe a separation to be inadvisable."[24] Cumming also visited the united tribes of the Kaskaskia, Peoria, Piankeshaw, and Wea Indians; these tribes experienced such a rapid decline in population that consolidation was necessary for their survival. According to Cumming, they successfully defended their rights and established permanent settlements in Kansas, perhaps in part because they joined together in the face of intruding whites who squatted on Indian land.

The practice of intertribal mixing gained so much prominence, even when discouraged by government officials, that Superintendent Cumming recommended that the government officially sanction such behavior. He wrote: "The custom of inviting individuals of other tribes to participate in their payments even in cases where no consanguinity [exists] . . . prevails among many of the tribes. . . . It therefore becomes a matter of policy to tolerate the arrangement they voluntarily entered into; and if tolerated, it ought, in my opinion, to be authorized by order."[25] Cumming recognized that the government's efforts to prevent certain tribes from intermixing were pointless, and under his leadership, the Central Superintendence succumbed to and reluctantly supported the Indian practice of tribal consolidation. As a result of Indian removal and migration, then, the blending of Indian cultures began well before the official arrival of white settlers in 1854.

"GOD WILL JUDGE IN RIGHTEOUSNESS"

The infiltration of religious missionaries and traders into the region during the 1830s and 1840s facilitated the syncretization of Indian and white cultures. One historian argues that the Kawsmouth settlement, a French/Indian trading post eventually known as Kansas City, was "the most promising theater for a mixed-blood colony."[26] The conjunction of the Missouri River and Kansas River provided a strategic and fertile location for the fur trade, for agricultural pursuits, and for bringing a Christian God to the many Indians who resided in and passed through the region.

The Baptists, Catholics, Methodists, Moravians, and Presbyterians all established missions amid the eastern Kansas Indians during the 1830s and 1840s. Since their earliest efforts during the seventeenth century, Christian missionaries had aimed to lift the "savages"/"sauvages" from their primitive state and lead them toward a godly, civilized existence. Though the Catholics were more numerous (and some might say more successful) than the Protestants at converting Indians to Christianity during the seventeenth and eighteenth centuries, by the early nineteenth century, Protestant missions far outnumbered Catholic ones in the Midwest and thus dominated the forces of acculturation in Kansas Territory.[27] Both Catholics and Protestants, however, shared decades of experience in dealing with Indians, and some of the Indians who moved to Kansas had lived among or near missions since their initial removal from the East.

Some Indians welcomed the arrival of missionaries in the area because they were conscious of the missions' intermediary role between the tribes and the U.S. government.[28] Missionaries such as Baptist Isaac McCoy, who lobbied in favor of creating a sovereign Indian state, could serve as effective treaty negotiators for tribes.[29] Reverend M. Pratt, a missionary among the Delawares, implored Alfred Gray, a government official, to stop the ratification of an injurious treaty. George H. Patterson, commissioner for the Delawares, received a letter from Gray stating, "I am deputed by Rev. M. Pratt . . . to do what I can to prevent the ratification of a Treaty recently made. . . . I am particularly requested to address you upon the subject and solicit your influence with Mr. Seward and other members of the Senate with whom you are acquainted."[30] The Delawares understood that Pratt's connections with the federal government could be used to their benefit, and they employed him to speak to Washington about their land rights.

However, the missionaries' primary purpose in the territory was not land negotiation but "civilizing" and proselytizing among the Indians. Education and religious instruction comprised the main channels through which this civilization process occurred. Missionaries arrived hoping to replace native tongues with English and native culture with white, Christian values and lifestyles. Some missionaries concluded that by merely placing Indian children in a "white" environment, they would naturally progress toward "civilization." J. C. Berryman, a missionary among the Shawnees, claimed, "From experiments already made, we are fully satisfied that there is no essential difference between red and white children; the difference is all in circumstances."[31]

Missions cultivated an environment in which Indian habits were discouraged, whereas "white" behavior was learned and encouraged. Missionaries provided classes for Indian youth and adults in English, farming techniques, and domestic arts. One early settler observed, "The girls learned to sew, cook, do house work and the boys worked on the farm, helped the blacksmith, did carpentry work and both sexes spent several hours each day . . . in the school room."[32] Elizabeth Morse, a Baptist missionary working among the Delawares, reported to Indian agent J. G. Pratt that the mission school enjoyed a significant amount of success during its first year. "The 'Kinter Garten System' has been sufficiently tested to warrant the belief that it may be adopted in schools of Indian children with entire success," she wrote. "They are rarely sleepy nor inattentive, even though the mercury rises to one hundred while being taught."[33] Indeed, the younger the children, the easier it was to wrest them from their Indian ways and supplant white customs in their place.

Though Indian children were perhaps more malleable than their adult counterparts, educating them still posed significant challenges for missionaries. These challenges frequently revolved around convincing parents to endorse the mission school and send their children to classes on a regular basis. Francis Lea, an Indian agent, wrote in his committee report, "Much cannot be expected from the Methodist mission among the Kanzas [Kaw] Indians, as it will take time to operate on their prejudices against schools."[34] Thomas Mosely, another agent, wrote of a related problem in his annual report: "The Indians are remarkably fond of their children, and it is a difficult matter to get them to send them far from home."[35] Elizabeth Morse's initially positive report to Agent Pratt lost its optimism when discussing the older children. "A few [children] remain with us the entire session, thus setting an example of constant study, which is very rare," she wrote. "*Coming* and *going* is the rule, *staying* the exception."[36] Similarly, missionary J. C. Berryman expressed frustration at his ability to educate Indian youth effectively, arguing that the "ignorance and prejudice, instability and apathy, of the parents, and all the little whims that can be imagined as being indulged in by so degraded a people, combine to hinder us and retard their own advancement in civilization."[37]

Because the success of mission schools proved inconsistent at best, missionaries employed a variety of methods by which they would "civilize" their Indian subjects. Proselytizing and spreading the Christian word and religion among the tribes met with mixed success, but many missionaries believed this task to be their most important. Jordan Johnnycake, likely a Delaware, thoroughly embraced the Christian theology preached by the Baptist mission, thus appearing to be "saved" from the damnation inherent in practicing his indigenous religion. "At the Judgement there will be all nations of men. God will Judge in righteousness," he wrote. "At that day Christ will say to the wicked depart from me. . . . I think that if death should come I think that I should find myself with the wicked. . . . I ought to repent of my sins and turn to God."[38] Though he practiced Christianity at the urging of Baptist missionaries, Johnnycake continued to judge himself as "unsaved."

The strong influence of evangelical Christianity in the area also shaped race relations between white settlers and Indians. Some abolitionist settlers, many of them known for their egalitarian ideas about white/black race relations, reserved much of their overt racism and racialized criticism for the "heathen" Indians. Often grounded in the very same evangelical Christianity that aimed to liberate the slaves, abolitionist theologians could not conceive of Indian spiritual practices as alternative vehicles to God's grace.[39] Similarly, those Indians who converted to Catholicism rarely measured up to abolitionists' ideals about godliness and service.[40] Thus, like the missionaries, Christian abolitionists encouraged conversion to Protestantism, and white settlers' diverse opinions of the local tribes often varied according to that tribe's degree of conversion to evangelical Christianity.

The Kaw, known to resist Christian teachings, received the brunt of white criticism and scorn. Abolitionist Clarina Nichols described the Kaw as "the lowest and most degraded tribe in the territory, who are beggars and thieves, but otherwise harmless." She remarked that "their faith is unchanged since the time when Pope wrote of the 'poor Indian'" and recounted a funeral of one of their members that included a grave laden with provisions, including the deceased's dog and pony. Sara Robinson, also an abolitionist, wrote in April 1855 that "the Kaw Indians are the most uncultivated of all," and contrasted them with the "civilized Shawnee." Robinson reported that one of her friends was forced to entertain some "unwelcome visitors," a group of Kaw Indians that demanded food and drink and rummaged through her friend's personal belongings. The Kaw lacked a mission in the area, and their resistance to Christianity and their "uncivilized" behavior clearly cast them in a negative light in the white community.[41]

On the other hand, Robinson described the Shawnee and Delaware Indians favorably, in part because those bands had readily converted to Protestantism by the 1850s.[42] She even indicated that on occasion white settlers joined these Christian Indians in worship. On April 8, 1855, Robinson and her husband attended the "little white church upon the rolling prairie," whose architecture reminded Robinson of "dear New England." Though the church's exterior conjured up memories of home for Sara, its contents were far from familiar. She "noticed the Indian worshippers" and "their odd-sounding dialect" and commented on the Indian women who arrived on horseback. The essential quality of the service, however, impressed Sara, and she concluded that the Indian interpreters' "quick and varied intonations . . . their graceful and most expressive gestures, singularly enchain the attention of the hearers, and impress upon them the substance of the discourse."[43] Christian Indians might dress and act differently, but at least they embraced the word of God—and, most important for Robinson, a white, Protestant God.

Though Robinson looked fondly upon these particular Kansas Indians, native peoples who accepted Christianity and who practiced the missions' agricultural and domestic arts engaged white settlers on fundamentally uneven ground. No matter how willing certain Indians may have been to learn English and to convert to Christianity, they did so only after their land had been invaded and their cultures disparaged by the very missionaries who sought to "save" them. Nonetheless, many tribes recognized that some missionaries could be helpful in their quest for fair treaties and could give them cultural tools with which to enter the white world and defend their rights. One of the ways many Indians engaged the white world in a mutually profitable and positive way was through trade. On this more level playing field, Indians, especially mixed-breeds, prospered and maintained a healthy living by trading their goods and services with white settlers and traders.

A LIVELY TRADE

Economic exchange between the white and Indian worlds produced a variety of results, ranging from symbiotic to antagonistic, but formal trade between whites and Kansas Indians often garnered positive results for both groups. White traders and fur trappers moved into the area to profit from the commerce in Indian goods and to sell provisions to the numerous white settlers who traveled on the Santa Fe and Overland trails. B. F. Van Horn and his wife, Elizabeth, arrived in the territory in 1857 and settled near Topeka, where they opened a store and enjoyed a "pretty lively" trade with the Indians.[44] Frank La Loge also arrived in Kansas Territory in 1857 and with his wife operated a "dug-out" store near present-day Salina, Kansas, until 1864.[45] They took advantage of their location on the Santa Fe Trail to sell wares to both Indians and whites.

Indians also took advantage of the increased traffic in the region by taking in boarders and providing basic supplies to serve the needs of settlers and Indians alike. In fact, many white settlers' first taste of life in Kansas was filtered through their overnight stays in Indian homes, and most settlers experienced positive interactions with their hosts and hostesses. Free-state and proslavery settlers alike frequented the Indian boarding houses that peppered the eastern border of Kansas Territory. Sylvester Clarke, a free-state settler, wrote to his wife that upon arrival in the territory, his party stayed near the Shawnee reservation in an "Indian Hut" owned by proprietor John Ham. He described his evening there in detail: "Our supper and breakfast consisted of bread and molasses and some tea— Our beds were previously spoken for by a prospecting company of bed bugs and mosquitoes. . . . In one department there were ten persons including Ham and his Squaw with several Papooses—thus we passed the first night amid the charming scenery of the Kansa Valley."[46] Sharing meals, bedrooms, and bed bugs was not uncommon in frontier Kansas; during the territory's early years Anglos and Indians at times inhabited the same literal and cultural spaces.

The social lubricant that most frequently facilitated these Indian-white economic and cultural exchanges was undoubtedly alcohol. Although prohibited by the U.S. government, the practice of exchanging alcohol for Indian goods continued to dominate economic exchange between the two groups.[47] This pattern persisted in Kansas Territory, and the Indian agents in the region lamented the negative effects of alcohol on the tribes' mental and physical health. Superintendent Cumming reported that "the Pottawatomies are in a condition which requires the united effort of their agent and best men now to shield them from temptations which seem too hard for them to encounter alone."[48] And agent Burton A. James noted that "the Sac and Fox Indians who have been wintering in the state of Missouri and Kansas Territory have as usual been drinking to excess."[49] In response to these problems, Cumming and his agents in the Central Superintendence developed programs designed to curb alcohol consumption among the tribes. He formed alliances with influential men within each tribe and discouraged alcohol consumption by promising financial benefits in return for temperance.

Cumming experienced mixed success with his temperance policies, however, in part because the constant influx of new whites often brought new sources of alcohol. "The condition of the smaller tribes without agents is comparatively good," he wrote, "but much evil is apprehended from their proximity to the white settlements. This however, is inevitable and they are now in a more favorable condition for the trial than some of their neighbors." Cumming acknowledged that it would be impossible to prevent the tribes from trading and socializing with white settlers, but he made every effort to eliminate alcohol from this equation. Writing to Commissioner Manypenny, he claimed, "I have the honor to report that efforts are now being made by the agents and a few influential men of the tribe to diminish the intemperance and debauchery heretofore so prevalent among the Miami Indians."[50] While government policy curbed alcohol consumption among some tribes, the problem persisted, especially as more and more white families arrived in the area with few resources with which to trade other than food and alcohol. Trading for frontier essentials, such as housing, often necessitated the use of alcohol as capital.

Much of the Indian trade took place in less formal settings, as white settlers satisfied their needs for housing and material goods in exchange for food and drink. These informal exchanges, often accompanied by alcohol consumption, sometimes elicited positive and lucrative results for both parties. Mrs. Fannie Kelly, an early settler, experienced a pleasant interaction with a band of Sioux Indians when she first encountered them on the Santa Fe Trail: "A party of Indians rode up to us appeared to be friendly each one of them shaking hands with each one of us they made motions for something to eat we gave them bread, sugar and tobacco which pleased them very much. I traded for a pair of moccasins with a yancton Indian named Wechedah. I did not feel very much alarmed as the Indians all the way along had been reported friendly."[51] Though Kelly's friendly trading partners proved to be interested in taking more than food and drink from her party (they ransacked the wagon train and kidnapped Kelly and other settlers a day later), many Indian-Anglo encounters sustained a congenial tone.

The McMeekin family experienced positive and productive interactions with their Indian neighbors after moving from Kentucky to the banks of the Kansas River in 1850. Hayden D. McMeekin established a trading post near the Pottawatomie reservation, about eighty miles southwest of Fort Leavenworth, and enjoyed "good success" for several years before moving to Leavenworth and opening the Planter's House hotel in 1855.[52] His daughter, Mary, harbored fond memories of her family's interactions with their Indian neighbors: "The Indians were very friendly, and frequently brought my brother and me presents of quail and birds which they brought in cages they made. Indeed they were too friendly, for they would walk into the kitchen and pick up anything they fancied."[53] Clara Harding Jordan, who grew up near the Kickapoo, remembered playing "peek-a-boo" with the Indian papooses but also recalls how her mother had to keep a store of buttermilk on hand to give to the Indians who frequently made unannounced and unwelcome visits.[54] Jordan and McMeekin observed that Indian-white friendships treaded on uncertain ground, as both parties navigated differing interpretations of concepts such as privacy and sharing. Unfortunately, misunderstandings and miscommunication sometimes undermined tenuous friendships and led to violent altercations.

Predictably, Indian and white Kansans did not always engage in peaceful forms of economic and cultural exchange; violent conflict often punctuated the two groups' initial interactions. Large-scale combat occurred in eastern Kansas before the 1850s, as government troops stationed at Fort Leavenworth and Fort Scott battled the Pawnees, Kaws, and Osages in preparation for the westward movement of white settlers. Wagon trains carrying supplies to and from these federal forts were particularly vulnerable targets for Indian attacks.

W. B. Royall led two trains from Kansas to Arkansas, and he reported to Brig. Gen. R. Jones that Indians attacked his party in June 1848. At five in the morning, approximately two to three hundred "warriors" descended upon Royall's unit. Both sides suffered losses, but Royall praised the U.S. soldiers' courage: "The enemy made an attempt to charge through the line of tents on Major Bryant's side of the camp. One Indian was killed there and dragged into camp with his shield and lance. The Indians endeavored to obtain his body, and tried several times to lasso him to carry him off, but our men were determined to have him; lances and arrows flew at our men, but they beat them off and kept possession of their trophies."[55] Indians are stereotypically remembered as having carried war "trophies," such as scalps, from battle, but this example indicates that white men kept souvenirs from the conflicts as well. These soldiers refused to return the dead Indian's body to his tribe and even risked their lives to keep possession of the corpse. Though the ultimate fate of the body was not recorded by Royall, perhaps the soldiers used it as physical proof of their professed superior military strength or even as a marker of white supremacy.

But possessing Indian bodies was not as important as possessing Indian land, and some soldiers stationed in the region blatantly thwarted Indian land rights in Kansas. In an 1854 report of the commissioner of Indian affairs, the Delaware agent reported that several officers of the U.S. army squatted on Delaware land. "I found the Delaware Indians much disturbed in mind," he wrote. "By their late treaty, all the land ceded by them to the United States . . . were to be offered for sale for their benefit a public auction. . . . Some reflections were cast on certain officers of the Army stationed at Fort Leavenworth for their conduct in relation to the Delaware Lands . . . that some of them were engaged in trespassing on the lands ceded by the Delawares to the United States in trust for their benefit."[56]

Captain Hunt, commander of Fort Leavenworth, confirmed the officers' trespasses and reported the incidents to the Delaware agent. The agent deeply regretted the practice, arguing that the army squatters had done more to damage Delaware-Anglo relations than any other group of squatters: "The Delaware Indians had been accustomed in all former occasions to look to the Fort for protection from trespasses of any kind, and the conduct of the officers on this occasion has therefore been the most fatal to the peace and interests of the Delaware."[57] The agent requested immediate military action to remove the squatters but only received a letter from the secretary of war stating the squatting incidents would be fully investigated.

Several tribes, such as the Delaware and Shawnee, continued to trust the government's good will, even as they watched their land and rights get trampled on by the "Great Father's" white children. Others, such as the Osage and Kaw, persisted in their challenges to the government and proudly asserted and articulated their differences with white settlers. The U.S. government often responded similarly to both groups and attempted to mold all Indians into a white, middle-class ideal of civilized, Christian citizens. Several cultural practices proved difficult to change, however, and the differences between white and Indian gender roles and sexual practices promised to be some of the most intractable.

THE BERDACHE AND OTHER GENDERED ANOMALIES

In the process of securing Kansas Indian territory for white settlement, members of the army and the federal government gained firsthand knowledge of their enemies, information they often found puzzling. W. B. Royall, involved in a violent conflict with the Osage in 1848, added an interesting postscript to his description of the battle, involving what may have been a "berdache" Indian who led the tribe into conflict. He wrote matter-of-factly, "We saw about one hundred yards from us during the fight a female who seemed to be their Queen mounted on a horse decorated with silver ornaments on a Scarlett dress, who rode about giving directions about the wounded."[58] If the queen was not a berdache and was in fact a female Indian, it is interesting to note that she appeared to have a significant amount of power on the battlefield, a traditionally male preserve among most Indian tribes and certainly among the Osage. Royall guessed that the majority of the Indians were either Osage or Comanche, and given the location of the attack, his presumption seems credible. Thus while blood spilled on the battlefield, gendered boundaries and, more specifically, white assumptions about Indian gender roles blurred among some Indian tribes.

Government agents recognized that Indian gender relations created several obstacles to their project of civilization/colonization, and they formulated their removal and reservation policies accordingly. Some Indian agents suggested that women and children be removed from their tribes and sent to mission schools, perhaps in an effort to destroy the community-based agricultural and social system over which Indian women asserted a significant amount of control. This struggle continued into the 1860s, when an Indian agent among the Sioux advocated "the removal of the women and children with a view to wiping out the tribe."[59] By removing Indian women from the picture, U.S. agents could strike a blow not only at the physical reproduction of the community's population but also at the tribe's food supply and the cultural reproduction of gender relations that ordered Indian society in a particularly Indian manner. The project of civilization thus launched a two-pronged attack on Indian economic and gender relations because the government realized (whether consciously or not) that the two systems supported each other in symbiotic ways.

Some settlers and missionaries in Kansas specifically pinpointed Indian gender relations and sexual practices as blockades to the civilization process. Clara Gowing met an Indian man, his two wives, and two "babes," and she noted that "polygamy, though not the general custom of the nation, is not ostracized."[60] John W. Whitfield, an agent among the Kaws, doubted the abilities of whites to change Indian ways, in part because they practiced polygamy. He wrote, "I am unable to say whether this people have been improved by the efforts of the missionaries, who have labored for them for the last thirty years. . . . So long as the custom prevails of one man being entitled to all the sisters of the family he may marry into, I can not see how we are to expect much improvement."[61] Unless the agents broke the Indians' will to perpetuate their polygamous ways, the missions and the government would make little progress reforming and "civilizing" the Kaw. After all, polygamy in and of itself was uncivilized because, among other things, it countered the white, middle-class ideal of the nuclear family.[62]

In addition to making the nuclear family obsolete, polygamy included a whole host of corollaries that further challenged the mission's goals. Agent Whitfield connected the practice of polygamy to the mission's inability to reform Indian gender roles and hence their civilization. Whitfield elaborated on his initial complaints: "They never permit their daughters to go to school; some man has a claim to them as soon as they are born. The boys are taken from school as soon as they are large enough to go out on a hunt."[63] Whitfield's observations clearly indicate that the Kaws maintained polygamy and its corresponding gender roles, which in turn preserved much of the traditional Indian way of life. After males reached hunting age, they had no need for academic or agricultural education because their responsibilities included hunting and defending their lands, not farming. Although Indian men might have seen the advantage of acquiring some schooling, perhaps to increase their ability to communicate effectively during treaty negotiations, they saw little need for agricultural training. Furthermore, Indian girls failed to embrace a white, middle-class education because as women who spent their days tending the fields and processing animal and plant products, they would have little use for the domestic "arts" classes offered by the missions. Clearly, some Indians responded to the missionaries' multipronged attack on their culture with a multilayered defense of Indian traditions that sustained much of their traditional economic and social relations.

BLEED AND/OR DIE

Though many tribes resisted the repeated attempts of the U.S. government and the Christian missions to change their cultures, the forces of whiteness continued to press the Indians to change. Some missionaries believed that the Indians' only hope for survival depended on their total conversion to the white world; white blood must bleed into red if Indians expected to endure the westward expansion of Anglo America. Thomas Johnson, founder of the Shawnee Methodist Mission, agreed that the Indians' only course of action was to adopt the substance of white society. He wrote to Agent Benjamin F. Robinson, "I am forced to the conclusion that, as separate tribes, they must in a few years pass away. The only hope is for the few who may become identified with the white population, and take their position in the walks of civilized society."[64]

Several congressmen endorsed Johnson's sentiments, arguing on the House floor that tribes must acquire white ways or die a slow and painful death via removal and/or disease. During a U.S. Senate and House debate on peace with the Indians, Representative John Sherman of Ohio illustrated the threat that accompanied the language of whiteness: "As our white population progress westward over the Plains they will either absorb the Indian population or kill it off. It may be hard; but such is the fate of all barbarous communities, all wild tribes, when they come in contact with civilized tribes. . . . The result is that tribe after tribe will gradually disappear, until. . . finally [they will] disappear entirely from the race of human beings. You cannot stop or change that law of nature."[65] While Sherman desired to portray Indians as the racial "other," as members of a wild, barbarous tribe, he simultaneously acknowledged their membership in the human race by similarly referring to the white settlers as a tribe, albeit a "civilized" one. Thus his assertion of the white man's evolutionary prowess also came with recognition of the "wild" man's potential for civilization; only through "extermination" could Sherman entirely deny Indians their humanity. If not killed, they would be "absorbed"—in other words, Christianized and civilized—into the white human race.[66]

Sherman and like-minded settlers amplified their own whiteness by darkening and animalizing the racial other.[67] For instance, during the "Senate Debate on Negotiating with Indians" in 1866, Senator James Doolittle explicitly equated Indians with the buffalo:

> Compared with us, they [the Indians] are a very feeble people. We are strong; we are a great nation. They are wandering nomads over the plains, with no more habitation than the buffalo has. They go with the buffalo. . . . They live upon the buffalo, and with the buffalo, and range over those vast plains. . . . Whenever we meet them we can conquer them and capture and slaughter them; but it is just as impossible, within any reasonable amount of expenditure to catch these Indians and reduce them to obedience by war as it is to catch the buffalo upon the plains or the blackbirds that fly over the plains.[68]

Doolittle recognized the difficulty of subduing the Indian presence by force alone. "Capturing and slaughtering" served its purpose temporarily, but he acknowledged the need for other means of addressing the "Indian problem" (undoubtedly turning toward Christian missions for an answer). Those they could not kill, they would civilize.

Though Doolittle wondered how the nation could rid itself of the "Indian problem," his speech illuminated how Indians' redness helped confirm whites' racial purity. "Compared with us" the Indians are "feeble," wrote Doolittle; compared with redness, whiteness and the nation built on a foundation of white supremacy were "strong" and "great." Without redness (and blackness), whiteness—and the white privilege of citizenship and the sense of national identity which it fostered—could not exist. Thus the expansion of the country and its national/racial identity depended in part on the ability of whites to construct redness and blackness as "other."[69]

Many settlers reinforced racial otherness by consistently referring to Indians as "red men." James Hindman arrived in the territory in 1857 and stayed near the Baptist mission before surveying the area for a proper claim site. One day he lost his way and stopped at an Indian cabin for directions. He found his way after "a dart of the eye, a point of the finger and a peculiar grunt from the red skin showed me the way which I soon regained."[70] Hindman's description of the "red skin" uttering a "peculiar grunt" suggests that, in his mind, he was communicating with a being that was somehow less than human. Hindman used the red skin to represent the Indian's essence as an animal-like being, incapable of using rational language and dependent instead upon physical gestures and grunts to communicate.

In fact, white descriptions of Indians often aligned them with the animal world, and posited beliefs that the Indians lived in a state of nature. Martha Chenault wrote to her mother, "The Sac and Fox Indians are wild looking people."[71] Similarly, missionary Clemmie Boon wrote to her sister and referred to the Indians as "wild children of nature" who lived in a "savage land." Boon, though living among these "savages," was not "entirely exempt from society," because one trader in the area had two half-white daughters; one of these daughters had even "married a physician, a white man."[72] The "half-breed" daughter, by marrying a white man, especially a white man of property and social standing, slowly stepped inside the privileged sphere of whiteness. As long as white blood blended with red, whiteness, and hence, civilized society, remained within reach for Indians and for the missionaries who lived among them.

AMALGAMATION AND CIVILIZATION

Perhaps the most effective and obvious method of infusing red with white blood was through cross-racial intermarriage and sex. One of the last opportunities to change Indian life, according to some, lay in physically and sexually amalgamating whites with Indians and forming multiracial families comprised of "half-breeds." Only with white blood coursing through Indian veins, this argument ran, could Indians become truly civilized. By marrying Indian women (and the vast majority of interracial marriages were comprised of Anglo men and Indian women), white men could not only father children with white blood but also encourage their wives to adopt traditional Anglo gender roles, thus further diluting the cultural power of Indian society.[73]

John Montgomery, an Indian agent among the Kaws, issued a favorable report of the mission's progress among the "half-breeds": "The half-breed Kansas, or the greater number of them, are industrious and intelligent, well versed in the English, French and Kaw languages, profess the Catholic religion, and have almost a thorough knowledge of the arts of husbandry." The "full-blooded" Kaw, however, received a less positive evaluation:

> When [the Kaw] were separated from the half-breeds [it] only retarded the progress of the civilization and christianizing of the former; from the fact, that there has been no change in the Indian customs and manners to those of the white man; and from the fact that there has been no white people or half-breeds among the full-blooded Indians since they were removed from the Kansas river to this place. The native Indians having no white people affiliated with their tribe have strictly adhered to their natural customs and pursuits of life.[74]

Montgomery criticized the government's policy of separating the "full-blooded" Kaw from their mixed-race kin and further indicted federal Indian policy and the mission process by endorsing the French program of civilization. He closed his report by saying, "The Canadian French, in my opinion, have done more to civilize the Kansas than all the schools and moral institutions that have ever been established for their benefit."[75] Montgomery implied that the French had done more to civilize the Indian by intermarrying with them than by any other method of conversion to white ways.

Several accounts detail Indian-French intermarriages in Kansas. Pierre Le Clerc married a Pottawatomie woman in Chicago, "after the fashion of the whites," but later separated from her and married another Pottawatomie woman in Kansas, named Musch-puck quai (according to the report, Pottawatomie custom only recognized Pottawatomie marriage ceremonies and thus ignored Le Clerc's first, "white" marriage). Le Clerc fathered children with both women, which caused some confusion regarding his inheritance and his children's entitlement to it and to Indian annuity payments.[76] One of his daughters, Fanny Beach, married a white man, Alexander Rodd, and together they raised four or five children. Thus the trend of red-white intermarriage that Le Clerc and his Pottawatomie wife began persisted in their family and further whitened and "civilized" their mixed-blood children.

If intermarriage alone could not achieve the desired results among the Indians, some believed that a combination of economics and sexual exchange would sufficiently bring civilization and whiteness to the Indians in Kansas. During his travels in the territory, Sylvester Clarke explored several of the Indian missions and reservations, and he concluded in his diary that civilization had indeed reached a small portion of the Indian population. He was particularly impressed with the Delawares: "These Indians are far in advance of the neighboring tribes in everything appertaining to civilization. . . . Commercial intercourse and intermarriage with the whites has nearly obliterated the peculiar characteristics of Indian life. The bow and the arrow [have] been laid aside to make room for the axe and the plow."[77] Commerce and interracial marriage had "nearly obliterated" the cultural differences between red and white, according to Clarke. Cultural and sexual boundaries between the two races would continue to blur as an increasing number of white settlers moved to the territory and intermarried with the Indian men and women in Kansas.

Some interracial unions forged the kind of partnerships that allowed both parties to navigate their multiracial identities in skillful ways that benefited the couple and their larger communities. In rare cases, these mixed-race marriages promoted the idea among both cultures that racial amalgamation was favorable not only to Indians but also to whites. Take, for instance, the marriage of Abelard Guthrie to Quindaro Nancy Brown, a Wyandot Indian woman. Quindaro Brown belonged to the Big Turtle Clan of the Wyandot tribe and was herself a product of an intertribal marriage between her Shawnee mother and Wyandot father. After Brown married Guthrie, the Bear Clan of the Wyandots adopted him into their group and named him "Tah-keh-yoh-shrah-tseh, which means the twin brain."[78]

The Wyandots apparently recognized Guthrie's acute ability to settle disputes between their tribe and the U.S. government, because they said he possessed the brain of both the white man and the Bear. Guthrie was involved with the Wyandots' treaty negotiations, in part because his wife's land covered a large portion of the region bordering the Wyandot and Delaware reservations. He named a nearby town Quindaro after his wife, "because we were wholly indebted to her exertions and influence with the Indians for every foot of land on which the town is built."[79] It appears that Guthrie was not the only partner in this marriage who possessed talents of arbitration.

Guthrie and his wife discussed land deals and credit with the leaders of nearby white settlements, even though Guthrie loathed the endeavor. He complained in his diary, "I have never suffered more anguish of mind than I have suffered within the last month on account of pecuniary embarrassments. . . . After all the old Indian life, with all its poverty and hardship is the happiest."[80] Guthrie suggested that before he and Quindaro had acquired so much property, life had been poorer but much happier. He implied in his diary that the free-state men whom he had trusted had swindled him and put him into near-poverty and perpetual debt.[81]

Although Guthrie may have loathed the financial transactions he conducted with his neighbors, his wife Quindaro appeared to integrate them into her social calendar, often conducting business while on social visits. On March 31, 1858, Guthrie recorded that his wife "went to widow Sarah Coon's and got $60 which I had paid her for an old improvement. . . . Mrs. Guthrie also borrowed $100.00 from widow Coon for me." Guthrie signed a note a few days later "in favor of Sarah Coon payable on demand."[82] Coon asked Mrs. Guthrie to sign the note as well, indicating that she trusted Quindaro's word. It appears that Coon, a Wyandot Indian, felt more comfortable making a transaction with a fellow Indian rather than a white man, even one with two brains. Guthrie's marriage to Quindaro proved beneficial to his ability to gain credit in the community.

The Guthrie marriage also served Quindaro and her tribe's needs. In October 1858 Guthrie lamented that "the Wyandot pay[ment] will not take place for some weeks and possibly not until next year; this act of bad faith in the Government, must produce much suffering among the Wyandots and many whites to whom they are indebted." While Guthrie's concern for the tribe's late payment was obviously connected to his own dependence on their money, he pursued the issue with government officials and addressed the tribes' needs. He responded similarly when the government defaulted on a Delaware payment. Guthrie met with the local chief, John Sirahass, to discuss their options: "In this evening's 'talk' with Sirahass who is now our head Chief, I proposed that as the payment was not made in October last as the treaty required, that the two payments of 1858 & 1859 be made at the same time, say in May 1859." The next day he drafted a new treaty that he hoped would address the Delawares' needs. He claimed that if adopted, "it will secure the Delawares from being defrauded by the harpies that are flocking to Washington in the hopes of securing slices of their land." Guthrie felt confident that the tribe would endorse his new treaty, "as some of them have long been my friends and neighbors."[83] His marriage to Quindaro and his membership in the wider Indian community lent credibility to his word and permitted him to lobby the Government effectively for Wyandot and Delaware rights.

It was in fact this cultural, economic, and sexual blending that enabled the Guthries to be successful in the tenuous borderlands of territorial Kansas. Although their marriage and success may be an exception, it can serve as one example of the benefits that red-white exchange could hold for some couples in territorial Kansas. However, it also articulates the hegemonic tendencies of whiteness and white values. The Guthries adopted many practices that would have safely placed them in the white middle class. They sent their two daughters to St. Louis for boarding school, and they employed several servants, one of whom was "a mixed blood of white, Indian and negro" and one who unfortunately spent more time drinking than working.[84] They also acquired a healthy tract of land that they continued to possess, even in the midst of railroad expansion and increasing indebtedness.

Guthrie's attitudes toward some Indian tribes exemplified the ways in which the discourse on whiteness infiltrated even multiracial homes. He complained of the Wyandots and their inability to accept the Great Father's paternalism graciously. He argued, "The envious and malicious disposition of the Wyandots so manifest in all their dealings with the white man, is one chief cause of their rapid decline. . . . I pity their errors."[85] Like the congressmen who preached the inevitable decimation of the Indian, Guthrie implied that those Indians who insisted on stubbornly defending their rights would eventually die out. He pitied them from his privileged racial and class position, a position ironically obtained by his marrying an Indian woman. Guthrie and others like him implied that only by engaging in the white man's world—his culture, his women, his religion—could any shred of Indianness survive.

REDNESS AND BLACKNESS

Many whites shared Guthrie's sentiments and believed that Indian resistance to white ways would ultimately lead to their demise. In fact, missionaries, lawmakers, and Kansas settlers used Indian resistance as justification for their removal; if the "hordes" could not be civilized, they would be disposed of without apology. Missionaries in particular endeavored to transform Indian culture, but even they lamented the Indian's potential for progress without a near-total conversion to white ways. Paradoxically, those Indians who refused to discard their redness only furthered the project of whiteness, because Indian resistance inadvertently bolstered the white settlers' resolve to either kill or relocate the remaining Plains Indians. Many whites throughout the country believed that "there was no way of stopping the spread of civilization; Indians had to join the march or risk extinction." After decades of previous removal, disease, and oppression, the Indians in Kansas were doomed to conform or die.[86]

The increasing sectional tensions in the region only worsened the Indians' chances of survival. In his diary, Guthrie lamented, "Alas the poor Indian, despised by those who use him and spurned by those he opposes and who have been his only friends. . . . How soon will thy sad fate be sealed[?]"[87] As arguments over the fate of slavery in the West heated up, Indians in Kansas were used and abused by settlers from both sides of the sectional divide. White settlers recruited like-minded political allies, and Indians inevitably became embroiled in the conflict, as Indian land became the stage on which the great drama of Bleeding Kansas would take place.

2

RUNAWAYS, "NEGRO STEALERS," AND "BORDER RUFFIANS"

ANTISLAVERY AND PROSLAVERY
IDEOLOGIES IN ACTION

During the spring of 1855 the Fugitive Slave Law received a unique test in Kansas Territory, a region that had yet to be officially declared as free or slave. On March 19 a black slave escaped from his master and fled from Westport, Missouri, toward Lawrence, Kansas, a new stop on the Underground Railroad. The slave never made it to Lawrence, however, because he met his unfortunate fate at the hands of a Shawnee Indian, who apprehended, shot, and wounded him and returned him to his master. The *Kansas Weekly Herald,* a proslavery paper published in Leavenworth, printed a story on the incident that claimed the slaveholder "expressed himself satisfied as far as the maiming of the slave was concerned, but only wanted to find the 'd—d Abolitionist' who persuaded him to escape." The *Herald* warned its readers of the "spirit that actuates these Abolitionists who decoy off slaves, and rob their neighbors of their property."[1] Even though the Fugitive Slave Law had fulfilled its designs in this particular case, slaveholders still questioned its effectiveness when "negro stealers" lurked in the tall Kansas prairie grass. As Michael Fellman has noted, "'Nigger-stealing' became the central symbol of all that was base in these northern invaders."[2]

The conflict between these "northern invaders" and the defenders of slavery, often referred to disparagingly as "Border Ruffians," began as soon as Kansas officially opened for white settlement and persisted throughout the territorial era. This antagonism both mirrored and exacerbated the larger tensions between antislavery and proslavery politicians and ideologues at the national level. The question of slavery in the West hamstrung political debate from the end of the Mexican War until the firing on Fort Sumter and overwhelmed politicians during the 1850s. Historian Michael A. Morrison argues that "the issues of expansion and slavery extension were critical to the destruction of Whiggery, the resonance of the Republican and fire-eater appeals, the disruption of the Democracy, the election of Lincoln, and the secession of the South."[3] In other words, the debate over slavery in the West was a primary cause of the Civil War.

Morrison and others examine this important and convincing thesis by exploring the political and intellectual debates that occurred in Washington, D.C., and other more eastern cities; but rarely have the causes of the Civil War been evaluated from points farther west or from the perspective of the settlers themselves. How did proslavery and antislavery settlers put their ideologies about slavery's expansion into practice in Kansas Territory? Did they truly embrace the tenets of Republicanism and fire-eating Democracy? If so, how? Both parties breathed life into these ideologies: Slaveholders and their proslavery allies, like some Shawnee Indians, used legal and extralegal means to ensure that slavery would take root in the Kansas soil, but their efforts could not combat the fierce resistance to these proslavery measures executed by slaves and antislavery settlers.

Nicole Etcheson's *Bleeding Kansas* begins to help us understand how Kansans interpreted and enacted popular sovereignty. One of the strengths of Etcheson's work is its close examination of the sectional events in Kansas and the related analysis of how policies that were formulated in Washington applied in the territory itself. Etcheson carefully narrates the political conflicts between proslavery and antislavery settlers, especially their leaders, but she only rarely examines how blacks, white abolitionists, or women influenced the sectional tensions. In her final two chapters Etcheson does include African Americans and a few abolitionists (a woman or two among them) as she argues that the Civil War's "upheaval finally executed the promise that liberty would encompass blacks."[4] She finds that the outbreak of full-scale war provided unprecedented opportunities for Missouri slaves to flee across the border to Kansas and to participate in the military fight against Confederate and guerrilla forces.

Etcheson's runaways, who flooded into towns such as Leavenworth and Lawrence during the war, were following a path that had been well marked by Kansas and Missouri slaves and abolitionists during the territorial period. These "Negro stealers" and slave runaways comprised an important vanguard of early citizens who challenged slavery and racial hierarchy. Too little has been said about the efforts of blacks and their white allies to initiate the emancipation process between 1854 and 1861. As Stanley Harrold argues in his book about the biracial antislavery community in Washington, D.C., these men and women, "simply by engaging in interracial cooperation . . . raised a radical challenge to the existing social order."

Furthermore, like Harrold's "subversives," antislavery Kansans posed a palpable and immediate threat to area slaveholders.[5] Slaveholding Missourians' greatest fear—losing their slave property to a free Kansas—was realized not in 1861 but much earlier.[6]

INDIANS AND AFRICAN AMERICANS

The debate over slavery in the West arose amid a national discussion of Indian rights and treaty negotiations, but the influence of these developments on the conception of free labor ideology has only rarely been examined.[7] Republicans who embraced Free-Soilism crafted an ideology that appeared diametrically opposed to slave *and* Indian labor systems. Free labor families depended on their own relatives' sweat and toil for their agricultural prosperity, not slave labor. In addition, white free laborers divided agricultural tasks by gender, keeping women and female children near or inside the home and sending men into the fields.[8] Many Indians, however, reversed this gendered division of labor as Indian women tended the fields and men stayed in the village or ventured outside its boundaries to hunt and fish. White settlers often perceived Indians, especially Indian women, as living in a state of slavery because they performed hard labor in the fields while Indian men seemingly lounged around and got drunk. These "squaw drudges" and "lazy braves" provided "counterimages and negative reference groups by which to demonstrate [white] superiority and rationalize dispossession." In addition, Indians appeared to be enslaved to nature, preferring to allow the earth to dictate planting schedules and locations rather than manipulating the land to fit human needs. Indian agricultural practices and gender roles contradicted the ideal vision of the free labor family whose (male) members farmed land enclosed by fences and boundaries created by man, not nature.[9]

Indians appeared content with their "perpetual enslavement," and their resistance to the free labor system further alienated them from white notions of "progress" and might have bolstered the idea that African Americans were more likely candidates for integration into a free labor society. Methodist missionary Jerome Berryman remembered that even slaves' condition was "greatly preferable" to the degraded state of "any" Indians. Similarly, Col. E. V. Sumner, stationed at Fort Leavenworth, compared white and Indian laborers and argued that even though white labor was more expensive, it would "be better economy to employ white men," implying that Indians were poor workers.[10]

Many northern whites believed that freed slaves, on the other hand, could easily be molded into effective free labor farmers, if they had not already been introduced to such practices under slavery. Historian Elliot West defines African Americans in the mid-nineteenth century as "insiders" because they were "enmeshed in white society" and were quite literally "inside the house" of many white southerners; Indians, however, "were far removed from white control" and remained "outsiders." West cites Frederick Douglass, who claimed that "the Negro [was] . . . more like the white man than the Indian, in his tastes and tendencies, and disposition to accept civilization. . . . You do not see him wearing a blanket, but coats cut in the latest European fashion."[11]

Similarly, historian Randall Woods has argued that "extreme prejudice against the Indian" in Kansas made many believe that "Negroes were capable of farming and laboring; at least they had sense enough to try and learn the white man's ways and to want to become assimilated."[12] Furthermore, unlike many Indians, enslaved African Americans in Kansas and Missouri often followed a white, middle-class gendered division of labor: Men worked in the fields and female slaves functioned as house servants and laundresses. According to Nicole Etcheson, "Since most Kansas slaves were women and children, and the average slave owner owned only one or two [slaves], many probably worked in the house as servants rather than as field hands."[13] It appears that white settlers in Kansas might have been more comfortable envisioning blacks rather than Indians as fellow free laborers because the latter kept defying the free labor ideal.

Furthermore, contrary to the often-cited racial hierarchy constructed by Thomas Jefferson in his *Notes on the State of Virginia,* by the early and mid-nineteenth century, some Americans placed Indians *below* blacks on a racial continuum. They posited Indians as less intelligent than blacks and believed that most Indians were stuck in a permanent "state of barbarism." Instead of Jefferson's hierarchy, some Americans embraced Senator Henry Clay's philosophy on the races, which he articulated in a speech to the Colonization Society of Kentucky in 1829:

> In surveying the United States of North America and their Territories, the beholder perceives, among their inhabitants, three separate and distinct races, of men, originally appertaining to three different continents of the globe, each race varying from the others in color, physical properties, and moral and intellectual endowments. The European is the most numerous; and, as well from that fact, as from its far greater

advance in civilization and in the arts, has the decided ascendency [sic] over the other two, giving the law to them, controlling their condition, and responsible for their fate to the Great Father of all, and to the enlightened world. The next most numerous and most intelligent race, is that which sprung from Africa, the largest portion of which is held in bondage by their brethren, descendants of the European. The aborigines, or Indian race, are the least numerous, and, with the exception of some tribes, have but partially emerged from the state of barbarism in which they were found on the first discovery of America.[14]

Some Kansans echoed Clay's sentiments, as the black and Indian presence in the region enabled settlers to compare the two groups; often, Indians failed to measure up to African Americans, even slaves.

Indians were perceived as stubborn, headstrong, lazy and violent, but blacks in Kansas were often described as passive, flexible, and even hard working. During a visit to a Seminole reservation in the area one settler, Charles M. Chase, noted, "I could not help but observe the contrast between the negro and Indian characters. . . . The natural character of the negro is submissive, obsequious; that of the Indian, stubborn, contemptuous. The one is by nature menial, dependent; the other haughty, defiant, and independent. . . . One will live and increase among Caucasians, because he is flexible, easily directed and used—is handy; the other will be driven westward, and soon cease to exist all together, because he is inflexible, and too fixed in his own ways."[15] Admittedly, these impressions were informed by racial stereotypes—generalizations at best and falsehoods at worst. But many settlers' perceptions, however racist, fell into one of two separate camps that perpetuated stereotypes about each group: Indians refused to change and would never be integrated into a free labor society, whereas blacks could and would learn to live in ways that supported republican ideas about the future of the expanding nation.

In fact, Kansas provided some reassurance that if the North went to war over slavery, emancipation would lead to agricultural prosperity and the successful expansion of free labor, even with the inclusion of black farmers and their families. Some African Americans appeared to wholeheartedly embrace free labor ideology in Kansas and served as examples of a future that included black free labor. One black family in Kansas farmed Alexander Johnson's (son of the Reverend Thomas Johnson) land even while Johnson spent the majority of the year traveling and living across the river in Missouri. Remarkably, these slaves not only remained faithful to their master and never sought their freedom elsewhere, but according to Johnson they also worked diligently.[16] In addition, they performed this labor without living under the daily threat of the lash—quite an example for surrounding whites about blacks' potential as free labor farmers. The Johnson slaves worked on the Kansas farm while their master lived with his wife in Missouri until 1861, when state law outlawed slavery in the region.

However, the Johnson slaves provide only one example of the potential of African Americans to fulfill the free labor ideal, and the fact remains that free labor ideology persisted in its exclusion of blacks *and* Indians from its vision of a Free-Soil republic. As historian Reginald Horsman made clear over two decades ago, "The United States shaped policies which reflected a belief in the racial inferiority and expendability of Indians, Mexicans, and other inferior races, and which looked forward to a world shaped and dominated by a superior American Anglo-Saxon race." Though some missionaries and policy makers may have believed that Indians had the ability to improve and join the ranks of civilized citizens, by midcentury most Americans believed that Indians were innately inferior and unable to transform their society or culture unless physically infused with whiteness through interracial marriage.[17] Similarly, although some abolitionists argued in favor of including blacks in discussions of free labor and the expansion of suffrage, most Free-Soilers refused to consider African Americans, whom they deemed racially inferior, as equal political and economic partners in their vision of a world beyond slavery.

A few abolitionists in Kansas, however, firmly supported the idea of enfranchising blacks and incorporating them into free-state civic and political life. Abelard Guthrie himself fought simultaneously for Indian and African American rights at the free-state convention in Topeka in the fall of 1858.[18] But before the theory of black free labor could be put into practice, African Americans had to attain their freedom. The struggle between proslavery and antislavery forces in Kansas focused on this central question: Would Kansas soil be preserved for free labor farming or would the southern plantocracy spread beyond Missouri's borders?

The history of slavery in Kansas reaches back to the preterritorial period. According to historian Kevin Abing, Reverend Thomas Johnson, who ran the Shawnee Methodist Mission, "introduced slavery into Indian country, perhaps as early as 1832."[19] Slaves also lived at Fort Scott and Fort Leavenworth in the 1840s; for example, Maj. Gen. George A. McCall, who was stationed at Fort Scott in 1844, owned at least one slave, a young man named Jordan. Soldiers at Fort Leavenworth such as Chaplain Leander Kerr and Col. Hiram Rich kept slaves of their own in addition to employing some who were hired out by their masters from Missouri. Maj. Richard W. Cummins, also an Indian agent, owned at least a dozen slaves and worked them at a farm near the Shawnee Methodist Mission before returning to Missouri in 1850.[20] But the largest group of enslaved blacks who lived in Kansas prior to 1854 resided on or near the mission, where Reverend Johnson kept slaves and Indians to labor in his fields and tend to his affairs at the Manual Labor School. As Abing has found, some of the most "acculturated" and wealthy Shawnee Indians, most of whom were of mixed blood, owned slaves; in an effort to become "civilized" it appears that many of the Shawnee emulated their missionaries' habits, including slaveholding. Some slaves also resided on other Indian reservations, where "half-breeds" such as Baptiste Peoria owned a female slave who served as his maid.[21]

In fact, it is within Indian country that the slavery controversy began heating up prior to 1854. Agent Cummins reported in early 1849 that the conflict over slavery would "be the cause of much evil among the Indians themselves," as some tribes split into factions over the issue. The more "progressive" mixed-blood Shawnee, for example, tended to support the "peculiar institution," whereas the more traditional tribes, and those who were served by the local Quaker and Baptist missions, opposed the practice. After the Methodist Church fractured into northern and southern divisions in 1844 and the Methodist Church, South, gained the right to control the Methodist missions in the area, some antislavery Indians withdrew their children from the Manual Labor School.[22]

Similarly, Thomas Mosely, an agent to the Wyandot Indians, discovered that there was "considerable excitement" among the Wyandot regarding the slavery issue, claiming that the nation was "fairly divided upon the subject." A group of Wyandots requested a missionary with "northern principles about slavery," and they burned part of a chapel owned by the Methodist Church, South. Both agents Cummins and Mosely believed that some of these antislavery Indians would refuse to uphold the fugitive slave law and would help runaways, making them even more vulnerable to attacks by white Missourians. Mosely wrote, "Difficulties and troubles [with the Missourians] will surely beset them thick." He reported, "The people of Missouri located in the immediate vicinity of the Wyandotts, entertain, and express daily, the opinion that the Methodist [Episcopal] Church north are abolitionists, and that their great anxiety at this time, to locate a northern preacher near the State, is to carry on their religious fanaticism with regard to slavery."[23] As white settlers began pouring across the border after 1854—some bringing slaves, others bringing antislavery ideals—the potential for conflict with the resident Indians only magnified. The application of popular sovereignty was thus complicated even further by the presence of Indians, who were also divided on the slavery question.

THE KANSAS FIRE-EATERS

Bleeding Kansas gave the nation a concrete, living example of how two different political visions could and did clash as ordinary men and women put broad theories such as popular sovereignty into practice. Proslavery settlers enacted their ideology quickly and definitively; they argued that white southerners had every right to bring slaves to Kansas, and they would ensure the protection of slave property by defending this right through a variety of means. Indeed, proslavery forces enjoyed several successes early in the territory's history: They elected (however illegally) a proslavery territorial legislature, passed a territorial constitution that included a strict slave code, and enlisted a vigilant cadre of settlers who enforced the laws that protected slavery in the territory.[24] A proslavery paper in Parkville, Missouri, just north of Kansas City, argued in favor of protecting slavery at all costs, in part because they believed the "peculiar institution" was endorsed by the Constitution. They chided the Free-Soilers and abolitionists in the territory, speculating that "by robbing the South of the rights secured by the Constitution, Free-Soilism seeks to drive the South out of the Union. . . . Under these circumstances it is evidently the duty of our Legislature to take steps to prevent the introduction of such treason."[25]

One important step white southerners took to mitigate antislavery influence on the border was to migrate to the territory and transplant southern political and cultural institutions that incorporated slavery. One Missouri newspaper on the border "noticed a family of emigrants pass[ing] through this city last week for Kansas Territory, taking with them three or four negroes." The proslavery paper approved, saying, "We like to see such families on the move, especially when they are headed towards Kansas."[26] According to the March 1855 territorial census, southerners comprised roughly 60 percent of the population. The census also counted 193 slaves and 151 "negroes" out of a total population of roughly 8525 settlers (about 4 percent); an 1856 almanac counted 242 slaves and 151 free blacks.[27] Other sources claim the number of slaves in the territory was grossly underestimated. John Speer, editor of the antislavery *Kansas Tribune,* remembered that he "called upon the venerable Dr. J. N. O. P. Wood at Wichita, a well-known opponent of the Free State movement, and compared notes on our personal knowledge of slaves in Kansas, and we counted over 400 and quit."[28] In 1859 John James Ingalls, future U.S. senator for Kansas, wrote, "It is estimated that there are five hundred slaves in the territory today" and declared, "Kansas may be a slave state after all."[29]

From 1854 to 1857 the number of slaves in the territory rapidly increased, from a few dozen to roughly four hundred.[30] The majority of slaves in Kansas emigrated with their masters from Missouri, Kentucky, and Tennessee; only a sprinkling came from Virginia, Maryland, Alabama, and Georgia. According to the Territorial Census of 1855, Missourians accounted for forty-six out of a total of sixty-three slaveholders.[31] The Kansas Emigration Society of Missouri sent the most proslavery settlers to Kansas, for they understood the importance of settling the territory with men sympathetic to their cause.[32] A proslavery convention that met in Lexington, Missouri, in 1855 passed a resolution that reveals the state's fears about a Kansas populated with abolitionists: "The Convention have observed a deliberate, and apparently systematic effort on the part of several States of this Union to urge a war of extermination upon the institution of slavery . . . [by] incorporating large monied associations to abolitionize Kansas, and through Kansas, to operate upon the contiguous States of Missouri, Arkansas and Texas."[33]

As early as 1855, Missourians realized that they could not colonize Kansas by themselves; they needed help from other, more populous southern states that were capable of sending slaves and masters to the territory. Missourians appealed to their southern brethren for assistance: "The time has come when she [Missouri] can no longer stand up single-handed, the lone champion of the South, against the myrmidons of the North. It requires no foresight to perceive that if the `higher law' men succeed in this crusade, it will be but the beginning of a war upon the institutions of the South, which will continue until slavery shall cease to exist in any of the states, or the Union is dissolved."[34] Many white southerners viewed Kansas as the "key to the southwest," connecting the future success of slavery with westward expansion.[35] They worried that if slavery stopped in Missouri, there would be no hope of it expanding elsewhere in the West. One Missouri lawyer, William B. Napton, revealed these concerns in his diary: "If we cannot carry slavery into Kansas, it is quit[e] obvious that we cannot succeed any where else. The result will be that no more slave states will be created. The majority of the North over the South will in a few years become overwhelming."[36] Men such as Napton argued that the whole South must be involved in the struggle to extend the western border of slavery, and they solicited assistance for their colonization project throughout the region.

Various emigration parties formed across the South to organize the proslavery settlement of the Kansas Territory. Kansas emigration meetings convened in many southern states, like one held in Griffin, Georgia, where "resolutions were passed calling upon the people of the slave-holding States to adopt such measures as would encourage Southern emigration to Kansas."[37] Maj. Jefferson Buford answered Missouri's call for help, and he led what eventually became the most infamous and vocal of southern emigration parties.[38] Buford sold forty of his slaves to finance the trip to Kansas and garnered financial and military support from his fellow proslavery brethren in Alabama, Georgia, and South Carolina. Before leaving Montgomery, Alabama, in 1856, Buford told the prospective emigrants, "Here is your cheapest and surest chance to do something for Kansas,—something toward holding against the free-soil hordes [who attack] that great Thermopylae of Southern institutions."[39]

Buford's implication that the "free-soil hordes" were intent on destroying the institution of slavery rang true for many Kansas slaveholders. At one point, several proslavery settlers found that their commitment to slavery made their homes targets for arson. John Montgomery, an Indian agent for the Kaw nation, warned local proslavery squatters that they had violated a federal treaty by building cabins and farming on the Kansas "halfbreed" lands. When the squatters refused to vacate the land, Montgomery, an opponent of slavery's extension, burned down roughly twenty cabins; antislavery homesteads on nearby Delaware lands, however, escaped his torch. The proslavery squatters appealed to President Franklin Pierce for a federal response to what they deemed "acts of lawless violence" against their "rights of property," and it appears that Pierce and the local government officials sympathized with their plight. The proslavery men, organized by a former Kentuckian, were able to rebuild their cabins on the Kaw lands, and the government eventually bought out the Kaw rights to the land.[40]

Proslavery emigrants learned that protecting their property, both real and human, required local and federal government allies. It also required a watchful eye, as slaves began running away and resisting their enslavement in a variety of ways. Some slaveholders seemed genuinely confused and surprised at their slaves' "betrayal" and "thought the negroes loved them so well they would never leave them."[41] But most proslavery men took immediate precautions to protect and control their human property, employing both legal and physical defenses.

The white southern community quickly took legal action to ensure the safety of its chattel by enacting one of the strictest slave codes in the nation's history in September 1855. Benjamin F. Stringfellow, organizer of the Platte County, Missouri, Self-Defensive Association, wrote in a letter to the *Montgomery (Ala.) Advertiser,* "They have now laws more efficient to protect slave property than any state in the Union."[42] Kansas's "Black Law" threatened severe punishments for rebellious slaves and their co-conspirators. The Laws of the Territory of Kansas stipulated the following:

> SECTION 1. That every person, bond or free, who shall be convicted of actually raising a rebellion or insurrection of slaves, free negroes, or mulattoes, in this Territory, shall suffer death.
>
> SECTION 2. Every free person who shall aid or assist in any rebellion or insurrection of slaves, free negroes, or mulattoes, or shall furnish arms, or do any overt act in furtherance of such rebellion or insurrection, shall suffer death.[43]

Clearly, proslavery Kansans feared slave rebellion and made the punishment of convicted slave rebels or their allies a primary concern. They shared this obvious concern with their southern neighbors. Notices of slave conspiracies and uprisings peppered the Missouri papers in the border counties, and a Covington, Kentucky, newspaper clipping found in one proslavery Kansan's scrapbook claimed, "Some of the slaveholders too, are in dread lest their slaves rise and kill them."[44] Indeed, just across the border in Missouri, one master met his fate in the fall of 1855 at the hands of his slave, who bludgeoned him to death with a hoe.[45]

Proslavery settlers were anxious about both black rebellion and white inspiration of said resistance. The Westport, Missouri, *Star of Empire* claimed, "Negroes never attempt to rise of their own accord: some white devil is always at the bottom of insurrection, and this community must provide for keeping out of it . . . [those] who want to see the slave cut his master's throat, and give money to encourage such crimes."[46] Because of these fears, the Kansas slave code pertained to white *and* black settlers. "An act for the protection of slave property" passed by the territorial legislature in 1855 declared that "any free person" who challenged the right to own slaves in Kansas in print or in speech committed a felony worth two years of prison time.[47]

Proslavery legislators attempted to deter any settlers from expressing abolitionist opinions, acknowledging the potential danger that such propaganda might create if read or heard by slaves. The Independence, Missouri, *Western Dispatch* feared that abolitionists would not only threaten the security of slaves in Kansas, but also in Missouri. The editors wrote, "We have seen with concern the efforts of the Abolitionists of Boston and New York by the importations of loafers and vagabonds into Kansas . . . with a view, as we believe, of . . . eventually operating in our own state against the institution of slavery and gradually undermining the value of our property by diminishing its security, and thus, in time, abolitionize the state."[48] To further aid proslavery Kansans in their fight against abolitionists, the territorial legislature also passed a statute that prohibited any person suspected of antislavery beliefs from serving on a jury in a case involving crimes outlawed by the slave code.

Legislators armed proslavery citizens with several legal tools to combat abolitionist settlement and incendiary speech, but they reserved the most extreme punishment for the infamous Negro stealers: "If any person shall entice, decoy, or carry away out of this Territory, any slave belonging to another, with intent to deprive the owner thereof of the services of such slave, or with intent to effect or procure the freedom of such slave, he shall be guilty of grand larceny, and, on conviction thereof, shall suffer death."[49] Though the codes threatened the death sentence, the more likely punishment for breaking any of the codes was hard labor. Stringfellow noted with irony that some white people convicted of opposing the code would be hired out for manual labor and could potentially work with a "ball and chain" next to a slave.[50]

Proslavery men continued to organize and pass local statutes designed to curb abolitionist activity in the region. A group of men headed by Lewis Burnes and J. H. R. Cundiff formed a squatters association and passed a series of resolutions that were aimed at intimidating antislavery settlers. The eighth resolution asserted that "we recognize the institution of slavery as already existing in the territory, and recommend to slave-holders to introduce their property as fast as possible," and the ninth warned that "we afford protection to no abolitionists as settlers of Kansas Territory."[51] Another group of proslavery settlers met in Westport, Missouri, and passed the following: "Resolved, that we will carry with us into the new territory of Kansas, every species of property, including slaves . . . that we desire to do so peacefully . . . yet, we notify all such [organized antislavery bands], that our purpose is firm to enjoy all our rights, and to meet with the last argument all who shall in any way infringe upon them."[52] Proslavery settlers, like their brethren in Congress, declared their rights as southerners and citizens to carry slave property into Kansas and beyond.[53]

When the local squatters' organizations and slave codes proved ineffective at stemming the tide of antislavery activism in Kansas, proslavery men frequently turned to vigilante tactics to enforce their rights. Tarring and feathering seemed to be a favorite tool of mob law among the Border Ruffians. The editors of the *Independence Dispatch* warned of a "Negro stealer" in the area, noting that "a white man . . . has, we have been informed, attempted to incite slaves in this city to leave their masters." They sent a message to "all such philanthropists, who are not desirous of sporting a suit of tar and feathers, to make themselves peculiarly scarce."[54] Reverend John McNamara, an Episcopal preacher who ministered to several proslavery communities, witnessed the tarring and feathering of an abolitionist who was also "Sold at Auction." A group of proslavery settlers kidnapped one Mr. Phillips, a known free-state man, and decided to "teach him a lesson." They tarred and feathered him and dragged him across the river to Weston, Missouri, where they cut off his hair and verbally harassed him. "They cut off the hair of his head, but his strength did not fail him—he was a Samson still," McNamara remembered. "His body looked contemptible but the soul of the man was there; they could not tar and feather that!" Next the mob demanded that Phillips sign a paper saying he would leave the territory immediately. He refused, and the ruffians brought forward a slave who was commanded to "sell" Phillips at auction. McNamara recounted the scene: "'How much, gentlemen, for a full-blooded abolitionist, dyed in de wool, tar and feathers, and all?' Laughs and jeers followed this sally of humor on the part of Sambo. 'How much, gentlemen? He will go at de fust bid.' A quarter-of-a-cent was bid and Phillips was sold!"[55] By tarring and feathering Phillips, the mob literally and figuratively blackened him, turned him into a virtual slave, and pretended to sell him at auction, thereby taking control over the abolitionist as they would over their own slaves. The act functioned to not only intimidate abolitionists but also bolster the mob's sense of their own whiteness and superior racial identity. "Sambos" and abolitionists were relegated to the auction block, whereas proslavery white citizens commanded the fate of their slaves and their white allies.

In another example of vigilantism, proslavery men once again "blackened" their white victim by branding him and sending him "down river." Reverend Pardee Butler arrived in Atchison amid the fervor of a recently passed squatters' resolution that declared slavery legal and vowed to preserve the institution at all costs. News of Butler's antislavery tendencies quickly reached the proslavery community, and several men held a meeting to determine what course of action should be taken against the antislavery culprit. A party visited Butler and demanded that he sign the proslavery resolutions. He refused, and after much discussion the ruffians agreed that the best punishment would be to banish him from the territory by using a most unconventional method. They set him on a log raft, gave him a loaf of bread, and painted the letter R (for "rogue") on his forehead before sailing him down the Missouri River.

After completing the banishment, the *Squatter Sovereign* of Atchison, Kansas, issued a warning: "Such treatment may be expected by all scoundrels, visiting our town for the purpose of interfering with our time-honored institutions, and the same punishment we will be happy to forward to all Freesoilers, Abolitionists and their emissaries. If this should prove insufficient to deter them from their dastardly and infamous propensity for negro stealing, we will draw largely on the hemp crops of our Missouri neighbors, for a supply of the article, sufficient to afford every jail-bird in the north, a necklace twelve feet in length."[56] The editors of the *Squatter Sovereign* threatened all abolitionists with lynching if they dared interfere with the South's "time-honored institutions." Similarly, the *Star of Empire* flexed its proslavery muscle, saying, "We warn abolition agents as they value their necks, to keep clear of Westport." The South stood ready to defend its ideology and its institutions with violence, in Kansas and elsewhere.[57] Their antislavery opponents and their slaves, however, were also ready to practice what they preached about abolitionism and Free-Soil.

RUNAWAYS AND NEGRO STEALERS

Much to proslavery settlers' dismay, vigilantism and slave codes failed to prevent a significant number of slaves from resisting their owners or to curb "Black Republican" agitation in the region. Slaveholders complained of their slaves becoming increasingly disobedient on their arrival in the territory, and they often attributed this unrest to abolitionist influence. The *Squatter Sovereign* reported, "A servant . . . [was] induced to believe that she 'was illegally held in bondage,' and that she was on 'equality with her owners'; since which time she has been unruly, and shows evidences of discontent."[58] The newspaper blamed the slave's resistance on "Negro stealers," but the direct quotations in the report might indicate that the slave woman verbalized her discontent on her own volition. Although pro-slavery settlers continued to nurture the myth of the contented slave by pointing their fingers at abolitionists, African Americans in Kansas clearly resisted their enslavement in a variety of ways.

Perhaps the most extreme action against slavery recorded in the territory was slave suicide, but even in this case proslavery men refused to believe that a slave would act without abolitionist "coaching."[59] The *Squatter Sovereign* reported that a slave woman named Lucinda threw herself into a river near Atchison and purposely drowned. Her master, Grafton Thomason, accused a local abolitionist, J. W. B. Kelly, of tempting her to commit suicide, but Kelly maintained that Thomason's cruelty and excessive drinking had driven her to death.[60] The incident initiated a confrontation between Thomason and Kelly in which Thomason tried to provoke a fight. But Kelly refused, saying smugly, "I do not speak with men who own negroes." At this, Thomason reportedly pulled Kelly out of his house, beat him severely, and dragged him to the center of town, where a proslavery mob was waiting to administer justice for the crime of inciting slave suicide.[61] After a brief discussion among the members of the vigilante group, when several recommended hanging Kelly, the majority ruled that he should only be tarred and feathered and exiled from the territory. Thomason and his cohorts refused to believe that the slave woman could have actively pursued her own destiny, that of death over enslavement, and continued to blame and punish the neighboring abolitionists for her crime and resistance. Through killing herself, Lucinda sent a message to her master and the slave community that enslavement was worse than death.

Not surprisingly, some white southerners feared the deaths of their slaves less than their own. In a speech to the Platte County Self-Defensive Association, Benjamin Stringfellow indicated the level of paranoia initiated by abolitionist emigration to nearby Kansas. "To induce a slave to escape, involves not merely to the master the loss of that slave . . . but it brings in its train far more serious consequences," he argued. "Other slaves are thereby induced to make like attempt; a hatred for their masters . . . is thus begotten, and this, too, often is followed by arson and murder."[62] Stringfellow asserted that his association formed precisely to "guard against such fearful evils" and worried that slaveholders in neighboring states like Arkansas would also become "victims to abolition energy" and slave violence.

One proslavery man from Indiana wrote to the *Kansas Weekly Herald* and warned its readers that he heard "a big buck Negro swear he would like to be in Kansas to kill a few proslavery men and Missourians."[63]

Proslavery fears of slave murder and violence were not unfounded. In their study of slave resistance, John Hope Franklin and Loren Schweninger assert, "There were more than a few overseers—and masters as well—who feared a possible violent response by the slaves. Their anxiety was more than justified." They chronicle the story of a Tennessee slave, Jake, who murdered his master with a knife when the master tried to reprimand him for being insubordinate. They also uncover evidence of a slave woman named Ellen who tried to poison her mistress by serving her a mercury-tainted apple. The ingenious Ellen had scraped the mercury off the back of a mirror, poured it into the core of the apple and roasted it. Had her mistress not cut up the apple prior to eating it and been puzzled by the strange contents, Ellen may have succeeded in poisoning her.[64]

Two slave women in Kansas, Aunt Cely and her daughter Patsy, both slaves of a Mr. Agness, were accused of poisoning their master, who died "mysteriously" in the fall of 1856. A neighbor who remembered the scene described the punishment meted out for the accused murderers: "They were both taken down to the saw mill . . . [and] were set astride the log and the saw started. When the saw got uncomfortably close Aunt Cely declared, 'To God I is innocent.' The saw was stopped and they were released."[65] One can only speculate whether Cely and Patsy were innocent or guilty of Agness's murder, but the white community's response to their indictment suggests that masters feared slave violence and retaliation. Though Cely and Patsy evaded execution, the reaction to their suspected crime demonstrates how slave owners attempted to control resistance through intense public intimidation and punishment.

Even the threat of such extreme punishment for slave crimes did not discourage many slaves from resisting their masters. Runaways caused problems for slaveholders throughout the territorial period, although the exact number of fugitives in Kansas has never been determined. Advertisements for runaways were published in local proslavery newspapers such as the *Lecompton Union*, in which George W. Clarke offered fifty dollars for the return of his slave woman, Judy. He guessed that Judy was "no doubt lurking in the woods or about Lawrence if she has not already secured passage on the underground railway to Chicago."[66] Clarke suspected that Judy ran to the Lawrence area, a known haven for Negro stealers, and other slaves undoubtedly followed suit. Col. Peter T. Abel of Atchison lost a slave woman, Aunt Nancy, when she "suddenly disappeared—permanently—much to the surprise of everyone." Aunt Nancy and Judy may have traveled on the local tracks of the Underground Railroad (UGRR) to Iowa and Illinois, for news of their suspected presence filled the Atchison, Leavenworth, and Missouri papers.[67]

Slaves in nearby Missouri also took advantage of the porous borders to their west and north, and proslavery papers reported on their escapes. The *Missouri Republican* published a notice in May 1856 claiming that "a larger number of Negroes . . . [than in years past] has made their escape" from the state during the previous winter and spring.[68] Historian Douglas Hurt finds that the escape rate in Missouri increased between 1850 and 1860 to 1 fugitive per 1,161, a rate that far "exceeded the national average of 1 runaway for every 4,919 slaves." Harriet Frazier concurs with Hurt and also claims that larger numbers of slaves began absconding in groups during the 1850s.[69] Slaveholders often attributed the increase in runaways to abolitionist agitation, and they worried that the entire state would be "entirely niggerless" if the abolitionists kept up their activity. The editor of the *Saturday Morning Visitor* of Waverly, Missouri, claimed that the "U.G.R.R. is doing a smashing business—to the owners of Negroes especially. . . . The whole country is 'lousy' with abolitionists."[70]

Escaping north on the Underground Railroad was a constant attraction for slaves in the area and its close proximity unnerved local slaveholders. Slaves who considered running away and otherwise might not have taken the risk by themselves found extra courage when they knew assistance and safety lay ahead of them on the road to freedom. Hurt acknowledges that "the pursuit of runaways often proved a fruitless experience, if a white guide led the escaped slaves."[71] John Bowles, a Lawrence resident, boasted that the UGRR there had facilitated the escape of "nearly three hundred fugitives" between 1855 and 1859 and noted that slaves were sure to find assistance in the area.[72]

One slaveholder, Duff Green, acknowledged the risks associated with keeping human chattel near these active UGRR stations and decided to sell his two slaves to a trader in 1859. While waiting for the steamer in St. Joseph to take them south, Green's slave woman decided to take her freedom and left the city with her daughter in tow. The slave woman was accompanied by another "colored person" to the home of Reverend J. H. Byrd, who then passed her off to George H. Evans, whose home was an official stop on the UGRR. Evans secreted her and the child on a platform that lay above the crossbeams of his small cabin, where they remained for two or three days. Slave hunters searched Byrd's home the day after the slaves left but found nothing, thanks to Mrs. Byrd's quick response and her big skirt. Before she greeted the slave catchers, she spied the slave child's skirt in the front yard (which had been dropped the previous night) and hid it under her petticoats.[73]

Slaveholders and slave catchers lost several slaves because of lax surveillance. In 1857 a slave woman named Ann Clarke escaped from her master near Lecompton and sought refuge at an UGRR station located about two miles east of Topeka. She remained there for six weeks until neighbors discovered her whereabouts and dragged her back to Lecompton. While waiting at a hotel for her master to arrive with a reward, the slave catchers sent Ann to the kitchen to "tidy up and eat her lunch."[74] Her "captors" imbibed some whiskey while awaiting their reward, and Ann took advantage of their altered state to escape from the hotel. Early settlers recounted her flight from the proslavery men: "It was then quite dark. She secreted herself in a thicket and laid there till morning. At dawn she rose, followed the ravine out onto the prairie, and looked about her. A man approached her from the west, a book under his arm. She felt assured that a book meant a Free State man. It was Dr. Barker of Lecompton. . . . She acosted [sic] him, and was told how to reach his house in safety." Whether Ann knew the man's book denoted his free-state status or not, she was careful enough to consider her contacts and connect with someone who assisted her escape. She returned to a UGRR station near Topeka, run by Barker. Two days later, "concealed beneath comforters in his waggon [sic]," Barker drove her to a boardinghouse in Topeka. Here she hid in the hogshead cellar at night and remained at the Scales' house until the UGRR community raised enough money and supplies to carry her to Chicago. Ann and her abolitionist allies left Topeka in February 1857 and traveled through northern Kansas and Nebraska to Iowa, from whence she traveled safely to Chicago.[75]

Though the slave catchers failed to retrieve Ann, proslavery men persisted in developing spy patrols to combat the success of runaways in the area. Mr. and Mrs. James B. Abbott operated a station on the UGRR from their home in southern Douglas County in 1857, and Mrs. Abbott concealed "two bright mulatto boys," aged fourteen and eighteen, for two days. On the second day the slave fugitives "very unwisely" revealed their whereabouts by venturing outside, and Mr. Abbott quickly transported them to the next station. He knew that the spy patrol would be close on the boys' heels, and in fact Mrs. Abbott's neighbors sighted lanterns circling around the Abbott claim that evening.[76] Once again, however, the UGRR triumphed and secreted the slaves to safety.

Fugitives and conductors on the UGRR carefully worked together to avoid detection, because both parties' livelihoods and safety depended on the successful transport of the runaways. In 1857 Mrs. Abbott received a "stoutly built colored man of 23 or 24" when Mr. Abbott was away on business, and she hid him away in the basement. When Mrs. Abbott suffered from an injury to her arm, she solicited the fugitive's assistance in cooking the evening's meal. "He had cooked for the river steamboats, and was very skillful," she remembered. "He made delicious chicken broth with milk. It was my first knowledge that milk could be used as an ingredient in chicken soup."[77] But their pleasant exchange of culinary ideas was interrupted by a loud knock at the door. Abbott recounted the story:

> He [the slave] started, but I told him to keep still and went to the door. Two men were there on horseback [and] they wanted dinner. I told them I had nothing cooked up, and was not fit to do anything more than was absolutely necessary on account of my lame arm, and that my husband was away in Lawrence. I told them they could go to the next house and I could assure them that they could get their dinner there. They evidently didn't like it, and hung on. I finally closed the door and they went off.

The woman remembered greeting the strangers confidently, not even flinching at the potential danger at her door. She successfully detained them at the time, but they persisted in searching for the fugitive slave with a bloodhound. The dog ran into the woods and Mrs. Abbott stepped outside to look for the men, whose horses she sighted in the ravine. She developed a plan to ensure the slave's safety:

> The axe was lying there and I told him [the slave] to take it. . . . I told him "now is your time. If that dog attacks you, knock him over with the axe. Don't make a mistake and allow him to get away. It is your only chance." He took the axe and started straight for the creek through the timber. I was all in a tremble. It was not but a little while when I heard that dog give a terrible yelp. . . . The boy did not return until after dark. He said he was so trembly [sic] that he missed the dog the first stroke, but the second finished him.[78]

The slave catchers left the property after hearing the dog's yelps and Mrs. Abbott's fugitive moved on to the next UGRR station. Thanks to Abbott's quick thinking and the slave's courageous response, the two escaped an altercation with the proslavery men and the slave successfully traveled north to freedom.

Not all slaves made it to Canada, and if they did, it was only after a long, protracted journey through Kansas, Iowa, and Illinois. But conductors on the UGRR in southeastern Kansas Territory proudly asserted that fugitives were "as safe here, as they would be in Canada." James Montgomery, an active leader of the Kansas UGRR, wrote to George Stearns, coordinator of the Kansas Relief Committee, "Two more [fugitives] have come to us since my last writing. If Mr. Bird were here, I think he would be disposed to take back what he said to me on our first meeting: and agree that fugitives may be protected in Kansas." The following year he added, "It will cost less to protect them here, than it will to send them to Canada; and besides, the principle is much better. 'He shall dwell among you, even within thy gates, in a good place where it liketh him best.' Deut.XXIII: 15, 16 does not allow us to send him to Canada against his will." Montgomery identified a few exceptional fugitives and sent them back to their native states to guide more runaways to Kansas. In the fall of 1860 he reported to Stearns, "We have several fugitives on hand and more are expected. . . . When a keen, shrewd fellow comes to us, we send him back for more. As yet they have not been followed by anything like a force."[79]

FIGHTING PREACHERS AND ANTISLAVERY VIOLENCE

At times the conflict among the UGRR conductors, the fugitives, and the slave catchers reached an intense, violent level. James Montgomery and others not only harbored fugitives but also provided them with the tools, including guns, with which to defend themselves against the slave catchers. One settler reported that slaveholders who chased their slaves into the territory risked their lives in doing so:

> The troublous times that have beset Kansas have proved to be a very good track for the underground railroad—numbers of slaves have passed through here on their way to Canada. They know their masters dare not follow to take them back until Peace is restored in Kansas. In the Delaware County near the border of Missouri, however, they have tried it but have met with such a reception they will hardly try again.

Four of them tried to take one of the runaways but he stepped into a house and in coming out the muzzle of a musket appeared first and they ran when the Negro came out.[80]

Two proslavery men attempted to kidnap a free black, but "he disarmed one of a revolver and drove them both off and that after being shot in the side though not severely injured."[81] Fugitives and abolitionists alike knew the power of the sword was necessary to support the power of the pen when encouraging slaves to escape.

One man who used the power of the sword was Capt. John E. Stewart, the "fighting preacher" of Kansas. A former Methodist minister, Stewart was a close associate of James Montgomery's, and Stewart and his wife ran a popular UGRR station just south of Lawrence. The couple facilitated the escape of dozens of slaves from the western border counties of Missouri. At one point, Stewart boasted that in less than six months he had "brought away from Mo. [Missouri] fourteen [slaves], including one unbroken family, of which I feel rather proud, & very thankful that I have been able to do so much good for the oppressed." Stewart reported that he had been involved in "considerable fighting" in the process of freeing the slaves and claimed that "sometimes our success depends upon the fleetness of our horses, sometimes on a steady hand, when the revolver cracks." Mrs. Stewart endorsed her husband's violent means, and said, "What a wicked Institution Slavery is. . . I feel that I should like to burn every slaveholder up. I believe, husband, it would be right for you to shoot them."[82]

The free-state man most famous for his violent conflicts with proslavery men was John Brown, a fanatical abolitionist who would gain even more notoriety for his armed invasion of the federal arsenal at Harpers Ferry, Virginia.[83] Olive Owen, whose parents' home served as a station on the UGRR north of Topeka, recalled that Brown brought sixteen slaves to her home in January 1859. He arrived at night with the slaves concealed in his wagon, where they remained until morning, when Mrs. Owen provided them with breakfast. They left the Owen station and headed for Holton, where they were "overtaken by a crowd of slave holders."[84] Brown sent to Topeka for help, but apparently he resolved the situation before any free-staters arrived. Horace Greeley reported the event:

As they [the slaveholders] were preparing to attack, Brown and his companions suddenly issued from the wood in order of battle, when the valorous posse turned and fled. Not a shot was fired, as they, putting spurs to their horses galloped headlong across the prairie and were soon lost to view. Only four men stood their ground and these were made prisoners henceforth. Brown ordered them to dismount and give their horses to the negroes. This command occasioned, not to say provoked, profane language on their part, whereupon he commanded silence saying he would permit no blasphemy in his presence.[85]

Brown forced the prisoners to kneel and pray twice a day on each of the five days they were held captive. Brown's actions indicate that he and his slave "companions" collaborated on their escape plan. Their pursuers were clearly caught off guard by the united black/white military front that "suddenly issued from the wood in order of battle." Brown understood the power of intimidation, especially when backed by rebellious slaves and radical abolitionists.

Brown's men and other radical abolitionists like James Montgomery led the fight in resisting the Fugitive Slave Law. The federal government dispatched troops to southern Kansas presumably to preserve the peace between the antislavery and proslavery settlers, but Montgomery argued otherwise. He quipped, "It is not the hanging of a few scoundrels that has brought the troops to this country: there is a 'nigger in the woodpile.' The 'nigger' *is* here, but Uncle Sam *can't get him*."[86] Benjamin VanHorn confirmed Montgomery's claim and remembered that the "government officials at [Fort] Leavenworth often sent United States soldiers out to hunt for and capture runaway slaves."[87] Part of "preserving the peace" in southern Kansas, it seemed, involved recovering runaway slaves. But in their quest for runaways the troops confronted a well-organized UGRR and recalcitrant slaves. Montgomery coordinated most of the southeastern Kansas UGRR efforts, and he received a positive report from one of his conductors in December 1860: "The Government already feels badly whipped; and . . . *no more Troops will even be sent to Southern Kansas; and I predict again that not another attempt will even be made to enforce the Fugitive Slave Law in this part of Kansas.*"[88] The conductor, Daniel R. Anthony (Susan B. Anthony's brother), concluded, "The Fugitive is as safe here as in Canada." Furthermore, he asserted, "Nothing less than a Regiment of troops—'Proslavery Troops' at that—in every county can compel us to send them forward."[89]

Montgomery relayed his own positive report to George Stearns and felt confident in Kansans' ability to evade the troops who enforced the Fugitive Slave Law. He wrote on December 11, 1860: "It isn't worthwhile for

Uncle Sam, or anybody else, to think of enforcing the Fugitive Slave law on us here; it can't be done." Montgomery's confidence stemmed from the warm reception he received in most Kansas homes. He recounted, "We have a home among the people; and our darkies too are welcome wherever we go. By shifting frequently we elude the troops, and this is thought better, under the circumstances, than fighting them."[90]

Some abolitionists and slaves went beyond merely resisting the Fugitive Slave Law and instead advocated outright rebellion. Immediately following the firing on Fort Sumter, some eastern abolitionists looked to Kansas for answers to the ensuing conflict between the North and South. W. W. Thayer of Boston wrote to James Montgomery on April 16, 1861, declaring, "If President Lincoln does not proclaim liberty to the slaves, then the work of insurrection should be hastened by private means. . . . We boys here are waiting to hear from Montgomery and his intended course." Thayer went on to encourage Montgomery to incite slave rebellion in Kansas and Missouri: "Now is the time. Providence seems to be calling upon the men ready for work to go forth and free the slave. . . . Organize your guerrillas and pursue a line of independent operations. . . . Do not let the time go by without one more attempt to start an insurrection. Insurrection *now* not only will liberate the slaves but will help save our liberties. I hope, I do hope that Kansas can do something." Thayer argued that slave insurrection was the only quick solution to the impending full-scale war. He urged Montgomery to start the process in Missouri, a key border state, and asked him, "Would not slave insurrection . . . destroy *all cause* for further war?"[91] Raising the specter of slave rebellion, a slaveholder's primal fear, undoubtedly caused many Missourians to examine carefully their commitment to the new war and to the institution the Confederacy supported.[92]

But even before Fort Sumter, Brown, Montgomery, and others who actively encouraged slaves to escape from their masters or suggested slave rebellion caused many proslavery men to seriously question their decision to populate Kansas with slaves. One Missourian recognized the danger in bringing his slaves to the territory. "I've got some boys [slaves] up hyar, and I expect I'll bring them down," he wrote. "Reckon property's a 'nation sight safer at home than among these mean, cantankerous abolition cusses." He went on to protest the interference of New England abolitionists in Kansas, arguing, "Let Massachusetts govern itself, and *we*'ll govern *ourselves*, I say. That's right and fair; and they've no right to interfere."[93] Slaveholders already feared slave rebellion throughout the slave states, thanks to memories of Nat Turner and others; the addition of antislavery violence in the expanding West merely exacerbated their fears.

THE SUICIDE OF SLAVERY?

The intense combination of slave resistance and abolitionist agitation proved a formidable force to be reckoned with for proslavery Missourians and Kansans. By 1858, especially after the proslavery Lecompton constitution failed to pass Congress, the presence of slavery in Kansas dwindled to an insignificant and unprofitable level.[94] Zu Adams, a state historian in the 1890s, wrote a brief essay that chronicled the proslavery issue in Kansas. She argued that "a large per cent of our actual slave holders came during the first two years of the settlement, with the honest intention of founding new homes in a new state, and brot [sic] with them their slaves as they brot their horses and cattle. When the partizan [sic] strife broke over and waged around them, they were alarmed and dismayed. Many of those who had come, hastened to remove their slave property to a safe distance."[95] Most slaves who continued to live in the territory after 1858 eventually emigrated with their masters or were sold to slaveholders in the Deep South, and many of the slaves who remained after that date either escaped north or demanded their freedom.[96] Proslavery Kansans either surrendered their rights as slaveholders or returned to the South where they and their right to hold chattel was still respected. James Montgomery proudly noted that the free-state efforts in Kansas had "*widened the boundary* between Freedom and Slavery by removing the slaves further South—leaving their place to be supplied by Free Labor."[97]

The expansion of slavery had been tested in Kansas, and the results did not bode well for the South. In her book on runaway slaves in Missouri, Harriet Frazier claimed, "In the endgame stage of slavery in Missouri, the presence in eastern Kansas of a host of abolitionists from upstate New York and New England made slaveholding in western Missouri a risky business."[98] Bleeding Kansas provided an arena for slaves and abolitionists to combine their strengths, and their collective activism demonstrated how difficult it would be to extend slavery beyond its current borders. Though slaveholders responded quickly to abolitionist and slave agitation, their efforts fell short of their goal of preserving Kansas and the West for slavery. Some argued at the time that the South committed the "suicide of slavery"—metaphorically killing itself by attempting to extend slavery west of Missouri.[99] But a thorough examination of abolitionist and slave resistance complicates this interpretation by illustrating how crucial black-white activism was to "murdering" the peculiar institution in Kansas. Slaves and abolitionists refused to allow slavery to triumph in Kansas, and their joint efforts demonstrated that antislavery ideology's primary concern, preventing the extension of slavery, would be defended by men and women in the West.

In fact, as Julie Roy Jeffrey has recently shown, antislavery and abolitionist women in the North played an integral role in attacking the power of slaveholders during the 1850s. What Jeffrey's "Great Silent Army of Abolitionists" does not include, however, are the very Kansas women who were central players in the drama that she claims helped energize the movement after 1854. Abolitionist women who inspired activism during the 1850s did so in part because they were made increasingly aware of how desperate the situation was in Kansas. Massachusetts abolitionist Elizabeth Earle recognized the gravity of the battle between proslavery and antislavery forces when she wrote in 1856, "The powers of slavery are no longer content with self-defence—they are active and aggressive."[100] Earle no doubt reflected on the bleeding in Kansas, and she, like her abolitionist sisters, knew that their great silent army had some powerful female soldiers there.

3

"ALL WOMEN ARE CALLED BAD"

WHAT MAKES A WOMAN IN BLEEDING KANSAS?

On April 19, 1858, Joseph A. Cody, a recent Kansas settler, penned a letter to his "loving" wife who lived in Ohio. He reported from the battlefields of Bleeding Kansas that "the great mass of people are desperadoes. . . . All manner of evil conjectures are a[float]." He seemed particularly disturbed by the status of women in Kansas: "All Women are called bad, no high minded man would suffer his wife to be poluted [sic] with the odor of this scum of earth, and no Woman that has the least particle of care for the opinions of this society could possibly live here." He implied that women who lived in the region were involved in criminal activities such as prostitution, noting that "even Mrs. Butts is accused of the worst crimes." Unfortunately the records do not reveal if Mrs. Cody eventually joined her husband in Kansas, though he wrote to her in 1859, "As soon as my house is ready, I leave for your arms," perhaps implying that he returned to Ohio to retrieve his wife and bring her to Kansas.[1]

If Mrs. Cody accompanied her husband to Kansas, she would have confronted a number of challenges to the traditional gender roles that shaped nineteenth-century social and economic relations between women and men. In addition to more typical frontier forces such as crude living conditions and Indian conflict, Kansas settlers confronted political upheaval and the imminent threat of sectional violence; these tensions pushed and reshaped the boundaries of Victorian gender norms. As a result, new gender identities formed as emigrant men and women adjusted their lifestyles to the war-torn border; gender bled as Kansas did.[2]

Free-state women, those who embraced the antislavery cause in Kansas, experienced the most profound shifts in gender roles. These women actively involved themselves in free-state activities and moved swiftly and gracefully between the public and private spheres, even though proponents of separate spheres ideology argued that women belonged in the home.[3] In fact, many female settlers attempted to fashion households reminiscent of those back east, but antislavery women rarely enjoyed the luxuries of a truly private space. Free-state women transformed their homes into antislavery meeting halls, ammunition "factories," Underground Railroad stations, and safe houses for free-state men fleeing southern aggression. This voluntary infiltration into the "private" sphere was peppered by involuntary invasions from Indians and more often, proslavery men who sometimes ransacked antislavery properties, harassed free-state women and threatened their husbands, fathers, and brothers with murder.

Rather than surrender to their fears, however, free-state women mustered the courage to join their husbands and brothers on the metaphorical and physical battlefields of territorial Kansas. When conflicts over slavery ignited the streets and public spaces of territorial towns, free-state women met their proslavery enemies head on, attacking their rhetoric with antislavery speeches, parades, and editorials and violently defending their homes and families if necessary. Because they adopted these new roles as politicians and domestic soldiers, they lent stability and political power to the nascent free-state community. Women's dynamic involvement in the free-state fight was an integral part of free labor's triumph over slavery in Kansas Territory.[4]

The role of proslavery women in territorial Kansas is more difficult to discern. First of all, few women accompanied their husbands in the very early years of proslavery emigration, which was dominated by Missourians. Some men crossed the border only to vote in the territorial elections and thus did not bring their families, whereas others who were "bona fide" settlers chose to leave their wives at home until they established a proper homestead. Southerner Jefferson Buford believed the wilds of territorial Kansas and the sectional violence posed too much danger for southern ladies, and he claimed that part of his mission in Kansas was to secure the area before their arrival. "Women and children should not be exposed there in tents in the spring," he wrote, "but the husbands should go first and prepare homes."[5]

The white southern women who did settle in the territory unfortunately did not leave much documentary evidence of their existence. Unlike some of the literate, middle- and upper-class Virginia women who engaged the antebellum political sphere and documented their actions, many proslavery women in Kansas, most of whom were from Missouri, may not have been literate, nor did they have a history of political involvement.[6] Furthermore, the local proslavery newspapers in Kansas and western Missouri rarely published articles or editorials related to southern women and their approach to the slavery question prior to the Civil War. Instead, when southern women appear in the local papers, the articles often focus on fashion or "character," as one editorial in the Parkville, Missouri, *Southern Democrat* demonstrates. Titled "Consistency of Character," in it, the author describes the ideal woman's intelligence: "Hers is not a masculine mind; it is peculiarly, sweetly feminine . . . they ['intelligent' ladies] set so gracefully and becomingly, that they never obtrude themselves into notice."[7] With advice like this, it is not surprising that it is difficult to "notice" southern women in Kansas, and their unfortunate silence indicates that a strong belief in patriarchy persisted among proslavery settlers in the territory.[8]

Patriarchy was less stable in free-state communities, however. Women such as Margaret Wood, an abolitionist originally from Ohio, broke down the boundaries between public and private, sometimes acting in ways that posed radical challenges to patriarchal ideals. However, these same women often justified their radical behavior with more conventional notions of women's superior religious and moral strength. By couching their activism in service to "God and Truth," they eluded accusations of improper womanhood and reformulated a gender code that endorsed female participation in sectional politics, even to the point of embracing violence.[9]

Contrary to what Joseph A. Cody observed, free-state women were not perceived as "bad women" by their political peers. Like the Garrisonian abolitionists, most of whom supported the expansion of woman's rights, antislavery men and women in Kansas cultivated a new ideal of womanhood that encouraged independence and bravery, rather than Victorian notions of feminine delicacy and helplessness.[10] Mrs. Wood gave a speech at a reception for the territorial governor that embodied the new gender ideology articulated by numerous free-state settlers. She asserted: "Woman's sphere is *wherever* there is a wrong to make right . . . It is here to guard our beautiful embryo State from the invasion of wrong, oppression, intemperance. . . . Yes, Kansas must and will feel that woman has an influence and that influence on the side of God and Truth!"[11] Free-state women's political activism not only bolstered the antislavery forces at home, but perhaps more importantly, publicized the events of Bleeding Kansas nationwide, pulling the disinterested public onto the battlefield with them and their families.

PIONEERS WITH A MISSION

Julia Louisa Lovejoy espoused a love of God and freedom as she tearfully departed her native New Hampshire for the Kansas plains in 1856. Although one could characterize Lovejoy as a reluctant pioneer, given the tentativeness with which she approached emigration, her diary reveals a strong commitment to moral reform that motivated her move to the West. Even as a young woman of seventeen, Lovejoy recognized that her faith and principles would carry her into uncharted waters:

> I am willing to leave my youthful friends,
> For the precious peace that Jesus sends
> To the souls of those, who obey His word,
> And leave all *beside,* to follow the Lord.
> Come! who will go along with me?
> The road is pleasant, as you may see,
> Its travellers united in harmony, and love,
> *We're bound for "Mount Zion," the City above.*[12]

Lovejoy did not anticipate at this early age that she would be "leaving all beside" to move to Kansas twenty-five years later, but her religious faith encouraged her to meet the challenge of the uncertain frontier in defense of moral justice and antislavery. In 1834 she married an antislavery Methodist minister, Charles H. Lovejoy, whose cousin, Elijah, was murdered by a proslavery mob in Alton, Illinois, three years later. The passage of the Kansas-Nebraska Act inspired both Julia and Charles to transplant their antislavery roots westward, and they traveled to Kansas in 1856 with a missionary-like zeal that some have called evangelical abolitionism.[13]

Similarly, Margaret Lyon Wood grew up in an intensely religious atmosphere. Her father served as a Presbyterian minister, and the entire family moved within Presbyterian and Quaker abolitionist circles in Mount Gilead, Ohio. Margaret Lyon became involved in the Underground Railroad through her father's antislavery connections and eventually met her husband through these very same associations. Samuel N. Wood was a Quaker and a conductor for the Underground Railroad, and Margaret became attracted to her future husband after hearing of his mythologized run-in with the southern border patrols. According to his biography, Sam Wood's wagon was stopped by the Kentucky-Ohio border patrol in 1849, and the guards inquired about the content of his wagon. Sam replied, "I've got a wagon full of runaway 'niggers' in the back."[14] The patrolmen laughed in disbelief and waved Wood and his cargo of runaway slaves across the border into freedom. Wood delivered the slaves to the Lyon home, met Margaret, and the two began a long and tempestuous life together (they were married in 1850).[15] After publicly proclaiming their commitment to abolitionism at a gathering held to protest the Kansas-Nebraska Act of 1854, they left Mount Gilead for the Kansas Territory one month after the act's passage.

Susan Wattles also hailed from an abolitionist background in Ohio. Based in Cincinnati, Susan and her husband, Augustus, traveled throughout the country, soliciting financial support for the establishment of a school for free blacks in southern Ohio. After opening the Free Colored School in Cincinnati, the Wattles migrated to Kansas and worked to establish similar institutions in the new territory. In addition to laying the groundwork for free black schools in Kansas Territory, Susan Wattles became actively involved in drafting various proposed state constitutions. Through her alliance with Clarina Howard Nichols, a Vermont native and antislavery and woman's rights advocate, Wattles became involved in a variety of political activities in the territory. She and Nichols initiated a mass petition drive to influence territorial legislators who might endorse an equal rights clause in the proposed state constitution that favored women. While Nichols sat in the legislative chamber in Wyandotte (knitting in hand), lobbying for the word "male" to be stricken from the bill of rights, Susan Wattles canvassed the Lawrence countryside, soliciting ammunition for Nichols's battle in the territorial legislature. Both women dedicated a significant portion of their lives in Kansas to political action and became integral parts of the activist circle of free-state women in territorial Kansas.[16]

Perhaps the most famous female emigrant to Kansas was Sara Tappan Robinson. Robinson gained notoriety in part because she was married to Charles Robinson, the first governor of Kansas, but she earned a prominent place in Kansas history in her own right because of her commitment to the antislavery cause and her authorship of the popular book, *Kansas: Its Interior and Exterior Life*.[17] Robinson, originally from Boston, traveled back to her native Massachusetts several times to lecture on the Kansas question. Charles Robinson alerted his wife in an 1856 letter that she was "getting quite noted to have [her] route marked by newspapers. It will soon be '*Mrs. Robinson* and her husband, the husband of *Mrs. Robinson*' etc. What can I do to keep even with you?" Robinson had little trouble "keeping even" with his wife; he held the highest post in the state government when Kansas joined the Union in 1861. He quipped lightheartedly about the reversal of gender roles that resulted from his wife's popularity, but he complained about the events that propelled his wife into the public sphere and longed for some domestic bliss. "I should love *very much* to see you in our *own house,* if we had one," he wrote. "When will this turmoil cease and we have quiet again?"[18]

The turmoil that enveloped the governor's home lasted for several years, and many free-state women, including Sara Robinson, recorded their experiences in the trenches of Bleeding Kansas in letters, diaries, poems, and autobiographical narratives. Their words chronicled the ongoing tensions between proslavery and antislavery settlers and publicized the experience of living in the midst of a border war. Many of these personal and published narratives traveled eastward to the settlers' extended families and hometowns, linking the events in Kansas with national concerns regarding the expansion of slavery.

REPORTING FROM THE TRENCHES

Women such as Sara Robinson and Margaret Wood moved to Kansas with a missionary zeal that inspired their commitment to antislavery activism in the territory and encouraged their involvement in the politics of Bleeding Kansas. Some of the most important effects of their free-state activism occurred outside the territory's borders, in the parlors and coffee houses of eastern cities and towns, where citizens of every political stripe learned about Bleeding Kansas through reports of these women's experiences. Free-state women kept easterners abreast of the important events that transpired in territorial Kansas, and their letters and editorials connected antislavery concerns in the West with those in the East. Historian Michael Pierson argues that Republican women's political activism peaked in 1856 in part because "the political debate of that year hinged on the extent to which families and private homes had been devastated by southern aggressors in Kansas." Free-state women who reported from the trenches and their eastern sisters who raised money for them and their families helped "convince the electorate that Democratic misrule had created a crisis in the [Kansas] territory."[19]

Julia Louisa Lovejoy interrupted her methodical diary keeping for three years to contribute to the free-state effort by writing numerous letters to newspapers in New Hampshire, Vermont, Massachusetts, New York, and Connecticut. The papers reprinted Lovejoy's letters and spread information about Bleeding Kansas throughout the Northeast. The proliferation of information on the Kansas Question sparked politicians' interest in the subject and motivated several legislators, most prominently Sen. Charles Sumner, to adopt the free-state cause as their own.[20]

Lovejoy's letters dramatized and personalized the Kansas conflict as she narrated outbreaks of violence and destruction in the territory. Writing to Concord, New Hampshire's *Independent Democrat* after an August 1856 attack on Lawrence, she warned, "A crisis is just before us, and if we fall our last petition is, that our blood may be avenged, and that our own New England, that achieved such wonderful victories in the Revolution of '76, will join her forces with our western brethren in the drama of '56, and ravage Missouri to its nethermost nook and corner, until every chain shall be broken and slavery die, without a resurrection!" Lovejoy recalled the revolutionary history of her native home and publicly declared her commitment to its legacy in Kansas. She continued, endorsing a full-scale attack on proslavery forces: "We never prayed for the destruction of men, made in the image of their Maker, but if they persist in killing and torturing our innocent citizens, let the sword be driven to the hilt!"[21]

Sometimes even private letters became public weapons for the free-state cause. Free-state leader Sam Wood fled the territory in the spring of 1856 and sought refuge from proslavery forces in Ohio with Salmon P. Chase, an antislavery politician and then governor of Ohio. Wood received a letter from his wife, Margaret, who remained in Kansas, and Chase requested that it be published in all of the Republican papers in the area. The letter "gave a graphic description of the gloomy situation in the Territory. Two more Free-state men—mere boys—had been wantonly murdered. The various companies of Southerners . . . had unitedly marched, eight hundred strong, upon Lawrence, pillaged and burned the Free State Hotel, stores, and many dwelling-houses."[22] Chase felt the published letter would serve as a useful campaign document in favor of the Republican Party's presidential candidate that year, John Charles Frémont. He recognized the power of these personal stories for promoting the free-state cause in Kansas and the Republican Party nationwide.

Horace Greeley, editor of the *New York Daily Tribune,* also realized the importance and political significance of personalizing the Kansas conflict for his readers. Greeley's paper solicited prominent abolitionist Lydia Maria Child to spearhead an effort to marshal support for Frémont and the Republican Party by publicizing women's experiences in Kansas. During the last week of October 1856, Child produced "The Kansas Emigrants," a daily column based loosely on the actual letters and published accounts she had received from female settlers in the area.[23] She skillfully and passionately lobbied for a free Kansas by weaving together fact and fiction in her account of a typical Free-Soil family's experiences in the borderlands of territorial Kansas. Child followed the fictionalized Bradford family from their home in New England to Kansas and chronicled their struggles with the environment and the famed Missouri Border Ruffians.

Child's story, though designed to galvanize support for the free-state and Free-Soil movements, also narrated a shift in the construction of gender. Child depicted her protagonist's transformation from a traditional New England housewife to an armed defender of free Kansas. Through her heroine, Kate Bradford, Child reconstructed a new ideal of womanhood that endorsed feminine independence, bravery, and violence in self-defense. Bradford defended her home and her family against ruffian attacks yet managed to maintain a feminine identity that withstood and accepted these more "masculine" tasks. Her husband, John, encouraged his wife's energy and autonomy, and Child emphasized how Kate's activities strengthened, rather than weakened the Bradford family.

Child's column, along with dozens of actual letters published in newspapers throughout the Midwest and East, produced a windfall of financial, emotional, and political support for free-state families like the fictionalized Bradfords. Elisabeth Shove wrote to Thaddeus Hyatt from Fall River, Massachusetts: "By an article in the Tribune . . . I notice that you are President of the National Kansas Committee and that Societies wishing to forward clothing to Kansas were at liberty to apply to you for information." Shove informed Hyatt, "The Ladies of Jesser Circle of this city are now interested in soliciting donations and sewing for the suffering ones of that ill fated country."[24] Dozens of Kansas aid societies formed, many of them exclusively female, in response to this publicity. In addition, female antislavery societies focused their efforts on Kansas, holding special meetings dedicated to discussing the Kansas question and to assisting the settlers there. For example, the Dover, New Hampshire, Anti-Slavery Sewing Circle "recruited seventeen new members, bought and distributed tracts, raised money for Kansas settlers, [and] called a citywide meeting on behalf of Kansas."[25] These antislavery and aid societies sponsored sewing circles, held auctions, and established monetary funds that funneled goods and money into free-state homes.

Women from Maine to Pennsylvania to Illinois joined together in supporting free-state emigrants in Kansas, and in doing so they solidified their commitment to antislavery causes in general. Helen Bushman wrote to

Hyatt that "some of the ladies of Norristown, Penn. have been assisting in the movement for the aid of the Kansas sufferers—we should like to forward our boxes (or barrels) of clothing next week."[26] Mrs. Maj. W. Mitchell of Freeport, Maine, asked, "What would be the best method of conveying a barrel of clothing to the Kansas sufferers," and Rachel Denison of Royalton, Vermont, inquired "whether a box of warm country-made clothing or its equivalent in money would be most useful."[27] Even individual women not connected to Kansas aid societies or antislavery groups became involved in the aid campaign. Mrs. J. H. Corwin of Newburgh, New York, reported that she sent "a barrel of clothing by barge . . . this evening which I shall pay freight on to be delivered . . . almost any free state family would need them all." Corwin wished she could send "a hundred fold more, but am sorry . . . what I send is from my own family. May God's blessing attend your efforts in the cause of humanity."[28] Julie Roy Jeffrey argues that Bleeding Kansas energized the antislavery movement, as previously disinterested women such as Corwin joined the cause to free Kansas.[29]

James Blood, area coordinator of the Kansas National Committee, a free-state relief agency based in Chicago, published a list of the numerous towns that donated items to the committee. Sixteen towns in Massachusetts contributed, as did six in New Hampshire, six in Maine, and two in Vermont. By 1860 the New York Ladies Kansas Relief Society had sewn and transported $707.65 worth of clothing to the territory.[30] The city of Boston alone provided sixty-four packages of clothing and/or provisions, and all towns together shipped roughly 275 barrels to free-state settlements. One contributor argued, "This supply is not a mere charity but a contribution of the North toward the support of her Free State soldiers, who have been bravely battling for the cause of freedom."[31] As late as 1861, free-state settlers continued to receive supplies from the East. W. J. Potter, pastor of a Unitarian church in New Bedford, Connecticut, for example, wrote to Thomas Webb that his congregation was busy gathering supplies for the "sufferers in Kansas." He proudly reported, "As the ladies are always the most zealous in such a cause we have undertaken to put up some boxes of goods and clothing, in preparing which they are now enthusiastically engaged."[32]

This well-organized philanthropic network of antislavery women and men helped sustain one of the most crucial roles played by free-state women in the territory, that of Underground Railroad conductor. Free-state women fed and clothed the often starving, half-naked fugitives, and the multiple shipments of goods from women's civic and church groups proved essential to the enterprise's success. Free-state women welcomed slaves into their homes, often feeding them and hiding them for months at a time. One settler remembered that Massachusetts-born Mary Jane Colman "aided in every way possible the negroes who came to Kansas as a place of refuge." Colman and her husband, Ezekiel, established a homestead near Lawrence that served as a stop on the UGRR.[33] Free-state women were responsible for preparing these UGRR "stations" for the unexpected arrivals, making sure adequate food, supplies, and even disguises were readily available. One man stopped at the Ritchie home in desperate need of a veil to disguise his female fugitive as his white wife. Mrs. John Ritchie, he recalled, "kindly loaned me her veil," and he continued on his journey north.[34]

Women's ingenuity also helped protect fugitives from capture. Richard and Mary Cordley harbored a slave woman, Lizzie, in their home in the fall of 1859. The Cordleys housed Lizzie for one dangerous night, after U.S. marshals had been dispatched from Missouri to extract her from a neighboring farm, where she had been hiding for weeks. Mr. Cordley worried about how to protect Lizzie if the marshals learned of her new whereabouts and searched the house. Mrs. Cordley and her companion, Mrs. Ward, devised a plan. Ward, known for her weak and sickly constitution, was set up in a "sick bed" and Mrs. Cordley played "the part of nurse." If the Marshals intruded the house, Lizzie "was to crawl in between the mattress and the feather bed and remain quiet there till the danger was passed." Lizzie told Mrs. Ward, "You need not be afraid of lying right on me with all your might." Lizzie understood that a few moments of discomfort outweighed the horror of being returned to her master. Lizzie's white allies never had to put their plan into action because before the marshals arrived, a wagon picked up the fugitive to carry her further north to safety.[35]

The boxes, barrels, and money that female aid and antislavery societies exported to Kansas sustained many free-state families who struggled with proslavery violence and bouts of poverty, starvation, and disease. Guerrilla warfare and the crudities of the frontier took their toll on many families, but free-state men and women used the support they received from aid societies and their families as a springboard from which to launch a political and military offensive against the proslavery forces. Like their antislavery counterparts in New England and Ohio, free-state women engaged in letter-writing campaigns, petition drives, and public displays of support for a free Kansas. Kansas women also went beyond their more eastern sisters by incorporating violence into their antislavery activism, at times even arming themselves to confront the "slave power" in Kansas. But they turned to violence slowly and somewhat reluctantly and only after political activism faltered.

STUMPING FOR FREEDOM

Female political activism in Kansas took several forms, ranging from conventional, indirect methods of participation to more overt and radical acts. Free-state women drafted poems and composed songs, wrote and signed petitions, and delivered speeches to mixed audiences that argued in favor of a free Kansas. Women who publicly stated their political opinions, whether by merely signing a petition or authoring a poem, did so at the risk of being accused of improper behavior for their gender. Female political action by its very nature implied that one rejected the notion that women's political power (if they had any) stemmed only from their influence on their husbands' political decisions. In fact, by drafting a petition or composing a song that lobbied for a free Kansas, each woman gave autonomous expression to her own political voice.[36]

Some women sustained the Free-Soil movement by writing songs and poems to comfort and reassure emigrants to Kansas of their weighty purpose. Though poems and songs may have been less controversial than petitioning or making public speeches, women effectively used these media to express their political opinions. Sara Robinson wrote the poem, "Kansas Emigrant Farewell" in 1856:

> Strong in the love of freedom, a brave true hearted band
> Far from the hearths and altars, of dear old Yankee land
> Go forth, mid prayers and blessings, mid affection's gushing tears
> And God's right arm defend you, ye sturdy pioneers . . .
> Go plant the tree of freedom, in the valley of the west
> And bid the poor and needy, beneath its shadow rest
> God's blessing on your journey, on the home where ye may dwell
> And on your Great Endeavor, brave pilgrims, fare-ye well.[37]

Robinson simultaneously praised and roused her fellow free-state emigrants with this poem, arguing that the Kansas pilgrims followed in their English ancestors' footsteps by seeking freedom in the name of God. "The tree of freedom" needed planting, and Robinson and others undertook this "Great Endeavor" to block slavery's extension west.

Like Robinson, Mrs. J. M. Winchell proudly noted the nation's history of defending freedom in the face of tyranny when she celebrated the Fourth of July 1855. She penned the following ode and sang it at an Independence Day celebration in Council City, Kansas:

Land of priceless liberty, loved and honored by the Free
Land we proudly claim our own, Land where God and Right are known
Thee we sing in grateful days, sing thy glory and thy praise
Hail the day, that gave thee birth—brightest fairest land on Earth[38]

Though Winchell's song commemorated the birth of the nation's independence from England, her song undoubtedly alluded to northern settlers' own quest for liberty in Kansas. Northerners in Council City likely related the nation's fight to their own fight with the proslavery settlers who passed laws made by a "bogus" legislature without their consent.

A group of women banded together to express their dissatisfaction with these "bogus" laws and directly challenged a proslavery man's right to rule their city. A "Petition of Ladies," signed by thirteen women, argued that the mayor of Leavenworth had failed in his duty as chief purveyor of civil law and order. Writing to the acting territorial governor, Daniel Woodson, they complained about being "driven from their homes by a band of armed men" and forced to flee their homesteads in fear of their lives. The women asserted that they arrived in Leavenworth with their husbands, fathers, or brothers, "prepared to endure the privations and inconveniences of pioneer life cheerfully," but claimed that it was impossible to live amid a "scene of general robbery and too frequently of murder." They pleaded with the governor to override the city officials' power and restore order: "We must and do doubt both the ability and inclination of the acting mayor of Leavenworth City to render protection to any citizens who may not be of the same sentiment as that advocated by himself and the bands of whose violence we have had to complain. Therefore we must and do rely solely upon your excellency to adopt such measures as will secure our present and permanent security."[39] These women demanded that Governor Woodson address their concerns immediately, and they directly challenged his proslavery sentiments by asking him to override his like-minded colleagues' policies. Though they placed their reputations (and perhaps their lives) at risk by publicly challenging the proslavery government, they insisted on pursuing their right to protection.

Some women asserted their political rights by signing their names on petitions written and signed by men. Four free-state women signed an otherwise male-dominated petition that firmly stated, "Believing that Kansas should be a free State, and that the proper way to insure it as such is to induce Free Soil Emigration and sustain it. . . . We whose names are affixed, agree to contribute in such amounts as may seem best for us . . . to relieve in part the many indispensable wants of a new settlement."[40] These women joined their husbands, brothers, and fathers in their support of Free-Soil emigration, and by doing so, implied their equality with men in this political project.

Some free-state women made the leap from words to action by publicly declaring their political convictions in speeches and parades. Independence Day celebrations appear to have been popular forums for female politicians to voice their opinions. Harrison Hannahs remembered that a Miss Whiting delivered an exciting address to a group of free-state women on the Fourth of July 1856 in Topeka. Whiting's speech was interrupted by the arrival of Colonel Sumner, who rode through the crowd and saluted Whiting and her audience as he dismounted.[41] A similar celebration took place in Lawrence, where Jonas Colburn reported to his wife that "the Topeka Company were drawn up in line to receive a Banner from the Ladies when the U.S. dragoons made their appearance and rode between the soldiers and the Ladies."[42] Perhaps the U.S. soldiers, who at the time were sent to enforce proslavery laws, understood the potential danger of men and women combining their resources to fight the proslavery forces and purposely separated the two "companies" with their horses.

Colburn noted later that year that the Ladies of Mount Oread (Lawrence) made forty-two waterproof coats and presented them to the free-state soldiers, "accompanied by a beautiful address from the young ladies." Mrs. Gates, the "adopted mother" of the Stubbs Company, delivered the address and Dr. Harrington responded to her words on behalf of the company. "Mother" Gates replied in turn and "made as beautiful and appropriate a response as it has ever been my lot to hear," concluded Colburn.[43] Gates led the Stubbs Company not only with words but also with a motherly spirit that was "beautiful and appropriate," perhaps indicating that Gates did not ruffle any feathers when she challenged traditional gender roles. Mother Gates left the fighting to her "sons," preferring instead to sew clothing and make speeches that lent feminine support to their masculine military efforts. Thus although Gates may have been treading on gender norms by speaking in public to a mixed audience, she did so under the cloak of motherhood, softening the impact of her potentially radical act.

Some free-state women went further than Gates and spoke openly about their political ideas and defied gender constructs that prohibited women from speaking in public.[44] Charles Robinson noted that his wife made quite a splash in the Chicago papers when she lectured on the Kansas question there.[45] Like Sara Robinson, Clarina Nichols traveled throughout the country to lecture and garner support for Kansas settlers. Reporting from Elmira, New York, Nichols wrote to Thaddeus Hyatt that in Pennsylvania she could not find "a house that would hold (standing) all the people who came to hear me on Kansas. The people are *awake*." Nichols suggested to Hyatt that he employ Susan B. Anthony to lecture and gather money for the free-state movement. She wrote that Anthony had "the executive ability and the experience admirably adapted to the work. . . . She has a brother in the Free State army in Kansas and if I take the post you propose I would solicit her as my right hand woman."[46] Though Anthony was too busy to join the speaking tour, Hyatt conscripted Nichols and other women to spread the word about tyranny in Kansas, and their lectures likely disturbed many audience members' ideals about gender and politics. Nichols remembered that several men verbalized their "conscientious scruples as to the propriety of women speaking in public," but she managed to deliver over fifty lectures in the fall of 1856.[47]

Some women's political opinions not only challenged traditional gender roles, but possibly disrupted their marriages as well. A free-state newspaper, the *Kansas Republican*, reprinted an account of one woman who expressed her opinions forcefully, even though they differed from her husband's. Several free-state emigrants boarded at the woman's hotel and recorded their spirited conversation with her: "Our landlady was not only a good cook, but a shrewd politician. . . . 'My husband,' said she, 'is a National Democrat,—would follow the party to perdition, I suppose—but I tell him that this National Democracy has been at the bottom of all our troubles here in Kansas.'" This woman not only had the gumption to share her political views with a group of strange men, but she boldly affirmed her disagreement with her husband. She persisted in this course and told them, "After suffering everything for three years, they ask us to *humble* to those bogus laws, and to go in and act with these National Democrats. For one, I would fight it out for fifty years, before I would do it."[48] The "landlady politician" refused to obey the laws passed by the proslavery legislature and even claimed she would "fight it out" before submitting to the lawmakers' position. One wonders what kind of fights occurred inside this woman's home, if in fact her husband defended the opposite political position.

RELUCTANT RECRUITS

Although these women embraced their new role as voices for Free-Soil politics and accepted the potential challenge their actions posed to their status as "true women," it appears that some free-state women and the majority of proslavery women were reluctant to challenge traditional gender
roles. Hannah Anderson Ropes traveled to Kansas in the spring of 1855 and
published an anthology of the letters she wrote to her mother while in the
territory. In *Six Months in Kansas, by a Lady*, Ropes demonstrates that she
adhered to Victorian gender norms whenever possible and left the defense
of her cabin and her body to free-state men. While at home with her sickly
daughter, she comported herself in keeping with the traditional model of
male protector and female victim. News of the "Wakarusa War" reached
Ropes in November 1855, and her male relatives instructed her in the gendered etiquette of war: "My orders are, if fire-arms sound like battle, to
place Alice and myself as near the floor as possible, and be well covered
with blankets. We already have one bullet in the wall, and, since that, one
struck the 'shakes' close by the bed's head and glanced off. Now, for the
first time, I begin to take an interest in Lawrence, as a city. . . . How well
her men bear themselves."[49] Ropes wondered how well Lawrence's men
"bore themselves" and their arms because she depended on their marksmanship for protection. Ropes cast women as passive, would-be victims
of southern male violence who relied on free-state men to shield and protect them.

The belief that women were helpless victims who were in need of
male protection pervaded the proslavery newspapers on the border. Several poems published in papers in the Missouri border counties construct
women as submissive and docile, and the authors appear to encourage and
laud these qualities. The "Farmer's Daughter," a poem published in the Liberty, Missouri, *Democratic Platform*, praises the ideal qualities of a farm
maiden: "The timid fawn is not more wild, nor yet more gay and free. The
lily's cup is not more pure, in all its purity. . . . There's none more pure and
free than she, the farmer's peerless daughter." Another poem, "To Kate
Upon Her Bridle," printed a month later in the same paper, affirms the
ideal white southern woman:

> In thy pure and gentle beauty, thou art standing by the side
> Of him thy young heart's chosen one—A proud and happy bride!
> Life should be full of beauty to one so bright as thou;

And may it ever prove to thee as fairy-hues as now:

But should the world grow weary and chill they heart-strings warm,

Thou'lt have a brave heart near thee, to shield thee from the storm.[50]

Both poems cast women as weak and dependent on men for protection from the pain and danger of the outside world. Kate leans on her groom's arm, never drawing on her own strength as long as she has a man to protect her, and she need never step outside her prescribed place by his side.

A poem in Westport, Missouri's *Star of Empire* provides "delicate hints for indelicate ladies" and instructs women to literally stay in their places unless given permission by a man to do otherwise. The poem derides women who assert themselves by asking and expecting men to give up their seats to women in churches and railcars. The author writes,

Never, girls, disturb a lecture, church or hall, where'er you go

. . . respect the rights of others—this is 'Woman's Rights,' don't you know.

Never ask a man abruptly to resign his chosen place;

if it's offered, thank him kindly, with a smile upon your face.

The author refers to women as "ladies" throughout the body of the poem until the above stanzas, when he directly addresses them and reprimands them as "girls." In an article in the same paper later that year, the author comments on the character of a lady: "She is all simplicity, a creature soft and mild; / though on the eve of woman-hood, in heart a very child."[51] According to these authors, ideal southern women were simple, obedient girls who dared not question their place in society.

Encouraging white southerners on the border to maintain traditional gender roles was an important project for these papers; with abolitionists looming in the West and threatening one of the South's foundational institutions, some comfort and reassurance could be found in conventional gender roles. Moreover, the few pieces of evidence that exist about proslavery women in the 1850s suggest that they responded favorably to the advice these papers gave their Missouri readers. Lucinda Ashton settled just north and east of Atchison, Kansas, in 1855. She, her husband, and the family slaves ran a farm, but even in the face of frontier hardship, "the dual-sphere ideology remained intact in the Ashton household." Lucinda supervised the domestic chores performed by her slaves, and she maintained a strict division between her own and her husband's family duties.

In fact, it appears that Ashton was wholly dependent not only on her husband but also on her slaves. When slavery was abolished, she complained about having to work and lamented that "there had always been someone to comb her hair and tie her shoes." Similarly, when Maryland native Ellen Bell Tootle married in 1862 in St. Joseph, Missouri, she entered into a strictly patriarchal relationship that was acutely obvious during her honeymoon trip across the Great Plains to Colorado. As the newlyweds traveled cross-country in a covered wagon, Mr. Tootle assumed that his wife was incapable of functioning outside her domestic sphere and insisted on supervising her every move, even her cooking. Mrs. Tootle recorded her experience in her diary: "Mr. Tootle says I can not do anything but talk, so would not trust me to make coffee."[52] Mrs. Tootle watched her husband make a bad pot of coffee, knowing that she could improve on his effort, but did not question his right to make it. These southern couples relied on the comfort of traditional patriarchal relations to carry them through frontier hardships and uncertainty. Better to drink bad coffee than disrupt time-honored institutions such as slavery and patriarchy.

Many women on the Kansas-Missouri border initially relied on the trusted standard of patriarchy for comfort and protection, but as news of atrocities committed by guerrilla forces instilled terror in the community, some women began to realize that they had to learn to protect themselves. Sara Robinson cited a particularly brutal example of the danger some women faced. She recounted an incident when a free-state woman from Indiana "was carried from her home a mile and a half, by four ruffians, her tongue drawn out of her mouth as far as possible, and cords tied tightly around it. Her arms were pinioned, and she was otherwise so wantonly abused, that for days her life was despaired of."[53] The ruffians' decision to tie this woman's tongue suggests that the men feared the power of female speech. Unfortunately, Robinson's account fails to disclose the mob's precise motivation for attacking the woman, but she mentions that "Atchison's ruffian band" had been attacking settlers in the area who criticized the recent murder of an abolitionist. So it is possible that this woman was similarly indicted. That she was "wantonly abused" probably indicates sexual abuse, a punishment in keeping with the men's desire to control this apparently unruly woman.[54]

The anxiety produced by these reports was heightened by free-state women's acute vulnerability to surprise ruffian invasions, but many women gradually learned to conquer their fears and began to confront the intruders with confidence. Wilson Shannon, a proslavery governor appointed by President Franklin Pierce, got drunk and entered one woman's home in search of her husband. Mrs. Hazeltyne recounted her story to Sara Robinson: "[Governor Shannon] staggered around, holding upon the furniture to keep himself from falling. He was busy feeling mattresses, peeping into closets, emptying trunks, looking under beds and used language which shocked those obliged to listen . . . he inquired of Mrs. Hazeltyne for her husband; upon her replying that she did not know where he was, the Governor of Kansas Territory replied, 'I'll cut his d—d black heart out of him, and yours too, madam, if you don't take care.'[55] According to Shannon, "taking care" meant obeying his orders, but Mrs. Hazeltyne defied Shannon and thwarted the gendered code of women's submission to men, especially those endowed with state authority. Hazeltyne obeyed a different code, one that placed her in the position of protecting her husband.

In fact, it appears that eventually many Kansans discouraged feminine submission and weakness, especially after experiencing encounters like the one above with Governor Shannon. One Quindaro, Kansas, woman chided her male cousin for seeking the perfect, obedient wife. She wrote, "I feel to remonstrate with you a little because you are waiting to have some earthly angel to drop into your home and become your dutiful wife. But such things are supernatural and the days of miracles are passed."[56] Rather than fulfilling the role of "dutiful wife," it seems that many free-state women spoke and acted as they desired, without respect for gendered propriety. Miss Kellogg, a schoolteacher in Lawrence, embroiled herself in a conflict between one of her male students and the boy's father. Sylvester Clarke recorded the event in his diary, calling it a "terrible excitement." According to Clarke, after Miss Kellogg disciplined a boy in her class by whipping him, the boy's father pursued and "insulted her, using threatening and abusive language. The citizens of Lawrence turned out en masse to protect Miss Kellogg, and . . . after considerable loud talk both parties quieted down and left the street."[57] Clarke described Kellogg as a "pretty, sprightly, [and] loquacious" woman, indicating that she most likely expressed her opinions openly, and her punishment of the boy indicates that she backed up her opinions with force. What is most fascinating about this event is the level of support expressed by the community for this brazen woman. Not only did they protect her from the boy's father and his threats, but they forced him to accept her decision to punish his son.

Another woman, Elvira Cody, elided definitions of the dutiful, submissive female when she traveled to Kansas as a single, unmarried woman and likely did so against her parents' wishes. Cody seemed impervious to the dangers that swirled around her in Bleeding Kansas. She wrote to her parents that Kansas was "a beautiful and excellent place to live" and assured them that she had "seen no hardships to alarm or discourage me in the least. Everything is novel, adventurous and delightful." She even noted that she saw "plenty of well dressed ladies everywhere—I am not the only adventuress I assure you."[58] Acknowledging that the frontier was not a typical destination for a young, single woman, Cody calmed her parents' fears with reports that daring ladies, and "well dressed" ones at that, abounded in the territory. Perhaps Cody and other free-state women were able to venture across gendered boundaries because the presence of Indian and black women reassured them that they were "civilized" white women, even if they did not adhere to traditional gender codes.

A short editorial in the *Kansas Republican* reinforces the notion that free-staters supported a conception of womanhood that embraced women's assertiveness, strength, and independence. The male editors advised, "Never shrink from a woman of strong sense. . . . You may trust her, for she knows the value of your confidence; you may consult her, for she is able to advise, and does so at once, with the firmness of reason and the consideration of affection."[59] Free-state women—women of "strong sense"— were eventually solicited for advice and assistance in the moral *and* military fight for Kansas's freedom.[60]

GENDERED DISGUISES

Though many free-state female settlers clearly transgressed traditional gender codes, they were able to capitalize on the perception that they, like their southern counterparts, still observed more conventional gender boundaries. Many women were able to protect their male relatives from dangerous proslavery men because of this misperception. Charles Chase wrote to the Sycamore, Illinois, *True Republican and Sentinel* about his experiences in the region during this turbulent era and challenged the idea that men always protected women. He reported, "In this country the old notion that men are the protectors of women has exploded, the tables are turned, men are now the weaker vessels and the woman the protector."[61] Women, by virtue of their perceived gender identity, projected an air of innocence and pacifism that often shielded men from harm. Some women accompanied their husbands on the dangerous trips between UGRR stations because their presence sometimes deflected harassment from slave patrols. Because white southerners believed women could not and would not partake in things military and masculine, they frequently overlooked free-state woman's role in the sectional conflict in Kansas.[62]

Northerners thus gained a military advantage and a degree of security by manipulating southern and national gender codes. For example, during the "Wakarusa War" in November 1855, free-state fighters ran out of ammunition and needed more gunpowder to defend their position. Their only remaining ammunition stores were located inside a guarded circle of Missourians, so they sent two messengers inside to solicit assistance. Margaret Wood and Mrs. George Brown answered the call of duty and rode in their buggy to retrieve the hidden ammunition: "Two kegs of powder were hidden under the buggy seat. Pillow slips were tied under their skirts, partly filled with the powder, bars of lead were concealed in their stockings, bullet molds, caps, gun wipers and cartridges stowed away in their waists and sleeves. So laden they were lifted into the buggy and they returned in safety to Lawrence, although they were halted and questioned by proslavery guards. Their only visible cargo was a work basket with knitting, a book, and some milk."[63] By using a disguise of naïve, feminine domesticity, Wood and Brown succeeded in convincing the men that their intentions were harmless. Their conscious co-optation of traditional gender constructions exemplifies many Kansas women's approach to free-state activism.

Like Wood and Brown, female spies used gendered disguises to facilitate the crossing of enemy lines and legitimize the presumed innocence of their missions. On May 21, 1856, proslavery vigilantes partially destroyed the town of Lawrence, the free-state settlers' nascent antislavery community, by burning the Free State Hotel and several other buildings and homes. Helen M. Hutchinson rode to Kansas City with "certain documents of value to the cause of free soil" on May 23, 1856, shortly after the Sack of Lawrence. She left the antislavery town "having secreted the papers about her person," and though intercepted by border patrols, she safely delivered them to Kansas City.[64] Her ability to evade suspicion related almost entirely to her seemingly innocent gender, and her services proved vital to the free-state war effort. Luckily for Hutchinson and her free-state allies, gender disguised her clandestine purpose and the battle plans were effectively transmitted.

Women's communication networks often carried news of impending proslavery invasions and facilitated free-state preparation for conflict. Tom Stearns's wife and her friends were known to "gather the news around and keep us posted," according to A. G. Patrick, who lived near the Stearns claim. Patrick and his male peers benefited from this advance information, and some left their claims to go into hiding on receipt of bad news. "The women one day gave us to understand that something was up, and possibly it would be advisable for us to be absent," they remembered.[65] When the ruffians arrived, they found no men present and the women professed ignorance of their whereabouts.

Kansas women often acted as decoys or created strategic diversions while "wanted" male free-staters remained hidden from their proslavery pursuers. In one instance, a group of proslavery men were searching for a free-state officer, Captain Walker, who had hidden himself in a ravine but had left his horse in full view his enemies. In an effort to secure Walker's safety and retain the horse, "Miss Dolly Thom," a free-state girl, confronted the men and protected both Walker and his horse. Hannah Ropes recounted the incident in her book, noting that the Georgians attempted to take Walker's pony, but Thom interfered: "With wonderful tact and coolness, the little girl went to the pony and put her arms round its neck. . . . 'Is that your pony, sis?' asked one of them. 'Yes, sir.' 'Well, we must have it; the governor told us we must take it.' 'It's my pony; you can't have it!' Here they threatened her, and . . . presented a pistol. The little girl did not relinquish her hold of the pony although she was nearly moved to tears."[66] Because Miss Thom pretended that the horse was hers, the Georgians could not bring themselves to take it. Using the "disguise" of a vulnerable young girl, yet conniving all the time, Thom beguiled the men, retrieved the horse, and protected Walker. Luckily for Thom, southern men observed their code of chivalry when dealing with young women and their horses.

Although chivalry restrained most men, others repeatedly transgressed the boundaries of southern honor, especially when free-state women failed to embody the ideals of true womanhood.[67] Proslavery "general" David Atchison, a former Missouri senator, orchestrated the Sack of Lawrence, and according to many accounts, his men committed random acts of destruction during the siege, although no settlers were killed.[68] For example, Sara Robinson's home was destroyed, and she witnessed several proslavery men fire their weapons at free-state women, threatening the "d—d" abolitionists.

But the Ruffians were not wholly indiscriminate in their attack, at least according to Robinson's report of the conflict. Her report implies that Atchison instructed his men to observe the gendered etiquette of guerrilla warfare. According to Robinson, he argued in a prebattle exhortation: "Boys! Ladies should, and I hope will, be respected by every gentleman. But, when a woman takes upon herself the garb of a soldier, by carrying a Sharpe's rifle, then she is no longer worthy of respect. Trample her underfoot as you would a snake!"[69] Whether Atchison actually said these exact words is impossible to confirm, but the message contained in the speech speaks volumes about how gender was used as a tool of war. The speech claimed that if a woman toted a gun, she no longer merited the chivalrous respect usually accorded the "weaker" sex. Violence against women who embodied traditional ideals of true womanhood was prohibited; antislavery women with guns, however, deserved the same treatment as their male counterparts and proved equally vulnerable to the proslavery attack on Lawrence. In an attack later that fall, one man reported that the Missourians "fired on the women and children, who came running into town."[70] Southern chivalry tempered male violence when passive, dependent females needed protection, but not when females asserted independence and carried guns to defend themselves.

DOMESTIC SOLDIERS

Proslavery men violently threatened free-state women, perhaps because some of these women carried guns and thus were no longer deserving of manly respect (or perhaps because they feared for their own lives). Many Kansas women actively engaged themselves in the process of self-protection and openly challenged patriarchal norms that championed men as woman's sole protector. One newspaper reporter quipped, "Prepare for an awful shock. . . . It is said the ladies of Lawrence are arming!"[71] The shock experienced by free-staters must have been brief, because they employed the ladies of Lawrence in a variety of military capacities, ranging from crafting bullets to shooting proslavery men. Free-staters refused to limit their military capability and effectiveness because of a restrictive gender code that discouraged women's participation in these masculine endeavors. Though necessity and the literal lack of "manpower" undoubtedly motivated these gender-bending activities, free-state men and women's willingness to transgress social norms should not be dismissed as incidental. Free-staters openly acknowledged that their mission necessitated radical measures, and they realized that such actions might scandalize the soft at heart.

As domestic soldiers, free-state women helped build and maintain a sufficient pool of firearms for the makeshift antislavery forces. Although they conducted their army work behind closed doors, Kansas women contributed greatly to the free-state arsenal. Several women gathered regularly at Sam and Margaret Wood's home to craft cartridges for Sharps rifle bullets. While bolstering the ammunition stores, "they tried to encourage and cheer each other, listening in the pauses of their conversation for the opening sounds of deadly conflict."[72] Though fearful of the "sounds of deadly conflict" and the men who initiated them, many free-state women eventually acclimated themselves to the daily threat of violence and channeled this fear into energy for the antislavery cause.

Susannah Weymouth recalled that her fear and hatred of the proslavery Missourians motivated her participation in the war effort. She settled in Kansas Territory in February 1855 with her husband, Henry Weymouth, who was part of the New England Emigrant Aid Company. When her husband was called to battle during the Sack of Lawrence, Weymouth added her support to the men in arms. She acquired a pattern to make bullet cartridges and "made a water bucket-full." She wished "every one would kill a man—not that I was a murderer at heart, but we were being murdered at every chance."[73] Weymouth justified her murderous desires and her status as an accomplice of war by arguing that the free-staters were merely fighting in self-defense.

After experiencing frequent confrontations with proslavery men, many free-state women bridled their fear of the Border Ruffians and defended their homes and communities with stubborn strength. Even Hannah Ropes, who initially hesitated to protect herself, warmed to the idea of self-defense and grew more comfortable with the small arsenal that her household maintained. Writing to her mother, she remarked, "How strange it will seem to you to hear that I have loaded pistols and a bowie-knife upon my table at night, three of Sharpe's rifles, loaded, standing in the room. . . . All week every preparation has been made for our defense."[74]

During the Sack of Lawrence, any and all weapons were used to defend the antislavery town. Mrs. Mandell readied herself with a pitchfork as she stood guard with John Brown, Charles Robinson, and George W. Brown at a makeshift fort east of town. Brown and Robinson carried Sharps rifles, but because they lacked sufficient guns to arm all the defenders, the remaining "soldiers" received pitchforks to use in the anticipated battle.[75] They kept watch at the fort for approximately two hours and apparently held their position with little or no opposition. Though Mandell lacked the firepower her male cohorts enjoyed, she remained committed to defending her town and its ideals with a pitchfork.

Other free-state women defended their homes with more conventional weapons, including shotguns. Kansas women familiarized themselves with guns, for their husbands frequently slept with one near their beds.[76]

In their husbands' absence, women used firearms to defend their homes and families. One fictional example of a gun-toting Kansas woman represents the reality for some female settlers in the territory. In a novel published in 1856, a Kansas widow asserts that she does not fear living alone, even in the wilds of Bleeding Kansas. "I keep a loaded gun at the head of the bed," she says, "and I'd shoot down the first person that entered my premises just as quick as I'd shoot a squirrel."[77] One Kansas woman, hearing rumors of proslavery raids in the area, prepared for the possibility of a ruffian invasion: "That morning she placed a rifle in the window, and told a young girl in the family, if she saw (Sheriff) Salters coming, to let her know, and she would shoot him before he reached the house."[78]

Another antislavery woman, Mrs. Speck, used a shotgun to defend her homestead and protect her husband. A group of proslavery Missourians marched to the Speck home with the goal of arresting Mr. Speck, but thanks to his wife they never collected their prisoner. While Mr. Speck and his father-in-law remained hidden in the fields beyond a nearby hill, Mrs. Speck confronted the men at the door and scuffled with them verbally and physically until one man forced his way inside the Speck home. The Missourian spied a gun and immediately grabbed it up. Mrs. Speck explained that the gun was a souvenir from her father who had used it to fight in the Revolutionary War. She pleaded with him to return it, but the man refused. In response to his refusal, Mrs. Speck "sprang back of the door where she had a double barrel shot gun conveniently concealed, snatched it up drawing the hammer, and bringing the gun to her shoulder ordered the captain to drop the old gun and get out instantly or she would fire." The proslavery man, surprised by Mrs. Speck's sudden show of military strength, dropped "the old Blunderbuss [and] went out through the door as if fired from the muzzle of the Blunderbuss itself."[79] Whether the captain actually fled the property because of Mrs. Speck's threats is difficult to discern. It is likely, however, that the captain and other Missourians who found themselves on the wrong end of a woman's gun barrel received a terrible shock. They not only stared down death, but death at the hands of a woman.

One settler observed an entire company of women readying themselves for war in May 1856. Phil Tower reported, "*Forty ladies of Lawrence enrolled themselves secretly, with the determination of fighting by the sides of their husbands and sons as soon as the combat commenced! Many of them had previously practiced pistol shooting, for the purpose of giving the invaders a suitable reception if they came again, as they came on the 30th of March,* to desecrate the ballot-box." Although it is unknown if these women were used to defend Lawrence later that month, Tower marveled at their eagerness for military action. "One young girl—a beauty of nineteen years—told me that she dreamed last night of shooting three invaders," he wrote.[80]

Some of the most intense, violent conflict between antislavery women and their enemies occurred during the Civil War itself, when William Clarke Quantrill invaded Kansas on August 21, 1863. Quantrill and his band of guerrillas completed what Davy Atchison and his followers had begun in May 1856—the destruction of that hated antislavery town, Lawrence. Quantrill officially targeted Lawrence *men* and their property in the attack, so many women tried to safeguard their husbands and families from harm. Mr. C. W. Cherry fled his property with Mr. and Mrs. Solomon and the Solomon's two children. As the guerrillas closed in and "bullets began to whistle about," Cherry and Solomon left the women and children behind to seek shelter on the next claim. Mrs. Solomon did all she could to buy them time to escape: "The guerrillas were close by and Mrs. Solomon stood in front of their horses and tried to stop them, hindering them long enough to allow [us] to get into a small field of corn over the hill. From that field they soon got into a larger one west of the Dulinski place, where they remained until Quantrill took his guerillas [away]."[81] Mrs. Solomon's bravery and gender protected her and her family from virtual death. Quantrill's men may have murdered innocent men and boys during the raid, but they drew the gendered line when it came to physically harming women.

One Lawrence woman literally threw her body on her husband's, hoping that her protected gender status would shield them both from harm. Unfortunately, her efforts to save her already wounded husband were not successful, because the "rebel forced a pistol between their bodies and killed her husband."[82] Another woman grabbed a rebel's horse bridle and "repeatedly jerk[ed]" it around to prevent the rebel's aim from meeting its target, her husband. Neither woman was able to save her husband, but their gender and the southern chivalry it elicited protected their own lives.

Two women employed quick thinking and intelligent deceit in rescuing their husbands and saving their families from Quantrill's attack. One watched the raiders torch her house, knowing that her husband was inside attempting to elude detection. She pleaded with the men to allow her to go inside and retrieve a carpet from back home that she cherished. Remarkably, she received permission to remove the carpet and "succeeded in bringing [her] husband out under it," saving him and his disguise. Another woman protected her entire family and their property by quickly painting "Southern" over the door of their homestead.[83] By playing on southern sympathies, these women managed to escape many of their neighbors' more unfortunate fates.

BAD WOMEN MADE GOOD

Violence animated the struggle between slavery and freedom before and during the Civil War in Kansas, and the "ladies of Lawrence" engaged in both the political and military conflicts that rifled the region during its first ten years of white settlement. Free-state women were crucial to both means of attacking slavery. One settler, remembering the bravery exhibited by pioneer Samuel Walker, quickly added, "No more heroic man ever lived than Samuel Walker, unless it was his wife."[84] Free-state women's willingness to defy gender roles by asserting their political identities and engaging in the verbal and violent defense of antislavery goals sustained a political and military project that eventually prevailed at the state and national levels. The nation followed Kansas, as Free-Soil triumphed over slavery.[85]

Governor John Geary, third territorial governor and twice governor of Pennsylvania, made an address to the people on March 12, 1857, in which he praised the contributions free-state women made to the state's survival. He gave "grateful acknowledgement to the peaceable citizens, and [to] the women of the territory—the wives, mothers, and daughters of the honest settlers—I am also under a weight of obligation."[86] Geary and others recognized that women's activism shaped the tenor of events in territorial Kansas and implied that the free-state cause could not have succeeded without their influence. One editorial lauded "Kansas women who . . . endured hardness as good soldier[s]," and argued, "Never too often or too graphically can their story be told who were the foundation makers in the building of the West."[87]

"The Women of Kansas—Brave as they are fair," adopted their new roles as politicians, reluctant recruits, and domestic soldiers without entirely compromising their gender identities as proper women.[88] By couching their activism in service to "God and Truth" and to antislavery justice, free-state women evaded accusations of improper femininity and reshaped the concept of nineteenth-century true womanhood to fit their needs. Free-state women forged new spaces in which they pursued the cause of antislavery, and they formed a political partnership with their husbands and brothers in pursuit of their goals. They made every sphere woman's sphere, evading the nineteenth-century doctrine of separate spheres that discouraged women's participation in things public and political.

In addition, by manipulating southern and national gender codes, many women furthered the military objectives of the free-state forces by disguising themselves under the cloak of innocent femininity. Whether it was to transport battle plans across borders or secret their husbands to safety, women used their protected status to escape detection and attack by pro-slavery forces. Though not always successful, these women maintained their reputation as "good women" and fought slavery in Kansas until its abolition.

The men and women who transformed true womanhood in Kansas also witnessed a shift in definitions of true manhood. The two changes were interrelated, as gun-toting "good women" forced some men to reassess what it meant to protect themselves, their women, and their way of life. What made a woman in Bleeding Kansas affected what made a man.

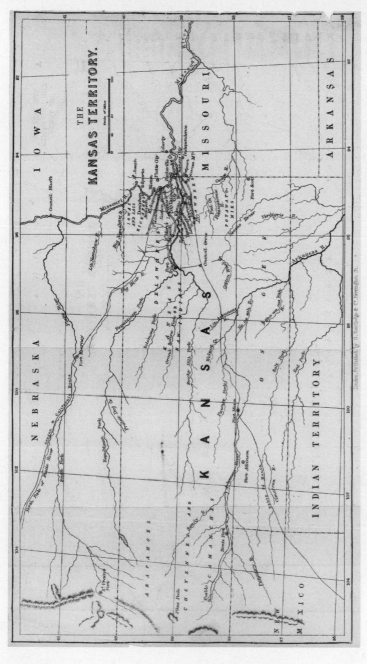

Map of Kansas Territory. The Kansas-Missouri border also served as the boundary between slavery and freedom in the 1850s. The principal towns of Kansas Territory and the locations of many of the border conflicts are shown in this 1857 map.

(Thomas H. Gladstone, Kansas; or Squatter Life and Border Warfare in the Far West, London: G. Routledge & Co., 1857)

Portrait of Isaac Brown and His Wyandot Wife. Isaac Brown and his
Wyandot Indian wife are just one of the many mixed-race couples that
formed in the Kansas-Missouri border region before the Civil War.

(Kansas State Historical Society)

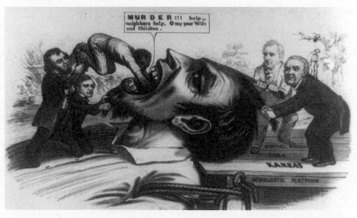

Forcing Slavery Down the Throat of a Freesoiler. This 1856 political cartoon
showed Democrats Stephen A. Douglas, Franklin Pierce, James Buchanan, and
Lewis Cass "forcing slavery down the throat of a freesoiler." But freesoilers in
Kansas, along with black runaways, made it impossible for slaveholders
to establish slavery in the region.

(Library of Congress)

Portrait of Sara Robinson. Sara Robinson, wife of the first Governor of Kansas, helped forge a new ideal of womanhood that endorsed women's participation in free-state politics.

(Kansas State Historical Society)

Portrait of John Brown. John Brown, the most famous "negro stealer," embodied a martial manhood that gained ascendancy in the late 1850s.

(Kansas State Historical Society)

LIBERTY. THE FAIR MAID OF KANSAS_IN THE HANDS OF THE "BORDER RUFFIANS".

Liberty, the Fair Maid of Kansas, in the Hands of the "Border Ruffians." This 1856 cartoon depicts Democrats William Marcy, James Buchanan, Franklin Pierce, Lewis Cass, and Stephen Douglas harassing the "fair maid of Kansas" who cries out, "Oh, Spare Me Gentlemen, Spare Me!" The feminized and vulnerable Kansas kneels down before the licentious looking Cass and President Pierce, as Douglas scalps a free-state man and Marcy and Buchanan attack and rob another Kansas settler. In the background, a free-state family laments the loss of their children as their house burns, while other scenes depict widespread murder and pillaging.

(Courtesy, American Antiquarian Society. Artist: John L. Magee)

The exact cartoon captions are as follows, from left to right:

[Woman in background]: Come husband let us go to heaven where our poor Children are.

[Man in background]: Ho! ho! She thinks I'm her husband, we Scalped the Cus and she like a D_mn fool went Crazy on it, and now she wants me to go to heaven with her, ha! ha! ha!

[James] Buchanan: Twas your's once but its mine now. "Might Makes Right," dont it.

[Franklin] Pierce: You may bet yer life on that, ole Puddin head. Come, Sis_sy, you go along wid me, I'll take Good care of you (hic), over the left.

Liberty: O SPARE ME GENTLEMEN, SPARE ME!!

[Lewis] Cass: Poor little Dear. We would'nt hurt her for the world, would we Frank? ha! ha! ha! he! he! he! ho! ho! ho!

[Stephen A.] Douglas: Hurrah for our side! Victory! Victory! "WE WILL SUBDUE THEM YET"

4

"FREE SONS" AND "MYRMIDONS"

WHAT MAKES A MAN IN BLEEDING KANSAS?

On May 26, 1856, the pages of the *New York Daily Tribune* overflowed with news about the "War in Kansas." The headlines warned of "Freedom" being "Bloodily Subdued" after proslavery forces attacked the town of Lawrence on May 21 and nearly destroyed the small antislavery outpost. Events in Washington, D.C., only exacerbated the increasing tensions between North and South when on May 22 Representative Preston Brooks of South Carolina brutally caned Senator Charles Sumner of Massachusetts on the Senate floor. Sumner had given a speech titled "The Crime Against Kansas" in which he admonished white southerners, particularly South Carolinians, for their behavior in territorial Kansas. Brooks refused to allow Sumner to slander his southern brethren and defended South Carolina's honor by attacking Sumner.[1] The *Tribune's* reporters painted literary pictures of Sumner's bruised body and the charred remains of the Free State Hotel in Lawrence for nearly a month after the incidents occurred.

One report of the Sack of Lawrence argued that the "free sons of the North" confronted the "myrmidons of Border-Ruffianism" in a bloody battle over the extension of slavery into Kansas Territory. Northerners charged that the Missouri Border Ruffians who attacked Lawrence acted "like wolves," hunting down their enemies in lawless, animal-like mobs.[2] Southerners countered these incendiary accusations by claiming that northern men simply lacked the manly courage and military skill necessary to defend themselves and their families.[3] According to these reports, southern men exceeded the proper boundaries of manhood by violently defying any code of civilized law, whereas northern men barely mustered the strength to protect themselves, let alone their property. In the context of fighting about slavery and free labor, white northerners and southerners also argued about what kind of men they were.

Proslavery and antislavery men battled over what brand of manliness would best serve the territory of Kansas and the nation itself. The southern version, one that endorsed violence and aggression, eventually triumphed over the northern definition, which championed self-restraint and moral fortitude. Thus even as they lost the struggle to make Kansas a slave state, white southerners won the rhetorical battle over the meaning of manhood on the eve of the Civil War.[4] The language of gender in Kansas articulated the tensions between the North and South, and through this lens, one can see how the gendered meanings of sectional conflict helped foreshadow the nation's movement toward the violence of civil war.

The political and physical conflict over slavery's extension also spawned a rhetorical battle over the meanings of manhood. Several scholars have constructed models of manliness in the nineteenth century that can be applied to northern men in Kansas. The "Masculine Achiever" and the "Christian Gentleman" both championed a man's ability to control his behavior, manipulate his environment, and maintain power over others. The "achiever" focused on man's domination of the marketplace and his external environment, whereas the "gentleman" disciplined his internal drives, such as sex and violence. The Masculine Achiever guarded his ideals and his property, through violent means if necessary, whereas the Christian Gentleman kept that violence in check and justified its occasional usage with religious morality.[5]

These characterizations of manhood are distinctly northern and middle class, and although they may describe the ideals of the majority of free-state men, they fall short in delineating white southern manhood. Many southern men may have subscribed to these models, but white men's behavior in the South was influenced first and foremost by the code of southern honor. Historian Nina Silber notes that "a strong tradition of chivalric and heroic behavior had taken root in the antebellum South, propagating a code of masculinity that affected the lives of all southern white men."[6] Defined by Bertram Wyatt-Brown as "a masculine ideal—aggressive, possibly rash, jealous of the family name, and protective of its women," southern honor supported strict notions of the patriarchal family.[7] The code of southern honor dictated rigid gender rules for both men and women and sustained a racial hierarchy that relegated enslaved and free black Americans to perpetual inferiority. Concepts of southern honor shaped ideas about gender, race, and social status, as these interwoven ideologies together governed social relations in the South.

These ideal types of northern and southern manhood, however, rarely coincided with reality, especially in frontier Kansas, where settlers' daily lives were punctuated by sectional violence and lawlessness.[8] A group of free-state men summed up the situation best when they declared, "We, the citizens of Kansas Territory, find ourselves in a condition of confusion and defenselessness so great, that open outrage and midday murders are becoming the rule, and quiet and security the exception. . . . The law . . . has never yet been extended to our Territory—thus leaving us with no fixed or definite rules of action, or source of redress."[9] Within such a hostile, anarchic environment, perhaps it is no surprise that antislavery men in Kansas gradually shed the doctrine of restraint and nonviolence as a marker of true manhood. As historian Nicole Etcheson notes in her research on vigilantism in 1840s southern Illinois, "Violence became the recourse of the law-abiding when there was no law."[10] One could therefore attribute northern men's turn toward violence as simply a product of the frontier itself.

But the frontier environment alone cannot explain northern manhood's eventual embrace of violence in Kansas. Faced with free-state women who wielded pitchforks and guns and proslavery men who accused northerners of timidity and weakness, free-state men gradually shed their reliance on notions of restraint and self-control in favor of martial manhood. Like their abolitionist counterparts in Boston, free-state men "struggled to balance rebelliousness and respectability," and in the process they successfully forged an ideal of manhood that embraced both violence and moral correctness.[11]

"GOD, GIVE US MEN!"

In 1855 Lucy Larcom wrote "Call to Kansas," a poem that commemorated the westward movement to Kansas, and won a fifty-dollar prize from the New England Emigrant Aid Company for her literary effort. Larcom began by calling forth "Yeomen strong" to "hither throng!" and settle the West in freedom's name:

> Bring the sickle, speed the plough,
> Turn the ready soil!
> Freedom is the noblest pay
> For the true man's toil.[12]

A "true man," according to Larcom, sought freedom and liberty, not monetary gain or political prowess, in return for hard work. Thus the New England Emigrant Aid Company, though primarily a money-making enterprise in practice, remained in theory and rhetoric a vehicle for "true men" and their families to establish a society based on the principles of antislavery and free labor.[13] True New England men pursued justice, civilization, and moral truth, regardless of whether wealth and power rewarded them for their endeavors.

Defending truth and justice required bravery, and Larcom continued by marking the courage these men must possess in order to survive the trials in Kansas:

> Brothers brave, stem the wave!
> Firm the prairies tread!
> Up the dark Missouri flood
> Be your canvas spread[14]

Larcom called on northerners to "stem the wave" of slavery and prevent its extension west, noting that as they moved westward they would have to tread through "the dark Missouri" river, whose banks were peopled with black slaves. As they traversed the prairies, northern men spread a white canvas that covered Missouri's blackness, transforming it into a place where "Father . . . there your sons, brave and good, shall to freemen grow." Proper northern men created a society in the West that not only embraced free labor but also was blanketed by whiteness. Such a tall order required bravery and a commitment to free labor ideology, values to which northern manhood increasingly aspired in the mid-nineteenth century.[15]

Sara Tappan Robinson, wife of the future governor, argued that in addition to brave and civilized male settlers, Kansas needed men who lived by Christian principles. She lobbied for a refined northern manhood, modeled after a family friend who just happened to be a minister: "We need such manliness among us, in this new, unsettled state of things; such men, with unwearying [sic] confidence in God, and the humanity of men; with whom the love for a distressed brother is more than one's faith in creeds, and whose faith is strong." Kansas needed men who resolved conflict nonviolently if possible and respected and lived to serve God. She pleaded with the Almighty to dispatch such men to Kansas: "God give us Men! . . . Tall men, sun-crowned, who live above the fog in public duty and in private thinking."[16]

In accordance with certain Christian teachings, the ideal northern man valued nonviolence and held pacifism in high regard, especially when backed by principles of justice and liberty. After a proslavery mob destroyed the press of the Parkville, Missouri, antislavery newspaper, the *Luminary,*

Samuel Pomeroy encouraged the editor, George Parks: "Be of Good cheer. . . . He whose cause is just is doubly armed—we are here for you. . . . Few in numbers but of strong faith and unconquerable courage! Strong in our adherence to principles strong in the Omnipotence of the right![17] Pomeroy assured Parks that although he was caught unarmed militarily and could not prevent the destruction of his property, he was "doubly armed" with a noble cause. "Heart, soul and purse"—not guns—supplied the ammunition for this battle, which northern men waged with "unconquerable courage" and "the Omnipotence of the right!"

Robinson noted the northerners' penchants for pacifism and implied that southerners, Border Ruffians in particular, failed to abide by such morals. "The people of Missouri call all eastern and northern men cowards, and are evidently disappointed at the calm determination of the people of Lawrence to protect themselves from mob violence," she wrote. "They do not understand how a people can be brave, yet quiet."[18] From Robinson's subjective viewpoint, she posited northern manhood and antislavery activism as "brave, yet quiet" and placed negative, excessively violent connotations on the proslavery men's actions.[19]

Even some Missourians regarded the quiet, pacifist nature of many free-state men as admirable. A newspaper correspondent for the self-proclaimed politically neutral *Missouri Democrat* met a free-state man on a steamboat whom he described as "quiet, gentlemanly and intelligent." The same reporter argued against using violence to make Kansas free, claiming, "One good man with a wife and family—one good Free-State bona fide settler—is worth more to Freedom than a dozen rifles."[20] Restraint from violence and the careful cultivation of free labor families ensured the destruction of slavery, not war.

As northern men attempted to shape their own version of the ideal free-state man, they often depicted him as a hard-working father who served as a mentor to his children and a moral exemplar to society at large. The *New York Tribune* claimed that the men of Kansas, "and preeminently those of Lawrence . . . are careful, industrious, orderly, moral *men*, who ask only to be permitted to earn their bread by honest labor, and rear their children to habits of temperance and frugality, and in the ways of intelligence, virtue and peace."[21] Historian Gunja SenGupta finds that Charles Robinson, the first governor of Kansas, typified this ideal by defending the "moral strength" of the free-state cause. Robinson argued that the free-staters were "fighting in defense of their wives, their children, their hearth-stones, and their family-altars" in addition to defending the free-state moral position.[22] Men such as Robinson sought to fashion a free-state masculinity and a free labor family that could serve as models of the ideal Republican citizen to the rest of the nation.[23]

Although northerners frequently touted nonviolence, free-state men also recognized the necessity of violence when forced to defend themselves, their families, and their principles. Kansas emigration promoters advertised for a particular type of man, a "moral hero" who refrained from reactionary violence yet bravely persisted in the fight for freedom. Writing to James Blood, member of the State Central Committee of Kansas (an emigrant aid society), George W. Hunt and Charles Stearns defined what they meant by "true men": "The class of men we most need are moral heroes, and not merely fighting bravadoes. We do not wish our war, to be conducted on the principles of Border Ruffianism—those of fiendish rage and savage cruelty. We therefore wish for men of principle and of course, for men of courage for moral heroes are never physical cowards."[24] True men, unlike Border Ruffians, used violence only when absolutely necessary and fought according to a commonly accepted code of war. Samuel Walker wrote an editorial in the *Missouri Democrat* that claimed free-state men "never acted but in self-defense," and maintained that "we banded together for this purpose [because] of the organized bands on the other side."[25]

A willingness to resort to violence in self-defense or in pursuit of justice comprised a central component of proper northern manhood. Amos Lawrence, whose name marked the famous antislavery town, wrote to his uncle, Giles Richards, and assured him of the free-state settlers' laudable goals and their appropriate conduct in war. "Those shining pacificators Sharpe's Rifles . . . in hands of *good and true* 'Free State' men have wonderfully cooled the ardor of the border Missourians," he claimed. "Our people will act *on the defensive only*."[26] Lawrence argued that free-state men used violence "on the defensive only," an assertion the record does not always support, but he was careful to present northern manhood in a way that fit the restrained ideal.

"OUR PARTY IS COMPOSED OF HONORABLE MEN"

White southerners who moved to Kansas also defended their mission with moral ardor and claimed that they used violence only when they had to protect themselves and their property, which often included their slaves. A correspondent for the *Missouri Republican* reported that the emigration parties to Kansas were "composed of honorable men" who were "not in the habit of pledging eternal friendship to robbers and murderers."[27] One man, writing for a proslavery paper, claimed that the "Sack of Lawrence" was "done with order and according to law" and praised the "Law-and-Order men" of Kansas and Missouri.[28] Proslavery manhood valued respect for the law and stood willing to prosecute anyone who disobeyed the southern version of "law and order."

Historian Philip Paludan noted over three decades ago that Americans, particularly those who lived in the mid-nineteenth century, cherished the democratic ideal of law and order: "Although hardly the sort of law and order that civil libertarians admire, vigilantism is 'as American as cherry pie' and springs from . . . the belief that individual Americans are responsible for the preservation of stability, that the law is an expression of popular sentiment, and that the people have the duty to maintain it even if procedural due process is not respected."[29] Paludan finds the attachment to "law and order" particularly salient in the North, but the same adherence to the principle can be found among southerners in Kansas. They often defended what northerners called "ruffianism" or vigilantism with the assertion that they were simply defending the law of the land. Michael Fellman argues that proslavery settlers "defined themselves as defenders of American institutions and of law and order. . . . They stood for home, church, private property, familial and community honor and male authority; they were the conservative party, guarding tradition from anarchic, invading northern radicals."[30]

In fact, the proslavery men in Kansas called themselves the "Law and Order Party," and according to their rhetoric, lawfulness reigned supreme during the various territorial elections that northerners argued were plagued by illegality and chaos. One Kansas settler with southern sympathies reported to Congress that the "people of Missouri acted upon the principle of self-defense," when they crossed the border in March 1855 to vote into power a proslavery territorial legislature. He argued that any violence they might have employed in the process of voting was necessary "to counteract the unusual and extraordinary movements which were being made at the north." He blamed the northern emigrant aid companies for the strife in the territory, not the Border Ruffians, noting that "the people of Missouri . . . were alarmed and very greatly excited at the unusual movements at the north and east, which they considered would engender civil war."[31]

Southern men, like northern ones, affirmed their manhood by engaging in activities and advancing ideals that touted law and order and the use of violence for self-defense.[32] Consequently, the Border Ruffian sought to maintain a harmless, honorable reputation as a proper southern man. One Missouri congressman, Mordecai Oliver, bolstered pride in his pro-slavery constituents and described the Border Ruffians as "men of wealth, intelligence, and high moral worth." Oliver defended the Ruffians against congressional attacks, arguing that they epitomized the best of the Old Dominion and the new West: "Behold the wide-spread fields, churches of every denomination, numerous school-houses, the high state of civilization and refinement; and then talk about the people of Missouri being 'border ruffians!'"[33] He persisted in this laudable description by emphasizing the Ruffians' gallantry and patriotism, noting in particular that they possessed the "nerve to maintain" their rights. Perhaps Oliver implied that the use of violence to defend Missourians' rights was part and parcel of a Border Ruffian's honor and manhood.

Similar to Oliver's depiction, an editorial in the *Richmond (Va.) Enquirer* portrayed the Border Ruffian as a simple farmer who defended southern rights with valor. The *Enquirer* argued that the "'border ruffian,' the farmer of the far South and West, is the noblest type of mankind. In his person is revived all the chivalry and generosity of the knights of the Middle Ages. He is the pioneer of a high and honorable civilization." Countering much less favorable interpretations of the Border Ruffian, this report compared him to the ancient Greeks and Romans who represented the pinnacle of civilized society. It was no accident that the Greeks and Romans also practiced slavery; the Border Ruffian merely perpetuated the legacy initiated by these ancient slave societies. The *Enquirer* claimed, "He is planting a master race . . . on a new soil; not buying up white men at the shambles, to remove them from slavery to capital in Boston, to make them, in a few generations, slaves to capital in Kansas. . . . Free men of the North! Go there [to Kansas]. But invite Southerners with their slaves . . .then the African will be menial, which suits his nature, and you however poor, a privileged and honored class." The Border Ruffian's identity relied in part on the existence of the "menial" African, who performed labor unsuited for privileged white men, enabling white southerners to achieve "independence," whether as yeomen or planters. The reporter noted the white farmer's freedom from enslavement to capital yet denied his inherent dependence on the labor of black men and women. The story closed with the assertion that if northerners joined southerners and permitted slaves to settle in the territory, "to be a citizen of Kansas, will then be an honour and a distinction, as once it was to be a citizen of Rome."[34]

A story in the *Kansas Weekly Herald,* a proslavery paper based in Leavenworth, reinforced southern manhood's connection to ancient Greek society.[35] The *Herald* asserted, "The prosperity of a nation mainly depends upon the *number, ability,* and *integrity* of her Great Men. . . . The mighty Roman Empire owed her greatness, power and wealth, to such men as Cicero; while Solon, Lycurgus, and Demosthenea [sic], caused the fame of Greece to resound through the world." The author worried that the nation's Great Men had been relegated to the history books, but then encouraged Leavenworth's men to resurrect the historical greatness rooted in ancient Greece and Rome. He argued that the key to asserting "great" manhood lay in fulfilling the divine mission to plant slavery in Kansas: "Must we believe that the position which we now occupy, as the practical expounders of popular sovereignty . . . will fail to arouse American minds, and bring upon the stage of action, men equal to the demand? No; There will arise among us, men of principle, men of intellect, who will lead us forward." Politicking to make Kansas a slave state according to the rules of popular sovereignty could reaffirm southern manhood's commitment to preserving the ideal of the "Great Man." And Kansas's great white men, like Greece's and Rome's, would own slaves and/or respect the right to own them.[36]

Given this apparent link between white southern masculinity and slavery, one can understand the necessity of slavery's expansion westward for the South and especially for Missourians. If southern honor epitomized "power, honor, and respect, for which riches and a body of menials were essential," then the possibility of achieving real economic success without slavery seemed daunting.[37] Slaves performed the necessary labor required in making a large profit, and owning slaves served as a status symbol that marked one's economic and social prestige. A man ruled over his castle and his dependents, and the more he ruled, the more power he possessed. By arguing against the right to own slaves, free-staters threatened the very foundations of southern honor and southern manhood. Though not all white southerners owned slaves, the threat that antislavery activism posed to even nonslaveholders persisted because slavery was integral to maintaining the larger system of white patriarchy that dominated the South's social and economic relations.[38]

Even though only the southern system of racial social control was grounded in slavery, masculinity among white men in both the North and the South rested on the laurels of white racial ideology. In the South, slavery secured and perpetuated the supremacy of white manhood, in part because it denied emasculated black men the privileges of whiteness, such as having the ability to protect wives and families from physical abuse.[39] In the North, Republican ideology may have touted free labor and free men, but it also explicitly excluded free black men from its political project in Kansas and elsewhere in the West.[40] Accordingly, any threat to white manhood in the North or the South can also be viewed as a threat to racial superiority. And because one's gender identity was closely tied to one's racial identity, the battle over slavery was also articulated as a battle between northern and southern manhood.

But before proslavery and antislavery men faced off militarily on the battlefield and rhetorically in the nation's dailies, they encountered numerous challenges and stresses to their gender identities on the Kansas frontier. The crude existence that characterized early Kansas settlers' lives reconfigured social and sexual relations between men and women. For northern men, the Kansas prairie and the sectional conflict might have challenged their responsibilities as heads of household, because free-state women engaged in economic and political pursuits that supplemented the family income. Free-state women also learned to defend themselves, thereby calling into question men's responsibility as sole protectors of women and children.

The absence of southern white women during the early years of settlement further complicated this dynamic for southern men, whose code of honor depended on protecting a passive, if not submissive, female population. The exclusively male world that characterized most of the early southern settlements also necessitated a shift in gendered responsibilities like cooking and cleaning.[41] By examining the ways in which northern and southern manhood adjusted to the unique environment of a bleeding border, one can set the stage for the acute conflict that ensued between these two groups.

"ALL THERE IS OF MANHOOD WITHIN ME WILL BE DEVELOPED"

Lydia Maria Child's serialized column, "The Kansas Emigrants," which ran in the *New York Daily Tribune* during the last week of October 1856, portrayed the lives of several New England families who had moved to Bleeding Kansas. John and Kate Bradford, the fictional protagonists of Child's story, endured frontier hardships and conflicts with their Missouri neighbors before establishing a successful free-state home. The Bradfords' cousins, Ellen and William Bruce, joined them in Kansas, but only after contemplating their purpose in life and their motivation for moving west.

William Bruce cited his Puritan forefathers' trials in the wilderness in pursuit of religious freedom and utopia as the precedent for his mission to Kansas. He connected this mission to the fulfillment of his responsibilities as a man. "My heart is set upon accompanying these emigrants," he declared. "I feel that all there is of manhood within me will be developed by the exigencies of such a career." His betrothed, Ellen, wept at the thought of her beloved fiancé leaving New England for Kansas, for she feared the insecurity and violence of the frontier and wondered if she had the courage to accompany him. The strength of William's faith and manhood, however, persuaded her to go with him to Kansas: "He had spoken so seriously of his sense of duty, that her womanly nature reverenced the manliness of his convictions; and she prayed that *his* courage to dare might be equaled by *her* fortitude to endure."[42] Ellen's "womanly nature" was inspired by William's manly confidence and valor, and the newlyweds decided to accompany the Bradfords to Kansas.

On arrival in the territory, the Bradford and Bruce families experienced numerous challenges to their gender identities. For Kate and Ellen "there was a need that the women of Kansas should overlook their own inconveniences and be silent about their own sufferings." For John, "knowing the reliable strength of [Kate's] character, [he] did not hesitate to confide to her his anxieties and fears for Kansas."[43] These women, traditionally expected to express pain and grief, silenced their anxieties, whereas their husbands openly expressed their fears and willingly shared the emotional and physical stress of frontier life with their wives. Thus the strain of daily life in Kansas necessitated a shift in the ways in which Mr. and Mrs. Bradford interacted.

The fictionalized account of the Bradford family illustrates a number of themes about gender roles that can also be found in other private and printed sources on early Kansas. First of all, emigrant aid companies such as Eli Thayer's New England Emigrant Aid Company (NEEAC) emphasized family migration to Kansas. One settler remembered Thayer's achievements in the following way: "I . . . saw how the genius and energy of Eli Thayer taught the North to win Kansas for freedom by organized emigration, against the sporadic hordes from the populous borders of Missouri who poured over the line to plant slavery."[44] Charles Robinson testified that one hundred men and seventy women comprised the first company that arrived in the territory in November 1854, countering the Missourians' accusations that single abolitionist males filed into the territory to vote and promptly left after stuffing the ballot box.[45] Whether based on fact or fiction, the perception prevailed among free-staters that New Englanders arrived in organized companies comprised of families, whereas Missourians crossed the border in all-male bands. Northerners challenged the Missourians' commitment to settling the state by highlighting the southern emigrants' unbalanced sex ratio. Perhaps northerners also wanted to demonstrate that the difference in northern and southern sex ratios implied that antislavery settlers would be able to recreate "proper" gender roles in Kansas, but all-male companies of Border Ruffians could not entertain such a possibility.

Second, family migration implied that women and men shared equally in the task of establishing new communities in the West.[46] Embedded in the NEEAC migration plan was an acknowledgment of women's ability to withstand frontier hardships as well as an admission of their importance in establishing free-state institutions such as the family home, church, and school. The inclusion of women in the migration and settlement process also implied that northern men were more willing to open their traditionally masculine domains of farming, home protection, and politicking to incorporate women. Indeed, one guidebook published in Boston defined the kind of woman necessary for success on the Kansas frontier: "When the wife is feeble . . . *she had better remain behind. . . .* If, on the other hand, the woman is the man, or is in truth *a help-mate, and can cheerfully submit to roughing it for a while* . . . let [her] be taken along."[47]

Proslavery propagandists, on the other hand, rarely emphasized family migration, and their emigration parties often attracted criticism from local settlers because of their paucity of women. South Carolinian Jefferson Buford claimed that women should stay at home until men secured a proper home for their families, and no women accompanied his emigrant group to Kansas. One newsman in Kansas attributed a warlike character to an emigration party from Mississippi, in part because the group lacked women. "I will mention that a company from Mississippi, of some twenty-two men, armed to the teeth, enrolled as a military company, not a woman with them, and not a vestige of peaceable or industrious intentions, arrived at Lecompton a week ago," he wrote.[48]

Southern men might also have appeared more aggressive and warlike because outward displays of manly violence served as a means of displaying their honor. If the duel exemplified the epitome of southern honor, then proslavery men must have endorsed the duel as a method of boldly illustrating the honor that resided within each southern man. Kenneth Greenberg argues that the concept of the duel is not limited to armed conflict or threats of such conflict; lower-class men used fistfights as a method of dueling and defending honor.[49] Proslavery men who crossed the border, the majority of whom lived a middle- and lower-class existence, likely expressed their honor and manhood by presenting a rough, warlike appearance. To their fellow southerners, arguing and fighting with other men proved that proslavery settlers maintained their honor in Kansas; to northerners, dueling behavior countered popular ideas of chivalry and southern honor, and many wondered if the Border Ruffians had checked their honor at Missouri's door.

"O, SOUTHERN HONOR! HOW HER GLOSS HAS BECOME DIM"

Though northern and southern men endured a number of frontier challenges to their social authority and adjusted their gender identities accordingly, the most extreme attacks on their manhood came from their respective enemies. Free-state women evaluated southern manhood according to a gender code that was based in some measure on notions of the Christian Gentleman, and they expected southern men to display chivalry and exemplify southern honor.[50] In her book *Kansas*, Sara Robinson reflected on her ideas about northern and southern manhood, and southerners repeatedly came up short of her ideal. She experienced firsthand the Sack of Lawrence as several proslavery men pillaged her homestead. They raided her closets and drawers, set her bed on fire, and destroyed letters and daguerreotypes that had been locked inside a trunk. Robinson castigated one of the perpetrators and questioned the viability of southern honor: "This man, so busily prying into bureau drawers and private correspondence, was one of the principal men in the 'law-and-order party.' O, southern honor! How her gloss has become dim, when her chief men, the self-constituted champions of southern institutions, attempt to gain their ends by stealing private correspondence, and pillaging a lady's drawers!"[51] Robinson wondered what kind of man would resort to such means to accomplish even more deplorable ends. Proslavery manhood stood under constant moral assault from women like Robinson, and much of the free-state propaganda claimed that southern chivalry was mere hypocrisy.

Hannah Ropes joined Robinson in noting the lack of chivalry displayed by southern men, especially Missourians. She wondered "how we, at the North, have always believed implicitly in the chivalry of the South. . . . It is not until we arrive in Kansas . . . that the truth really dawns upon us. Mother, there is no indignity to be mentioned which has not been heaped upon us." Ropes castigated the Missourians, citing examples that proved southern chivalry had waned in Kansas. She argued that the Ruffians "shoot at defenceless people with as much cool indifference as they would at partridges or prairie chickens," and she feared that not "a single cabin [was] safe from outrage anywhere."[52]

In fact, few examples exist of women actually being harmed by southern men, but many Kansas women felt vulnerable without the guarantee of chivalry to protect them from southern aggression. One such woman questioned southern chivalry after sitting next to a southern man on a train. The two struck up a conversation about the events in Congress that week, which focused on Preston Brooks's brutal caning of Charles Sumner on the Senate floor. When the southerner stated that he had no sympathy for Sumner, the woman promptly replied, "Sir, it seems to me that you are an advocate of ruffianly violence against unsuspecting and defenceless men for the utterance of their opinions upon a great public question; and as I have no assurance that you will not put your theory in practice upon myself, if I venture to express my sentiments . . . I do not feel it safe to sit so near you." In theory, southern chivalry assured women of a certain amount of respect and protection from southern men, and in practice it did provide many women with that protection. But after "Bleeding Kansas" and "Bleeding Sumner" some northern women wondered if chivalry would continue to shield them from harm. In its report of Sumner's caning, the *New York Tribune* argued, "No meaner exhibition of Southern cowardice—generally miscalled Southern chivalry—was ever witnessed."[53]

Some free-staters not only challenged the validity of southern chivalry but also placed proslavery men on the boundary between man and animal. They often equated Missourians with animals and accorded them savage-like qualities. Historian Michael Fellman notes that poor Missourians were also called "Pukes" by free-state settlers: "To Northerners, it seemed clear that the Pukes were indeed savages, beasts who had to be expunged if free white civilization were to be implanted." A *Chicago Tribune* journalist described these "Pukes" as "a queer-looking set, slightly resembling human beings, but more closely allied to wild beasts."[54] Similarly, Hannah Ropes depicted the Border Ruffians as "a horseback people; always off somewhere; [they] drink a great deal of whiskey, and are quite reckless of human life. . . . They ride fine horses, and are strong, vigorous-looking animals themselves." She concluded her evaluation by arguing that "the west portion of Missouri is mostly inhabited with a partially civilized race, fifty years behind you in all manner of improvements."[55]

Julia Louisa Lovejoy used language that was particularly illustrative of this process of constructing the Missouri Border Ruffian, or Puke, as the violent, savage "other."[56] Lovejoy commented on their violent habits and emphasized the moral, civilized response of her northern, middle-class brethren: "The Free State men, are shot down by pro-slavery villains, as beasts of prey . . . the dogs of war, are let loose. . . . All is commotion. Murder, unwhipt by Justice, stalks abroad, at noon-day. . . . This is an awful crisis, and unless heaven interpose, we shall be swept away, by an overwhelming army, led on by the whiskey-demon, to *deeds* of the blackest hue!"[57] Lovejoy implied that murder "whipt" by antislavery justice was perhaps less reprehensible than proslavery murder. But proslavery settlers, influenced by the "whiskey-demon," committed "deeds of the blackest hue." Were these deeds in reference to carnal transgressions like rape? Or was Lovejoy implying that if the free-staters lost their struggle, Kansas would fall to slavery and thus be forced to engage in a sin of the "blackest hue?" In either case, Lovejoy castigated the proslavery men for their apparent efforts to convert the free soil of Kansas into a southern plantation, where she believed the sin of slavery encouraged violent proslavery men to rape and pillage without restriction.

Even decades later, the Border Ruffians' reputation for violence and animalistic behavior endured. Reporting on the area's tempestuous history, the *Kansas City Star* published "The Border Ruffian Chameleon" in 1916, a story that asked its readers to "imagine a picture of humanity who can swear any given number of oaths . . . drink any amount of bad whiskey without getting drunk and boast of having stolen half a dozen horses and killed one or more Abolitionists." The report claimed that the Border Ruffian "has, however the happy faculty of assuming a very different aspect. Like other animals, he can shed his coat and change his colors. In the City of Washington he is quite another person."[58] Thus the Ruffian, although posited as a simple, honorable farmer by southerners, assumed a very different persona when characterized by northerners; in the North the Border Ruffian was more akin to an animal than to a quiet farmer.

In the end, northerners criticized southern manhood primarily for its connection to slavery. One northern woman implied that any man who committed the sin of slaveholding, whether in theory or in practice, lacked manliness. "Every man at the South . . . who had any *manhood* left, would desert their shameful and ignominious cause and enlist under the banner of freedom and justice," she argued.[59] This woman encouraged southern men to salvage their manhood by embracing the antislavery movement.

MOCKING NORTHERN MANHOOD

Southerners vehemently resisted any attempts to attract men to abolitionism, and they retaliated against these efforts by questioning the manliness of northern men. Male abolitionists throughout the country were criticized by southerners for their feeble manhood. The *Baltimore Patriot* questioned Wendell Phillips's manhood and accentuated his association with "unsexed" abolitionist women: "Perhaps if a civil war should come, Mr. Phillips would be surrounded by a life-guard of elderly maiden ladies, and protected by a rampart of whalebone and cotton-padding."[60] Those men who resisted the extension of slavery in the West suffered similar accusations. While describing a congressman who considered accepting the Crittenden Compromise (a bill that would have prohibited slavery in Kansas but permitted its extension south of 36° 30′), one proslavery newspaper referred to the "coqueting and coyness on the part of the attractive Mr. Giddings and sundry other belles . . . at the advances of Mr. Crittenden."[61] The story continued to criticize Crittenden's supporters by referring to them as "duennas," or ladies in waiting. The reporter implied that men who supported the Free-Soil movement in Kansas mimicked feminine behavior, and he nullified their manhood because of their willingness to compromise on the slavery question.

Congressman William R. Smith of Alabama characterized free-state men as cowardly, treasonous, and sly, and he defended the bold actions of proslavery men during the Kansas territorial elections. On the floor of the House, Smith argued that "there have been outrages in Kansas, deliberate and designed, which are without parallel." He clarified which actions he found most appalling, citing those "which are committed in the dark by the quiet but deadly maneuvering of those ingenious peace men who, with a puritanical devotion to human liberty, utter speeches which are slobbered all over with treason."[62] "Peace men," men who furtively advanced their agendas in Kansas, fared much worse in Smith's opinion than did the Missourians because "there is more devil in a sneak than in a bully." Smith lauded the proslavery men for their aggressive, violent defense of proslavery ideals and insinuated that northerners lacked the gumption to assert their Free-Soilism openly, thus resorting to less daring and more covert modes of expression. Perhaps Smith meant to imply that northerners were less manly because they failed to follow the southern gendered etiquette of resolving conflicts via the duel. If a true southern man had a problem with another man, he did not sneak around and surreptitiously assault his enemy but called him to a duel and confronted him with confidence.

One southern newspaper agreed with Smith's sentiments, claiming that some northern men not only lacked manly self-assertion but also were wholly out of their league when it came to the stuff of war. The *Journal of Commerce* reported, "When Eastern clergymen undertake to play bowie knife and pistol with 'Border Ruffians,' they are pretty sure to get worsted. Their strength lies in the arts of peace and the principles of religion. Had they stuck to these . . . the pride and passions of the South and South-west would not have been roused."[63] In other words, if these eastern clergymen had adhered to their proper brand of manhood and not invaded the southern male domain of "bowie knives and pistols," then the South might have allowed their coexistence on the Kansas frontier. But northerners eventually engaged southerners on the same playing field, challenging them to an actual and metaphorical duel, a battle between North and South.

Considering how important the duel was to southern concepts of masculinity, any implications about northerners' inability to handle firearms or their reluctance to use violence certainly indicates a criticism of northern manhood.[64] Some southerners repeatedly critiqued free-staters' poor marksmanship and their unwillingness to use guns to resolve social or political conflicts. One congressman from Missouri noted the free-staters' apprehensions about using force in the territorial conflicts. Speaking about the men who comprised one of the emigrant aid companies sent to Kansas in 1855, Representative Mordecai Oliver argued, "I take it that no men who would allow themselves to be herded upon steamboats, and shipped to the place of destination for a particular purpose, under the control and management of an association of men, would have any particular desire to indulge in the exercises incident to physical strife with deadly weapons."[65] Oliver portrayed the members of the emigrant party passively, comparing them to cattle (or slaves?) who were forced to Kansas to pursue a goal not of their own making. As drones, controlled and managed by other men who imposed their own ideas on the emigrants, these male settlers shied away from taking up arms to defend free-state ideals.

Another southern commentator criticized northern men for their reluctance to use guns and their inability to use them effectively. He conceded that northern men outperformed southern men in some tasks, but marksmanship was certainly not one of them. The Missourian claimed, "[Northern gentlemen] do excel us in the manufacture of wooden clocks and such like enterprise . . . but history has not shown, not even in the history of Kansas, that they are our masters in the polite art of rifle-shooting, either in skill or willingness with the weapon." The man euphemized gun violence as a "polite art" and proudly asserted his southern and western brethren's prowess in shooting rifles and their willingness to use gun violence to defend their ideals. Northern men, he argued, "may find that they have mistaken their vocation if they expect to conquer Southern and Western men in the open field." He attacked Puritan men in particular, and asked, "Would it not be better to cross the Puritans with a race of men who will use weapons when they are put into their hands?"[66]

It appears that southerners reserved their most trenchant critiques of northern manhood for New Englanders and the men associated with the northeastern-based emigrant aid companies. The editors of Leavenworth's *Kansas Weekly Herald* repeatedly depicted New Englanders as less than manly, even as freaks of nature. In one article, the author described a gathering of the Lawrence "Emigrant Aid" men and demoted their manhood to the level of prehistoric man: "It is more amusing than instructive, to observe the little knots of sharp-eyed, thin-nosed, poaked-stemmed bipeds, that are constantly gathering like spawn in a frogs pond; and to listen to their verbal essays about Abolition, Maine Law, Bloomer, Spiritual Manifestations, Mesmerism, or whatever their fanaticism directs their attention to for the time being."[67] In this quotation, northern radicalism, ranging in focus from abolitionism to mesmerism, stands out in stark contrast to southerners' practical, ordered traditions like slavery and patriarchy. In fact, the South's "benevolent paternalism" served civilization's needs more effectively than "free" labor, for under its aegis white male "slaves" were forced to work as mindless cogs in the North's factories.[68]

Like the free-state settlers, the proslavery editors of the *Weekly Herald* constructed their own identities as civilized, refined settlers and even criticized fellow proslavery settlers when they tarnished such an image: "We are astonished that the intelligent Editor of the [*Squatter*] 'Sovereign' should have made use of the low and debasing word D—d in speaking in defense of Mr. Donaldson's rights. . . . We most cordially endorse the sentiments of the *Squatter Sovereign*; but we deprecate the profanity of its language."[69] The *Herald* editors "cordially endorsed" the opinions of the

Squatter Sovereign, yet they censured their comrades' use of "vulgar language."[70] As the *Weekly Herald* and the *Squatter Sovereign* quibbled over the proper behavior to be exhibited by true southern men, some of their northern counterparts wondered whether free-state men had any manhood left at all.

"WE HAVE LOST THE NOBLEST ATTRIBUTES OF FREEMEN"

Northerners debated and criticized their brethren in Kansas about what kind of masculinity they displayed. A few northerners were not surprised by either the repeated attacks on Lawrence or Senator Sumner's beating, and some implied that the North lacked the nerve and manly courage to prevent such southern outrages. An editorial in the *New York Daily Tribune* quipped that "the North has always lacked manly self-assertion. . . . So long as our truly civilized and refined communities succumb to the rule of the barbarian elements in our political system, we must be judged by the character and conduct of our accepted masters." One *Tribune* reporter argued, "Let them [Ruffians] seize and imprison, ravage and destroy; if the American People do not rise to the rescue of the free-state men of Kansas, they will deserve to be execrated to the last syllable of time."[71]

Another reporter related Sumner's beating to the violence in Kansas and connected these incidents to the North's inability to control its own affairs. The report claimed, "If, indeed, we go on quietly to submit to such outrages, we deserve to have our noses flattened, our skins blacked, and to be placed at work under task-masters; for we have lost the noblest attributes of freemen, and we are virtually slaves." Other reports articulated the theme of virtual slavery by claiming that the free-staters and the northern politicians had become the subjects of a "slave oligarchy" that forced innocent citizens to submit to tyranny.[72]

Free-state manhood faltered in Kansas, leaving many men humiliated by the northern settlers' inability to protect and defend the Free-Soil cause and the families who populated the area. One editorial in the *Tribune* bullied Kansans into violently defending their state against the extension of slavery by citing a southern source that criticized northern inaction. Reprinting a story from the *Lexington (Mo.) Express,* the paper cited a Missourian's opinion of Kansas male honor: "As a Southern man, loyal to the State I live in, I would say that [a] Northern man must be base and destitute of all honourable feeling who believes in acquiescing in such a measure."[73] Even some southerners could see why the North must respond to the outrages committed by the South, and the *Tribune* aimed to use this kind of persuasion and intimidation to rally northerners to support freedom in Kansas with arms as well as words.

Though many northern abolitionists continued to eschew violence, at least one man repeatedly opposed nonresistance.[74] John Brown organized and led an attack on proslavery settlers who lived near Pottawatomie Creek, brutally killing and physically disfiguring five men on the night of May 24, 1856. Claiming vengeance for the Sack of Lawrence and other attacks on free-state settlers, Brown and his men (among whom were four of his sons) systematically rounded up and executed some of the men they believed responsible for the proslavery depredations in Kansas.[75] Though Brown denied being present at the Pottawatomie Creek murders, several witnesses identified Brown and his sons as the chief executors of the bloody deeds.[76]

The extreme brutality of the Pottawatomie Creek murders and the national response to that massacre illustrates several aspects of the conflicted discourse over manhood at midcentury. Most free-staters and northerners condemned the attack, arguing that Brown exceeded the proper boundaries of antislavery activism in murdering and, especially, in mutilating his victims. George W. Brown, editor of the *Herald of Freedom* (and no relation to John Brown) criticized Brown's antislavery methods, claiming that "his policy was one of blood, which the best minds labored to counteract."[77] Brown acted against the grain of most free-state men's ideas about antislavery activism and manhood by turning to violence quickly and offensively. Though he cloaked his violence with claims of Christian justice, most Christian abolitionists were reluctant to embrace Brown's methods.[78]

Southerners, of course, were outraged by Brown's actions, which turned out to be a prologue to his 1859 raid on Harpers Ferry. Although the South attempted to undermine Brown's significance by labeling him a butcher and a traitor, the murder of five proslavery men by a white abolitionist undoubtedly struck fear into the hearts of all southerners.[79] One popular song, "Old Man Brown, a Song for Every Southern Man," warned in its chorus that "Old Osawatomie Brown . . . [will] run the niggers away."[80] From some planters' perspectives, the "South was under siege," and Brown's actions in Kansas and at Harpers Ferry confirmed their worst fears about abolitionism. Soon after the raid, Edmund Ruffin, a fire-eating Virginian, claimed that northern abolitionists, "designed to slaughter sleeping Southern men and their awakened wives and children."[81]

In contrast to the majority of opinions about Brown, a few northerners, most prominently men such as Ralph Waldo Emerson and women such as Lydia Maria Child, lauded Brown's behavior in Kansas and supported "by any means necessary" retaliation to proslavery aggression and expansion. Child confided in Col. James Montgomery that he and Brown were two of the only men who truly understood the weight and import of halting slavery's expansion. She eloquently expressed her enthusiasm and support for Montgomery and his Jayhawker troops, like-minded men then stationed in Kansas who were known by many for their blatant disregard for the fugitive slave law and for ransacking proslavery property. She wrote, "Your name is peculiarly endeared to me by the accounts I have often had of you from my beloved relatives. . . . They sympathize with all that is good and true; and since John Brown's spirit ascended to Him who gave it, I think no man has more of their respect than your honored self." Child praised Montgomery's stalwart tactics, likening them to Brown's, and encouraged further resistance to the fugitive slave law, even if such resistance meant boldly defying the U.S. government. She went on to support the violence of civil war by arguing, "Better this fierce ordeal, than the drowsy degeneracy preceding this war."[82] According to Child, manly aggression and violence in pursuit of antislavery justice deserved a great deal more respect than the "drowsy degeneracy" of pacifism.

Like Child, Emerson valued Brown's vigilance and portrayed him as a martyr to liberty. When Emerson heard Brown speak in March 1857 he wrote that "one of [Brown's] good points was, the folly of the peace party in Kansas."[83] Soon after this meeting, Emerson and thirty other Bostonians heartily endorsed Brown's military plans for Kansas and formed a committee to financially support and advise him. For Emerson and the Kansas Committee, Brown was neither savage nor unmanly, but rather, a moral hero who deserved the utmost respect and praise.

Inherent in the support and criticism of Brown lies a judgment about his manhood, which, because of his notoriety at midcentury, exemplifies two conflicting meanings of manhood before the Civil War—one that sanctioned violence and one that advocated self-restraint. Stephen S. Foster, a self-proclaimed pacifist, praised Brown's methods and said, "I think John Brown has shown himself a *man*, in comparison with the Non-Resistants!"[84] Similarly, Emerson emphatically endorsed Brown's tactics and encouraged other northern men to take up arms against slavery. "I am glad to see that the terror at disunion and anarchy is disappearing," he wrote.

"Massachusetts, in its heroic day, had no government—was an anarchy. . . . Every man throughout the country was armed with knife and revolver and it was known that instant justice would be administered to each offence." Historian Michael Fellman finds that other northerners endorsed Emerson's concerns and notes that the "freedom-loving moral manhood achieved in the American Revolution, subsequently gone flabby as unchallenged slavehounds desecrated that true national spirit, could now be regained in Kansas." For Foster, Emerson, and other northerners, their manhood, indeed humanity itself, carried with it the obligation to pursue moral truth and justice, which in this case meant literally combating slavery.[85]

"THERE CAN BE NO PEACE UNTIL YOU RISE UP"

The growing sense that war was a necessity rang true with an increasing number of northerners as the events in Kansas and around the country proved to many that violence was the only effective response to southern aggression. One newsman reported from St. Louis that the means to peace between the proslavery and free-state forces was war: "Little can be done here by men of moderate opinion. . . . There can be no peace until you rise up and in a mighty exercise of power, put an end to the fell spirit of slavery propagandism." Much of this push toward violence implied that northerners needed to reconfigure their definition of true manhood to incorporate violence—preemptive and revolutionary violence, not merely violence in self-defense. After the sack of Lawrence, the *Cleveland Herald* announced, "Let it be distinctly understood, then, that men!—Men!! . . . are needed and must come, or Kansas is lost!" The North had not sent the "right kind of men" to Kansas, and they now needed to dispatch the men and "the means to use and carry on all the arts of peace."[86]

The most infamous tools used by free-state men to carry on the war in Kansas were Sharps rifles, which some referred to as "Beecher's Bibles." By 1856 many in New England became convinced that settlers must employ violent means to accomplish the free-state goals, and sympathizers in the East sent numerous shipments of Sharps rifles to Kansas in late 1855 and 1856.[87] According to one of Henry Ward Beecher's biographers, Beecher believed that "since the conscience of the southerner was destroyed by slavery, the Bible was of little use and only force could make him uphold the laws." Accordingly, Beecher and his parishioners raised enough money to send more than fifty Sharps rifles to Kansas "for defense of the state."

Beecher received much criticism for his endorsement of violence in Kansas, but he continued to "wave the torch of bleeding Kansas" and argued that to attack slavery in Kansas was to perform the "most Godlike work of religion."[88]

Eventually, the North heard many cries for war, and some even embraced its arrival. One of the most vocal advocates for war had originally harbored a staunch commitment to pacifism and nonresistance only to be converted to violence while living in Kansas. Charles B. Stearns, the Kansas correspondent for the *National Anti-Slavery Standard*, refused to consider a military response to ruffianism until he experienced the firestorm of war firsthand: "When I came to Kansas, little did I dream of ever becoming a soldier. . . . Not until the war had existed for ten days did I arm myself, and then only in consequence of becoming convinced that we had not human beings to contend with. I always believed it was right to kill a tiger, and our invaders are nothing but tigers. . . . I made up my mind that our invaders were wild beasts and it was my duty to aid in killing them off."[89] Stearns constructed the Border Ruffians as wild animals, arguing they were not even human and were most certainly not proper southern gentlemen. Stearns not only justified using violence against these "wild beasts" but also argued that the Border Ruffians deserved nothing less than total destruction at the hands of proper northern men.

As southern men lost their humanity and assumed animal-like qualities in northern eyes, the "free sons of the North" somewhat ironically met the challenge of the "myrmidons of border ruffianism" in a battle to the death. Rather than lobby for a manhood that restrained itself in the face of provocation, free-staters began to find the utility in cultivating an ideal of manliness that stood ready and willing to strike the first blow. Abolitionist William Lloyd Garrison's *Liberator* argued, "The alarming situation of the Kansas settlers is urged as demonstrating the worthlessness of the principles of peace; because . . . returning good for evil, the martyr-spirit, [is] derided as folly and madness against 'border ruffianism.'" Free-state men would be mad to think that refined manhood could combat the savagery of ruffianism. What became proper, instead, was the kind of manhood they had once criticized in their enemies—one that took an eye for an eye without first asking permission. The *Topeka Tribune* announced in August 1856, "We are glad that the issue is thus finally reduced to one single, starting point, annihilation. We are ready."[90]

Seen through a gendered lens, the Sack of Lawrence was a virtual prelude to Fort Sumter. Proslavery and antislavery men provoked each other verbally and rhetorically until they finally confronted each other on southern terms—on the battlefield. The South and the North would seek to prove the superiority of their respective societies in part through asserting the prominence of their manhoods. In the process they engaged in a grand duel that led hundreds of thousands of men on both sides to their deaths.

5

"DON'T YOU SEE OLD BUCK COMING?"

MISCEGENATION, WHITENESS, AND THE
CRISIS OF RACIAL IDENTITY

On November 21, 1856, the *Weston (Mo.) Argus* mocked the candidacy of John Charles Frémont for president of the United States in the recent election. Capitalizing on the pervasive white fear of miscegenation, the editors argued that Frémont's election would have resulted in the amalgamation of the races. "Don't you see old Buck coming?" they asked. "The friends of the amalgamation of the White and Black races are earnestly requested to support the following very Black Ticket." Republicans chanted, "Free Kansas, Free Men, and Frémont!" but the *Argus* wrote, "Free Kansas! Free Niggers! And Frémont. Black Republican Ticket. UNADULTERATED NIGGER!" Frémont's presidency, they claimed, would have encouraged the racial mixing not only of blacks and whites but also of Indians and whites. They warned, "Hurrah for Free Kansas . . . Beecher's Revolving Rifle, Under-Ground Railroad . . . *a slight sprinkling of catawba.* . . . They say the 'Union shall be Preserved!' but we say 'Let the Union slide!'" The editors feared that Indian and Negro blood would taint the white racial purity they so cherished and defended, and they alerted their readership to the threat of sexual predation that would have resulted from a Republican victory.[1]

The presence of "Bucks" (male African American slaves) and "Catawbas" (Indians) among the few white settlers who lived in the Kansas-Missouri border region had always threatened the foundation of white supremacy that Anglo setters worked to establish through legal and extralegal means on the nation's expanding western borders.[2] With the arrival of slaveholders and their African American chattel and the resettlement of thousands of Indians to eastern Kansas in the early 1850s, whites undoubtedly felt the weight of racial "otherness" on them and their families. Historian Elliott West notes, "Expansion [west] was double trouble. It not only sped up the old conflict between North and South. By complicating so hugely America's ethnic character it raised new questions on the relations between race and nation."[3] To compound the dual threats of redness and blackness in the West, settlers in the borderlands of Missouri and Kansas confronted the possibility that slavery, an institution intimately connected to issues like white supremacy and racial identity, would either be abolished (white southern fear) or extended further west (white northern fear).

Ironically, although they approached the sectional conflict from opposing sides, the majority of white settlers in Bleeding Kansas fought against one another in pursuit of the same goal—white supremacy. Antislavery settlers charged that slavery perpetuated interracial sex and amalgamation and thereby threatened whiteness; not only did white southerners and their slaves live and work together, they claimed, but slavery gave masters the right and opportunity to sexually abuse their female slaves on a regular basis. As Lydia Maria Child wrote in her introduction to Harriet Jacobs's slave narrative in 1861, slave women suffered "wrongs so foul" at the hands of their owners "that our ears are too delicate to listen to them."[4] But Charles Robinson, future governor of the state of Kansas, summed up best the free-staters' negative opinion of amalgamation: "I am not a friend of amalgamation of the African and anglo-Saxon or Indian races, and never have been; and the fact that negro slavery is the principal cause of this amalgamation in the United States, is to me a very strong argument against the institution."[5] Robinson and other antislavery settlers discouraged amalgamation and the expansion of the peculiar institution that facilitated, even encouraged, racial mixing.

On the other hand, proslavery advocates such as the editors of the *Weston Argus* claimed that slavery ensured the separation of the races and any challenge to the "peculiar institution" was by nature a challenge to racial segregation and white supremacy.[6] A proslavery settler who lived in Wyandot City verbalized many southerners' fears when he testified that the free-state men and women from the East intended to abolish slavery *and* amalgamate the races. Speaking about the New England Emigrant Aid Company in particular, he claimed, "The company's object was to make Kansas a free State and ameliorate the condition of the negro. After forming a free State, with free suffrage, by amalgamation of the Indians with the negroes . . . amalgamation with the whites would be an easy matter."[7] Thus although pursuing different means in regards to solving the conflict over slavery, northern and southern emigrants to Kansas envisioned similar futures that relegated African Americans and other people of color to inferior social positions and prohibited interracial sex.

Kansas settlers' arguments over slavery distilled a larger trend in the national discourse about racial identity, miscegenation, and whiteness. Their anxieties over the meaning(s) of freedom and slavery, citizen and foreigner, "self" and "other" reflected national insecurities about racial identity that stemmed from a midcentury increase in racial and sectional tensions, Indian wars and treaties, and an unprecedented rise in immigration to the United States from non–Anglo Saxon countries. Because the idea of popular sovereignty implied that democracy itself would be tested in Kansas, the blending of these peoples, cultures, and ideologies profoundly shaped how white settlers conceived of themselves as citizens in the rapidly expanding and changing republic.[8]

As Kansas bled, its settlers battled over what kind of state and nation they would inhabit, and they established social institutions that at once undermined and reinforced a national system of white supremacy. The free-state movement helped abolish slavery in Kansas Territory, but antislavery ideology and its proslavery corollary coalesced to fuel a system of racial segregation and white supremacy that would persist in Kansas and elsewhere in the nation. Whether Kansas entered the Union as a free or slave state, the principle of white supremacy would govern the region's social and cultural institutions.

RACIAL IDENTITY—NOT EXACTLY BLACK AND WHITE

The recent historiography on interracial sex, racial identity formation, and whiteness is too vast to survey here, but several key studies lend important insight in to the crisis of identity formation in antebellum Kansas.[9] Historian Neil Foley's discussion of the "white scourge," which he defines as whiteness itself, helps explain the complicated, multifaceted nature and function of whiteness. He argues that whiteness was "not simply . . . the pinnacle of ethnoracial status but [also] the complex social and economic matrix wherein racial power and privilege were shared, not always equally, by those who were able to construct identities as Anglo-Saxons, Nordics, Caucasians, or simply whites."[10] As Foley and others have demonstrated, poor whites were repeatedly denied the "wages of whiteness" even though their skin color should have racially linked them with their wealthier, "whiter" peers.

Political ideology in Bleeding Kansas served much the same purpose as class did in Foley's Texas. Except for extreme racial egalitarians such as John Brown, white Kansans wanted desperately to define themselves as white, but both northerners and southerners claimed they were "more white" than their opponents. Having the wrong politics about slavery in Kansas could be as bad as working side by side with Mexicans and blacks in the cottonfields of central Texas—in each case, certain whites were associated more than others with people of color. Foley connects poor whites' inferior racial status to their close association with Mexicans and blacks and to their reproductive habits, noting that "poor whites who competed with blacks and Mexicans as sharecroppers came to be racially marked as inferior whites whose reproductive fecundity threatened the vigor of Nordic whiteness."[11]

A similar phenomenon existed in Bleeding Kansas. Free-staters argued that proslavery whites worked, lived, and even slept with their black slaves, and southerners claimed that antislavery whites welcomed free blacks into their homes and their conjugal beds. Leavenworth's *Kansas Weekly Herald* wrote that antislavery settlers came to Kansas specifically to "steal negroes" and take "to their own bed and their own arms, a stinking negro wench."[12] Close occupational and interpersonal relations with people of color and reproductive habits that threatened the "vigor" of white purity, then, left certain whites outside other whites' definition of whiteness. Perhaps more than anything, interracial sexual relations jeopardized one's whiteness, and northern and southern Kansans agreed that miscegenation, especially between whites and blacks, gravely threatened white racial identity.

The majority of whites in the mid-nineteenth century spoke out against miscegenation—in theory—but the preponderance of mixed-race offspring in the South and among free black populations in the North proves that whites did not always practice what they preached about interracial sexual unions. Historian Martha Hodes finds a paradox in the way southern whites responded to what she calls "illicit" sex in the South: "For whites to refrain from immediate legal action and public violence when confronted with liaisons between white women and black men helped them to mask some of the flaws of the antebellum southern systems of race and gender. Yet paradoxically, any toleration of such transgressions meant that those flaws would also be exposed, especially in the evidence of free children of partial African ancestry."[13] The paradox in southern attitudes about interracial sex lies in white southerners' attempts to ignore its existence—for to acknowledge it was to affirm that white men did not enjoy complete patriarchal control over women and blacks.

At stake was not only racial identity but also gender identity, as miscegenation simultaneously revealed patriarchy's strength—white men's seemingly unfettered access to sex with women of color and white women's powerlessness to prevent their husbands, fathers, and brothers from engaging in these transgressive unions—and its potential weakness, especially when white women and men of color formed consensual sexual unions. There are few examples of interracial sex between white women and men of color in 1850s Kansas, but reports taken during the Civil War indicate there were cases on the border and in other southern states. James Redpath, an associate of John Brown's, and Richard J. Hinton, also an abolitionist, gave the American Freedmen's Inquiry Commission (AFIC) sworn testimony about the surprising frequency of sex between white women and their slaves in Missouri. One doctor who lived in Kansas at the time but had previously resided in Missouri told Hinton that "a very large number of white women, especially the daughters of the smaller planters, who were brought into more direct relations with the negro, had compelled some one of the men to have something to do with them." Another testimonial focused on planters' daughters in Missouri who "were envious of their brothers who 'got a flashy education, which they completed in the slave quarters and the bar-room.'"[14] Hodes argues that this sort of evidence illustrates the power white women enjoyed over their male (and female) slaves and indicates a weak link in the chain of patriarchy on southern plantations.

Hodes's analysis, however, focuses almost exclusively on black-white sexual relations, leaving out an important component in the assemblage of white fears and ambiguities about miscegenation in the mid-nineteenth century—namely, red-white sexual unions.[15] Even scholarly discussions that consider the construction of white racial identity in general (and not miscegenation's place in that construction) rarely include Indians in their interpretations of American racial cosmology. For example, pathbreaking studies on whiteness by David Roediger, Theodore Allen, Toni Morrison, and Eric Lott rarely if ever interrogate redness and its relationship to blackness and whiteness.[16] Historian Philip Deloria proves to be an exception to this rule in his book *Playing Indian,* in which he uncovers the intimate connection between white ideas about Indian racial traits and culture and "white" American rituals and cultural practices, such as the Boston Tea Party. Though Deloria's book focuses more on late-nineteenth- and twentieth-century manifestations of white Americans' fascination, attraction, and abhorrence of Indian culture, *Playing Indian* builds on the early- and mid-nineteenth-century roots of red-white racial interaction and cultural exchange.[17]

By piecing together these various theories about racial identity formation in the nineteenth century, we can use them to analyze and comprehend the complexity of the multiracial frontier of antebellum Kansas. Any comprehension of race relations in Kansas must originate in a tripartite analysis, one that examines red, white, and black together. As Elliott West claims, the tension over westward expansion "was partly about Free Soil, the question of whether southern slavery, with its nonwhite peoples . . . would spread to the West. But equally pressing were questions about nonwhite peoples already there."[18] Northern and southern white settlers in Kansas may have endorsed similar racial ideologies and practices—in fact, the antiblack and anti-Indian racism they often shared certainly reinforced each other—but they often disagreed about how to accomplish this common goal of white supremacy. One of the areas in which they agreed most frequently, however, was in their approach to the "civilization" and/or removal of Indians in Kansas. White settlers in Kansas forged a common white racial identity in opposition to Indian people and culture.

"THE RED MAN [HAS] BEEN COMPLETELY OVERLOOKED"

To illustrate the unity of northern and southern ideas about white supremacy, one need only to look at the Kansas settlers' interactions with Indians and their repeated abuse of the Kansas Indians' civil, economic, and political rights. Commissioner of Indian Affairs George W. Manypenny issued an annual report to Congress on November 22, 1856, that criticized the settlers in Kansas for their behavior toward Indians: "In the din and strife between the anti-slavery and proslavery parties with reference to the condition of the African race there, and in which the rights and interests of the red man have been completely overlooked and disregarded, the good conduct and patient submission of the latter contrasts favorably with the disorderly and lawless conduct of many of their white brethren, who, while they have quarrelled about the African, have united upon the soil of Kansas in wrong doing toward the Indian!"[19]

Given Manypenny's support of the colonization and relocation of Indian tribes, a process that had consistently involved violence against them, his critique of the settlers in Kansas was surprising. But Manypenny apparently drew the line in Kansas Territory, feeling that the settlers there had transgressed the acceptable boundaries of "civil" and "legal" Indian removal and relocation. Indeed, one could conclude from his report that common whiteness enabled the settlers to transcend their opposing free labor and proslavery ideologies by uniting them against the Indians.

Manypenny recognized an important common theme regarding antebellum ideas about race from his observations in Kansas. While many northerners vehemently opposed black slavery and especially its extension west, many also joined their southern "enemies" in a firm belief in white supremacy and the practice of white racism against all peoples of color. This shared racism helped foster a collective identity as white people. Though at times this identity was fractured by gender, class, and regional differences, whiteness allowed northerners and southerners to form a bond that united them in opposition to Indians and blacks. Whiteness also gave the early Kansas settlers, as "civilized" Christians, the moral imperative to civilize, remove, or exterminate the native "savages"; it gave them a common ground on which to affirm the inherent inferiority of African Americans and Indians.[20]

Inevitably, white Kansans evaluated their Indian neighbors based on the Indians' adherence to and association with whites and their culture. As shown in chapter 1, those tribes who had adopted the trappings of white "civilization," such as the Delaware and Shawnee, were often praised by white observers; on the other hand, those tribes, such as the Kaw and Kickapoo, who maintained tribal and cultural sovereignty received the brunt of white criticism. Indians who intermarried with whites or eschewed their native culture and embraced "white" habits received favorable, though frequently racialized and romanticized, evaluations from their white neighbors.

Several "half-breed" Indians surface repeatedly in the sources for their industriousness and, not coincidentally, their adherence to white norms. Pascal Fish, a Shawnee "half-breed," ran a boardinghouse ten miles east of Lawrence, and Charles Bluejacket operated a store near the Wakarusa River. Both men entertained numerous white guests and impressed them with their knowledge of English and their familiarity with white customs.[21] Samuel Pomeroy, an antislavery settler, negotiated several land deals with Pascal Fish and his brother, Charles, and described them as "half breed Shawnees—*educated*—*honest*." He wrote that "both are *Methodist Preachers* . . . [should] become citizens and have the right to hold and transmit their lands. . . . Pascal and Charles Fish are *Excellent* and *honest men*."[22] Pomeroy wanted the Fish brothers to become citizens for selfish reasons (he wanted them to sell their land to his antislavery land consortium, not the competing proslavery one). But the rhetoric he used to argue in favor of their claims reveals what made a "good Indian," even if Pomeroy's private opinion of the Fish brothers remains more elusive.

Mixed-race people who ran boardinghouses often received praise from their white guests as well as from political supporters. James Hindman stayed at Pascal Fish's boardinghouse one evening, only to tarry the next evening at Mr. Smith's, whose wife was a Pottawatomie Indian. Located near the Baptist mission and the Pottawatomie reservation, Hindman spent the night at Smith's home and described Smith's wife as "an intelligent half Pottawatomie native."[23] He recorded in his diary that they were "kind and hospitable" and that he enjoyed his stay at the Smiths. Mary Lawrence McMeekin sometimes accompanied her father, an Indian agent, on his annuity payment trips, when they lodged with Joe LeFlambeau, a mixed-race man who had two wives and two sets of children. Though LeFlambeau challenged white norms with his polygamous habits, he ran his household in ways that impressed the McMeekins. Mrs. McMeekin, Mary's mother, commented on how smoothly the peculiar household conducted itself: "Ma said they got along beautifully; the first wife's word was law, and the younger obeyed her as a daughter."[24] Though strange on some accounts, those Indians who served white needs and who mimicked white norms were often admired by their white neighbors.

But praiseworthy comments about "half-breed" Indians were sometimes characterized by the same racist stereotypes as more derogatory descriptions. A Kansas correspondent for the *New York Daily Tribune* attempted to describe his Indian hosts, but faltered because of the indeterminate nature of their racial origins. The reporter stopped at the house of "an [Indian]— no, not exactly an Indian, but a Pennsylvania Dutchman who had married one," and recorded the scene for his readers: "The establishment was a compound of Indian life and Dutch civilization. Two coffee-colored, buxom damsels, my host's daughters, were busied about domestic matters, and a half dozen little boys, of different ages, were illustrating this queer compound of human nature."[25] The "Dutch man" (common slang used to describe German, or "Deutsch," men) was not quite an Indian but wasn't a white man either, for he had married an Indian and fathered two mixed-race daughters, described as "buxom damsels." The reporter questioned the man's racial identity and fell into the racist habit of describing the man's daughters, both clearly women of color, in sexually provocative ways. In addition, he claimed the man's sons represented a "queer compound of human nature," implying that these particular products of interracial marriage were abnormal, even bizarre. Thus even benign interactions with mixed-race households provided fodder for racial stereotyping and the profession of white supremacy.

Indians who resisted the white civilizing mission were especially criticized. One settler, Charles M. Chase, visited the Sac and Fox reservation in 1863 and recorded these observations for the *True Republican and Sentinel,* an Illinois paper: "The government has by treaty, built a large number of good strong buildings on their land, most of which are now occupied by the Indians who partially take care of the land. . . . Among them there is occasionally a good farmer but most of them are lazy. There are but few whites in town." Chase described the majority of the Sac and Fox Indians as being lazy, even though the government had provided them with "good strong" buildings in which to live and instruction on how to farm "properly." He referred to the tribe as a bunch of the "wildest looking Indians" he had ever seen and claimed they were "too indolent to advance without a power behind them."[26] Chase believed that white power—the presence and constant influence of white civilization—could change Indian ways and lift them out of a state of savagery. But without this white presence ("there are but few whites in town"), redness and the intractable Indian culture would not change.

Indeed, according to many white observers, proximity to whites and their culture or intermarriage with them proved to be the watermark for civilization among the Kansas tribes. Rev. Thomas Johnson, who presided over the Shawnee Indian Mission, developed a theory regarding the government's approach to the Indian "problem." He suggested a policy that foreshadowed what would become official Indian policy in the mid- and late nineteenth century:

> For many years my mind has been directed to the probable destiny of these remnants of tribes west of Missouri; and I am fully satisfied that they can never be extensively improved as separate nations, and that the time will come when it will be best for our Government to . . . buy up the surplus lands belonging to these tribes, leaving a reservation in each tribe for those who are not willing to live among civilized people, and let the enterprising part of each nation hold property in their names, and live among the whites . . . and at a suitable time, when they were found qualified for it, let them have citizenship with the whites.[27]

Johnson summarized a belief in the persistence of racial differences between Indians and whites that many settlers, missionaries, and government officials held. Those Indians who were willing to relinquish their redness—their native, "savage" habits and ways of life and "live among civilized (white) people," maybe even intermarry with them and literally whiten their offspring—could prosper in the United States and even achieve citizenship (which at the time was reserved almost exclusively for free, white men). Johnson reiterated these sentiments a few years later, arguing that "the only hope is for the few [tribes] who may become identified with the white population and take their position in the walks of civilized society."[28]

Similarly, John Montgomery, Indian agent for the Kaws during the 1850s, argued that the "half-breed Kansas . . . are industrious and intelligent, well versed in the English, French and Kaw languages, profess the Catholic religion, and [have] almost a thorough knowledge of the arts of husbandry." Montgomery evaluated the "full-breed" Kaw less favorably, however, finding that there had been "no change in the Indian customs and manners to those of the white man." He blamed the full-blooded Kaw's retarded path to civilization on the fact that there had been "no white people or half-breeds among the full-blooded Indians since they were removed from the Kansas river to this place."[29] For both Montgomery and Johnson, intermarriage with and proximity to white settlers promised positive change for Indians and ultimately, for whites, because the white race and its culture would triumph over redness, proving once and for all that white supremacy reigned.

Adopting the trappings of whiteness even promised beauty for one Indian girl who was taken away from her reportedly abusive Indian mother and raised by a white couple, the Elys. One Ely family member described the girl's remarkable transformation from savage Indian to civilized, "almost white." Mrs. Ely remembered, "She was supposed to be about 10 years old . . . [and] as she learned to read and write and speak good English she became very goodlooking."[30] As the Indian girl amassed the tools required of her to function in a white world, she also acquired beauty. As she grew even older and undoubtedly distanced herself even further from her Indian past, the now-attractive Indian girl received several suitors. The few Indian suitors who courted her proved inadequate, however, and she told her white family that they spoke only "foolishness" with their native tongues. She preferred the white language and culture and eventually married a white man, continuing on her path to whiteness by adopting white habits and committing herself legally and sexually to a white man.

Interracial marriage and sex between whites and Indians appears to have been viewed as a necessary evil, if not a natural byproduct of westward expansion, when dealing with Indian-white relations on the frontier. The neutral, sometimes positive portrayal of Indian-white sexual liaisons served the needs of white missionaries and Indian officials who believed that miscegenation was the quickest, if not the best means of civilizing the intractable red man. One article in the *Kansas Weekly Herald* flippantly recorded the following: "When Gen. Whitfield, Indian agent, visited the Cheyennes, and a few other wild tribes of Indians, to pay their annuities, last fall, they informed him that the next year he must bring them one thousand white squaws and the balance they would take in money."[31] Rather than give the Kansas tribes money, the government could provide the Indian men with white women. Ultimately, both government money and white women could accomplish the same goal: civilizing/whitening the savage Indian.

Another reason why Indian-Anglo marriage and sex may have appeared rather benign to most whites is that the vast majority of these interracial unions were formed by white men and native women.[32] Contrary to the example given by the *Weekly Herald,* white women rarely married Indian men, thus maintaining traditional patriarchal relations as both white and Indian women remained under white, male control. White, male patriarchy was not threatened by Indian women who intermarried; in fact, intermarriage bolstered patriarchy because these native women not only served white men's domestic needs but they also sometimes facilitated the transfer of Indian lands into white, male hands. Furthermore, marrying Indian women emasculated Indian men, as native women's fathers and brothers lost control of their female relatives to white men. Interracial sex in these instances shored up white patriarchy, as Indian women served both individual male needs and the larger needs of the white nation to conquer Indian lands and peoples. In sum, a reliance on conventional gender roles helped mitigate the effects of unconventional sexual behavior and racial mixing.[33]

"THE WHITE RACE WILL NEVER BE ENSLAVED!"

The apparent tolerance of red-white interracial sexual relations in Kansas stands out in stark contrast to the abhorrence of black-white miscegenation. In addition to the potential threats black-white interracial sex posed for patriarchy, particularly when white women and black slaves were the involved parties, the most salient reason for whites' disapproval related to the institution of slavery. The children of Indian and Anglo sexual unions rarely, if ever, lived as slaves, but miscegenation law protected white property rights and patriarchy by ensuring that all children produced by white men and enslaved black women were designated as slaves. Since the seventeenth century, American law had dictated that the child born from a union between white and black would carry the status—free or slave—of his/her mother. Moreover, even though the child of a white mother and black father was technically free, that mixed-race child carried the taint of slavery, as slavery and blackness became equated in the national consciousness.[34]

After 1850 and the passage of the Fugitive Slave Law, the "one drop rule" left everyone with "black blood" coursing through their veins vulnerable to enslavement in the U.S. South.[35] For example, free blacks in Kansas were vulnerable to capture by slave patrols, like the free black man who was kidnapped by Missourians and taken to jail in Independence, Missouri, where he awaited his fate as an "escaped slave."[36] Blackness had for so long been equated with slavery that laws like the Fugitive Slave Law merely reiterated what had been previously assumed: To be black was to be viewed as a slave in the United States. Missourian Benjamin F. Stringfellow articulated this assumption in a public letter to the *Weston Reporter* in August 1854. He told his fellow whites, "Stay in States where Negro slavery is established, there your color—the color of your sons and daughters—will be respected—there the white race will never be enslaved!"[37] Because blackness and slavery determined one another causally in the national psyche, whites feared that any "black blood" in their veins could and would strip them of their rights as free men and women.

White settlers acknowledged that a bit of "red blood" mixed with white was not as damaging to whiteness as "black blood." Redness connoted a more complicated history; Indians might be mistreated and discriminated against because of their race and culture, but they were rarely enslaved in North America after the seventeenth century. Red-white miscegenation would never result in the increase of blackness and hence the expansion of slavery. Indians might even be able to neutralize some of the negative threats of expanding blackness by adding a bit of beauty to it. One Kansas settler described a mulatto woman as beautiful because she had "a little Indian blood in her."[38] So although civilization rhetoric characterized Indians in Kansas as racially inferior, it rarely marked them as a threat to white liberty. Only blackness received such attention.

"SLAVERY SEEKING TO FORCE ITSELF UPON HER"

Civilization rhetoric not only encompassed descriptions of the various native peoples and cultures that inhabited the West but also referred to the land itself, the "wide-open" spaces that quickly filled up with white settlers. The propaganda and rhetoric that enticed settlers to emigrate perpetuated already popular ideas about civilizing the savage frontier and bringing culture and social institutions to the untamed region. Glenda Riley notes that women in particular "were reminded that, as carriers of Christian civilization, they had much work to do in the West." In addition, civilization rhetoric produced racialized, gendered, and sexualized meanings as masculine, white settlers impregnated Kansas's dark, virgin soil. In Senator Charles Sumner's words, "It is the rape of a virgin Territory, compelling it to the hateful embraces of Slavery; and it may be clearly traced to a depraved longing for a new slave state, the hideous offspring of such a crime." Even discussions about the land illustrated the nation's simultaneous fascination with and aversion to interracial sex and racial mixing.[39]

Scholars have only recently explored the gendered descriptions of the land and of states and nations, but many agree that female iconography and feminized language have commonly characterized nature and national symbols throughout American history.[40] The usage of the feminine pronouns "she" and "her" to describe Kansas was common in the media, literature, and in personal correspondence. Abraham Lincoln referred to Kansas with feminine pronouns in a series of letters and speeches he delivered after the passage of the Kansas-Nebraska Act in May 1854 reinvigorated his political voice. He proposed, "If Kansas fairly votes herself a slave state, she must be admitted, or the Union must be dissolved."[41] Criticizing Illinois senator Stephen A. Douglas's support of the Kansas-Nebraska Act, Lincoln retorted, "It is argued that slavery will not go to Kansas and Nebraska. . . . This is a *palliation*—a *lullaby*. . . . Slavery pressed entirely up to the old western boundary of [Missouri], and when, rather recently, a part of that boundary, at the north-west was, moved out a little farther west, slavery followed on quite up to the new line."[42] Lincoln warned that if they failed to stop slavery in Kansas, the institution would continue to spread westward until no land remained for the free, white laborer. Similarly, the

New York Daily Tribune claimed, "No State can shield her soil from the withering tread of the slaveholder and his human chattels. . . . The plow is turning up her virgin soil and the blithe sower preparing to scatter his seed."[43] Antislavery rhetoric like this portrayed slavery as a predatory force that spread westward, conquering innocent, virgin land with impropriety and relentlessness.

The *New York Daily Tribune* endorsed Lincoln's free, white soil ideology and warned its readers of slavery's predatory danger to Kansas and the nation as a whole. Writing after the proslavery attack on Lawrence in the spring of 1856, the *Tribune*'s Kansas correspondent asked, "Who does not know that it is slavery, and nothing but slavery, which has brought all this horror upon Kansas—*slavery seeking to force itself upon her,* first by gigantic fraud at the polls; next by the most infernal enactments through a bogus Legislature; and at last by butchery and arson in the settlers' homes?"[44] Reminiscent of the rhetoric used by Senator Charles Sumner in his "Crime against Kansas" speech, a masculinized, racialized slavery metaphorically raped the feminized Kansas and the white settlers who inhabited Lawrence by invading their homes and committing crimes on their property and persons.

Reports of the Sack of Lawrence repeatedly demonized the Missouri Border Ruffians, and many of them cited the negative, "blackened" effects that proponents of slavery left in their wake. The *Tribune* described the remains of downtown Lawrence as "a charred and blackened waste," where southern men were "intent on the transformation of Kansas into a breeding-ground and fortress of Human Slavery."[45] The *Tribune* article noted the necessity of breeding to the success of slavery. Perhaps the reporter recognized that extending slavery into Kansas would require breeding between male and female slaves and the "breeding" of the Kansas soil and the cotton or hemp seeds that would together produce a cash crop for the region's farmers. Using language that referenced the central importance of sexual reproduction to the perpetuation of slavery undoubtedly raised questions about interracial sex between white masters and their black female slaves, a practice abhorred by many northerners

The *Tribune* announced that the "black deed was consummated on Wednesday last," almost implying that the Border Ruffians cajoled and wooed an indifferent Lawrence until she no longer resisted slavery's advances; the Ruffians then "consummated" the unhappy marriage between slavery and Lawrence's antislavery citizens by invading the "virgin" town. The *Tribune* went on to declare that slavery's evil reached beyond its black roots and now threatened white settlers: "*It is the free white people of Amer-ica on whom the bonds are now to be cast,* for an aristocratic Slaveocracy must trample on their privileges and sacred rights before they can succeed in their object."[46] Slavery had the potential to rape white female settlers and/or the feminized land and blacken it all by casting the darkness of slav-ery over the free-staters and their land.

The *Tribune* raised the specter of white slavery repeatedly, arguing that "the South has taken the oligarchic ground that Slavery ought to exist, irre-spective of color." The shield of whiteness would no longer protect whites from being enslaved if the South gained control in Kansas—all people would be vulnerable to slavery. An advertisement for Sara Robinson's au-tobiographical book *Kansas* compared Robinson's work with *Uncle Tom's Cabin* and claimed that what truths Stowe unveiled about black slavery, Robinson revealed for white slavery. According to the ad, *Uncle Tom's Cabin* "shows, by fiction, what Slavery does for black people," whereas Robin-son's *Kansas* illustrates the "outrages" slavery has "perpetrated, through the organization of the United States Government, upon white men and women."[47] The federal government, backed by a proslavery president and local hirelings, threatened the freedom and, consequently, the whiteness of free-state settlers in Kansas.

One 1856 article, "Who Are and Who May Be Slaves in the United States," recognized the mutability and manipulative nature of color/race and its equation with slavery. Author George Weston argued that even peo-ple with coloring similar to the "pure Caucasian" could be enslaved, cit-ing southern laws that determined slave or free status according to the status of the mother, regardless of the child's paternity or how "white" he or she looked. Weston noted the importance of miscegenation to the maintenance of slavery and to the development of white slavery: "The fe-male slaves, exposed of necessity to the unbridled lusts of the whites, are made the instruments through whom the Caucasian race is itself reduced to the condition of servitude. . . . This is both the law and the fact as to Southern Slavery. The blood of orators, statesmen, generals, and even Pres-idents, flows in the veins of thousands, who are bought and sold like mules and horses."[48] He revealed the role miscegenation played in increasing the enslaved population with people of mixed-race backgrounds and even re-ported on a "white negro," Phil, whose free, white father had impregnated his enslaved mother. Though Phil was "nearly white, with eyes blue," he was destined to endure a life of servitude because of this irrational and im-moral law. The *Tribune* articles exploded common tropes about miscegenation and race to reveal the potential and actual dangers that slavery posed in Kansas and for the nation if the "free sons of the North" failed to take immediate action.

A Lawrence paper, the *Republican,* urged free-state men to act quickly and decisively in response to southern atrocities in Kansas and described the state as an innocent victim caught in the middle of a battle between civilization and savagery. "Rampant Pro Slavery [power] will exalt its horn against Righteousness and try again the virtue of ruffianism to prevail against civilization," the paper argued. "The barbarians will hang anew upon the border, ready to complete the conquest they began so well."[49] The proslavery power's "horn," could be interpreted as being a musical instrument, raised and blown loudly to signal the beginning of battle, or it could refer to an animal horn prepared for puncturing an enemy. Considering its pairing with "righteousness" and "virtue," two terms often associated with sexuality and moral character, the horn serves as an imposing, threatening, masculine tool of destruction. Kansas, on the other hand, remained vulnerable and faultless, waiting for northern men to defend its (her) honor and reputation.

The *Republican* and its readers, such as Hannah Ropes, gendered Kansas as an innocent, feminized victim and warned of the probable "darkening" effects of southern deceit and aggression; Ropes wrote to her mother that the "dark line of Missourians" stood ready to pounce on Lawrence and blacken her.[50] If northern men could ward off such an invasion and not succumb to the forces of evil, however, the *Republican* promised a moral and military victory: "Kansas at no distant period, will be welcomed by her Free Sisters to her place among them, with no stain of bribes in her hands and with no soil of meanness upon her garments."[51] To maintain Kansas's innocence and preserve her whiteness, northerners must harness the power of civilization to conquer the southern barbarians.

The media gendered not only Kansas but also the concept of freedom. In "A Song for the Time," published in 1856 in the *Tribune,* the author refers to freedom by name and uses non-gender-specific pronouns until the final stanza; then the author genders freedom. Not coincidentally, the final stanza also highlights the events in Kansas:

> For Freedom? ha! The cheering sight,
> From Kansas see her driven;
> She fights, she fain's, she falls!—at will
> See Slavery smite her!—stark and still

> She lies. And now on Bunker Hill
> Toombs calls his slave roll, loud and shrill,
> God rules—who doubts—in Heaven![52]

Slavery drove freedom from Kansas and perhaps even killed her; she fainted, fell, and lay still at the end of the poem. Though slavery had proven victorious in this life, however, the author questions its success in the next life and fundamentally challenges the moral character of the institution and those who support it. "God rules . . . in Heaven," not slavery, and those who impugned freedom in Kansas would pay for their sins in the afterlife.

"PROSLAVERY DOGS OF WAR"

Antislavery settlers such as Hannah Ropes and Julia Louisa Lovejoy moved to Kansas in an effort to shelter the innocent, feminized land from the "dark clouds" that crossed the border from Missouri and other southern states. Lovejoy asked in her diary, "Will Kansas, ever be redeemed, and saved and become a land where Sabbath-breaking and licentiousness and dishonesty are unknown? How has this fair land, been stained with *blood*, shed by a Cain-like murderer's hand, that *now* crieth to heaven for vengeance, and will not *long* be delayed."[53] Lovejoy lamented the "bloody atrocities" committed by the "proslavery dogs of war" and wondered if the men who "hailed from the land of the Puritans" could triumph over those who had for years "inhaled the air of the Sunny South, where the *miasma* of slavery taints and mildews every *finer* feeling of the human heart."[54] Her distinction between the two opposing groups is telling; she relates the New England emigrants to the Puritans, undoubtedly emphasizing and referring to their "pure" religious practices and morals (but perhaps also to their "pure" racial make-up), untainted by "the miasma of slavery." Southerners, on the other hand, inhaled impure air, air that colored everything and everyone it touched—air that produced "dogs of war." Lovejoy thereby juxtaposed the two groups on religious and perhaps racial grounds, questioning southerners' racial identity along with their morals.

Several antislavery reports from Kansas constructed proslavery southerners as savage beasts, and in so doing, questioned their racial identity by comparing them with animals. Charles Stearns, the Kansas correspondent for the *National Antislavery Standard,* called the Border Ruffians a pack of "wild beasts."[55] Like Stearns, the Reverend Pardee Butler (remembered for being tarred, feathered, and floated down river on a makeshift raft by a proslavery mob) wrote to abolitionist James Redpath about his experiences in Kansas and constantly referred to his attackers as dark, savage beasts. Describing his first encounter with the Ruffians, he painted a vivid, undoubtedly sensationalized picture of his confrontation: "If I can picture to myself the look of a Cuban blood-hound, just ready with open jaws to seize a panting slave in a Florida swamp, then I imagine we have a correct daguerreotype of the expression worn by these emigrant representatives of the manly-sentiment, high-toned courage and magnanimous feelings of South Carolina chivalry when first they scented—in their own imagination—the blood of a live Abolitionist."[56] Butler compared his South Carolinian enemies to Cuban bloodhounds, panting in a Florida swamp, salivating after the scent of a runaway slave. The Cuban reference elicited fear about race and amalgamation, because those who argued against the annexation of Cuba during the 1850s frequently used racist discourse to affirm their opposition. The United States' white identity was threatened enough by people of color within its current boundaries; the last thing the nation needed was to acquire and/or amalgamate with a nation of color.[57] Indeed, the comparison to a bloodhound alone implies that the southern Ruffians were more akin to animals than humans. Butler could even be insinuating that free white settlers risked enslavement and, hence, the surrender of their whiteness, if they allowed Border Ruffians to hunt them down like black slaves.

Butler continued his description of the Border Ruffians by fortifying his references to slavery, blackness, and savagery. He wrote, "I was given into the hands of my South Carolina overseers to be tarred and feathered. . . . One little sharp-visaged, dark featured, black-eyed South Carolinian, as smart as a cricket . . . seemed to [be] the leader of the gang." Again Butler constructed himself as a virtual slave, tarred and feathered (darkened) by his captors, the leader of whom sported a black eye and dark features. Butler raised the specter of blackness as a threat to the North's racial identity and used blackness as a tool to question his attackers' racial identity. Slavery anywhere, it seemed, threatened white identity everywhere. The mob finally left Butler alone, but only after they "shrieked and yelled like a pack of New Zealand cannibals" as they departed.[58]

Northerners repeatedly questioned southern racial identity by aligning southern men with black, less-than-human, or savage beings. Antislavery men like Johnston Lykins, who described a Border Ruffian he met as a "large, dark-skinned stuttering man," capitalized on northern fears about the extension of slavery, blackness and miscegenation to disparage their southern opponents.[59] Ironically, however, southerners used similar tools to combat their northern foes, arguing that it was the North, not the South, that perpetuated savagery and threatened white racial identity.

BLACK HEARTS AND BLACK REPUBLICANS

White southerners retaliated with their own brand of racialized and gendered civilization rhetoric; they claimed that proslavery settlers ensured, rather than threatened the establishment of white supremacy in Kansas. The *Richmond Enquirer* argued that the southern Border Ruffian was "the pioneer of a high and honourable civilization," who was "planting a master race . . . on a new soil."[60] According to the *Enquirer,* members of the master race would plant their white seeds in the savage Kansas soil and slavery itself would help preserve freedom and democracy for all white men. As historian Michael Fellman astutely noted over a decade ago, Missourians feared that their social and cultural worlds would be undone if "Black Republicans" settled on their western border. If these "nigger-stealers" gained control of Kansas Territory, the proslavery *Weekly Herald* argued, "Our white men would be cowards, our black men idols, our women amazons."[61]

Like their northern counterparts, southern settlers and propagandists played on fears of blackness to disparage their opponents. They repeatedly described abolitionists and free-staters using the color black and often equated them with black people, arguing that their sympathy for black slaves implied their similarity to them. Governor Shannon, a proslavery territorial governor, referred to one free-stater's heart as "black." According to Sara Robinson, Shannon "inquired of [a] Mrs. Hazeltyne for her husband. . . . 'I'll cut his damned black heart out of him, and yours too, madam, if you don't take care,' he yelled."[62] Shannon, angry and suspicious that Mrs. Hazeltyne had kept her husband's whereabouts a secret, threatened free-staters and their black hearts with extermination.

According to proslavery rhetoric, some abolitionists had "black hearts," others joined the "Black Republican" party, and still others had skin of the "ebony hue." Democrats consistently referred to their Republican rivals as "Black Republicans." Democratic representative T. L. Harris from Illinois gave a speech in Congress that betrayed his colleagues' opinions of free-state men and their supporters: "The Black Republican press of the North, and the Black Republican preachers, with that reverend rifleman—Henry Ward Beecher—at their head, have declared from their pulpits that they will carry freedom into Kansas."[63] Another member of Congress, Missouri representative M. Oliver, called the *New York Tribune* the "leading organ of [the] Black Republican party," and the proslavery *Missouri Republican* repeatedly criticized the actions of the "Black Republican party of Kansas."[64] One reporter in Washington, D.C., claimed the Crittenden Compromise, a bill that would challenge the proslavery Lecompton constitution, was the "darling object of the black-republican heart." Furthermore, this reporter compared the Crittenden Compromise's supporters to "belles of the pure ebony hue," implying that antislavery congressman were not only less white, but less masculine than their proslavery counterparts.[65] By consistently naming antislavery men and women as members of a "black" party who had black hearts and skin, white southerners attempted to at once radicalize the Republican project and the party's members.

One antislavery man whom proslavery settlers sometimes referred to as less-than-white and less-than-human was John Brown. Especially after his 1856 attack on slaveholders near Pottawatomie Creek, Brown rarely looked white in photographs, nor did accounts of his actions describe him as being white. Photographs and daguerreotypes highlighted his dark, ruddy complexion and unruly hair, often depicting his eyes as slightly crazed pools of fire. During the congressional investigation of the Pottawatomie murders, John Doyle, who lost his father and brother in the massacre, described Brown as "dark complected" and depicted the entire raiding party as men who "were of sandy complexion." In her testimony, Mahala Doyle, John's mother, disparaged the motley crew that rounded up her husband and son and claimed Brown left their property after giving a "wild whoop."[66] Whether dark or sandy, Brown and his men's murderous behavior marked them as savages, more like "wild, whooping" Indians than civilized white men.

In the proslavery *Kansas Weekly Herald*, a southern settler wrote a poem that explained the "Origin, history and progress of Abolitionism" and simultaneously indicted, demonized, and "othered" the free-staters and their ideology:

> Before time began, but how long we can't tell; a mighty Archangel, in heaven did dwell
> The Son of the morning, and glorious was he; But higher in glory, he wanted to be.
> Throughout the world he is known by many a name, but Abo-li-tion, we find is his true name

To abolish the order of heaven he tried; And in his presumption its Sovereign
defied.

In the pride of his heart, he aspir'd to gain a higher position in heav'n to
reign.

But for his ambition, he quickly was hurl'd, far, far, down below, from the
heavenly world

To very hot quarters, in which to remain; forever in torment, in sorrow, and
pain

But in process of time, he made his way out; and for a new world, he strait-
way took his rout

Into Eden's fair Garden he enter'd one morn; the picture of envy, wrath, malice and scorn.

To try to abolish whatever he could; in this new world discover, fair, lovely
and good.

He sat himself down full of anguish and pain, with malice and hatred to
madden his brain.

He contrasted the beauty and grandeur all round,

With the horrors and gloom of his own burning ground;

The ambrasial sweets as they pass'd on the gale, with the hot sulph'rus va-
pors he had to inhale

Then he said, as he sigh'd—"this is all very well, but if i don't make this a
provence of hell,

It will be, because, I lack power, and not will;

But softly—my passions—I bid you be still;

For yonder comes one of this newly form'd pair; how graceful her form; how
enchantingly fair!

I'll assail her at once; all my arts I'll employ; this beautiful being—that I may
destroy

In revenge for my rout; and expulsion from heaven; to the regions of torment
to which I am driv'n! But stop! I must change me, and be mighty civil

Lest she may discover, that I am the Devil.

And though I am from the dark regions of night; I'll appear in her eyes, as an
angel of light.

I must act well my part, to secure my prey or in deeper disgrace, I'll be
driven away.

Stay, I'll enter that serpent, it suits my disguise they say it is cunning deceitful and wise.

And with its assistance, exert all my power, to turn into sorrow and wo, this
fair land.[67]

This poem elucidates many of the themes explored in this chapter and also captures the essence of the conflict between antislavery and proslavery ideology. To begin with, the proslavery author accuses the fictive abolitionist/devil character of disrupting the natural order between master and slave, a hierarchy ordained by God. The author blames such blasphemy on the abolitionist's ambition and egotism and casts him into hell for questioning the slave owner's patriarchal authority and hence God's omniscient authority.

The abolitionist (Lucifer) then adopts the guise of a snake and enters the "Garden of Eden." Here presumably the author is referring to the free-state migration, and the raging debate over the expansion of slavery into the untouched, divine gardens of the western frontier. While in territorial Kansas, or some other slave-owning Garden of Eden, the abolitionist attempts to reform the system by turning it into a free labor "hell." But he "lacks power" and loses sight of his goal of abolitionism, when he becomes attracted to a southern woman (Eve).

This Eve-like woman, undoubtedly a white, innocent plantation mistress, was duped into submission by the abolitionist/serpent's disguise. The author implies miscegenation as he hints at the abolitionist's less than lily-white racial heritage ("though I am from the dark regions of night, I'll appear in her eyes as the angel of light"). In addition, the poem darkens the abolitionist and constructs him as the devil himself. The concluding reference to the serpent reinforces the theme of miscegenation and suggests that the serpent, with powers that are "cunning, deceitful and wise," could defile the southern lady. Abolitionism and the inevitable consequence of miscegenation, the poem declares, would destroy the natural, divine order of slavocracy, disrupt the southern Gardens of Eden, and desecrate southern white womanhood. The author paints the abolitionist as a racial, sexual, and ideological other and, as the very Devil, casts him into the caverns of hell.

Proslavery men metaphorically blackened their opponents with words, and they literally blackened them with tar, often turning to tarring and feathering as a favorite means of enforcing their supremacy and their whiteness.[68] One proslavery mob tarred and cottoned a young free-state man, dragged him across town, and left him at the doorstep of his family's homestead. The proslavery "party" of Leavenworth called a meeting on April 30, 1855, to endorse tarring and feathering and other vigilante tactics used by their fellow proslavery brethren. The members, led by Judge Payne, passed several resolutions, one of which specifically referred to the tarring of a suspected abolitionist, William Phillips: "1st. That we heartily endorse the action of the committee of citizens that shaved, tarred and feathered, rode on a rail, and had sold by a negro, William Phillips, the moral perjuror."[69] These proslavery men went beyond blackening their opponents' skin and sold Phillips on a mock auction block as if he were a slave.

In addition to associating abolitionists with slaves, the proslavery newspapers also implied that they permitted and even encouraged miscegenation. Atchison's *Squatter Sovereign* published a story that predicted the "Effects of Abolitionism": "We copy the following marriage of a 'Buck Nigger' to a White Woman. . . . Such occurences [sic] will be frequent here, should the Northern fanatics succeed in excluding the institution of slavery." The *Squatter Sovereign* fanned the flames of miscegenation hysteria by reprinting the wedding announcement of this interracial couple from the *Abington (Conn.) Standard*: "Scorning the conventionalities of society the fair bride has set a noble example of practical amalgamation. This was no childish fancy or result of fanaticism working on youthful enthusiasm. The bridegroom had arrived at the mature age of fifty, and the bride thirty-three. Both have tied the silken cord of Hymen with a partner of their own race, and so will be able to speak experimentally on the advantages of one or the other plans."[70] This article most certainly frightened the *Squatter Sovereign's* readership, because it openly announced a mixed-race marriage and noted the sexual implications of such a union. Furthermore, the *Sovereign* implied that such unions would be commonplace if more abolitionist New Englanders, like the couple from Connecticut, were allowed to settle in Kansas.

But anxiety surrounding interracial marriage and sex was not reserved for proslavery settlers; antislavery papers, like their proslavery counterparts, carried stories filled with accounts of miscegenation and population growth spurred by nonwhites. The author of one story in the *Republican* worried that native white families no longer married and reproduced in tandem with immigrants: "More than four sevenths of the marriages in Massachusetts are among the foreign born. . . . Here is our intolerable stupidity once more; having children is left to the Irish!" The author blamed native whites' extravagant spending habits and women's reluctance to fulfill their wifely duties for the difference in marriage and birth rates. He lamented, "Once was the time when a wife was a 'help meet'; now in thousands of cases you can change the 'meet' to 'eat' and make it read more truthfully."[71] Instead of focusing the problem on immigrants and their "savage" habits (as much conventional wisdom did), this reporter blamed white, middle-class men and women. If these whites failed to change their marriage and reproductive habits, they would ensure a nation populated by not-so-white foreigners, like the Irish.

So although the most acute white anxiety stemmed from black-white interracial sex and blackness, white fear about miscegenation and the racial other attached itself to a variety of sources. The Irish, African Americans, some Indians (particularly the "uncivilized" and full-blooded tribes), Border Ruffians, and Abolitionists all took their turn as racial others in Kansas Territory. White settlers grappled with each other for the exclusive right to claim whiteness and to formulate a white identity that maintained its purity and racial integrity.

COPPER-COLORED SONS, MEN OF AFRICA, AND OTHER CHALLENGES TO WHITE SUPREMACY

In contrast to the northerners and southerners discussed here, a few pieces of evidence indicate that some settlers in Kansas embraced not only abolitionism but also racial equality. Sara Robinson articulated many of her immediate peers' sentiments when she explained why abolitionist women joined the movement to abolish slavery in Kansas: "Could she see this great country [Kansas] . . . thrown open to the foul inroads of slavery, so that no woman with black blood in her veins could be a welcome inmate of her father's house, feel safe in the protection of a husband's love, or, in caressing the children God gave her, call them her own, and make no effort in their behalf? No. It was not thus, thank God! Men felt and women felt."[72] Similarly, Thomas Webb wrote to James Montgomery about coordinating relief efforts for the fugitives who flooded into Kansas from Missouri and Arkansas and argued for equality in their treatment: "Where distress exists I do not stop to . . . inspect his complexion; whatever his color, white, black, or red, whatever his status, bond or free, neither he nor his family must . . . be left to starve or freeze."[73]

One settler, Erastus Ladd, criticized Rev. Thomas Johnson for his bigoted views toward African Americans and highlighted the irony embedded in a man who simultaneously worked for the betterment of one "colored race" while degrading another: "This Johnson is the distinguished slave-holding missionary of 'good will'. . . to the *copper colored* sons of the American forests, but not to the 'men' of Africa with darker skins, or even of skins as light as his own, if a particle of African blood permeates their veins, even if most of the rest of that blood should be his own. The Rev. Mr. Johnson's mission is to the skins of a peculiar color and not to the *souls of men*."[74] Ladd not only chided Johnson for his slaveholding but also noted that he might in fact be enslaving and discriminating against his own off-spring. By implying that Johnson's "white blood" ran through some of his slaves' veins, Ladd's comments demonstrate that even those Kansas settlers who advocated equality among the races capitalized on the fear of miscegenation to reveal the hypocrisy of proslavery men like Johnson.

This small vanguard of abolitionist settlers challenged slavery and white supremacy in Kansas, and it was their radicalism that attracted black leaders such as Frederick Douglass to Kansas's cause. In his abolitionist newspaper, the *North Star*, Douglass proposed a "Plan for Making Kansas a Free State," which suggested an exodus of one thousand free blacks into the territory.[75] His proposal, however, met with firm opposition from the mainstream antislavery groups in Kansas. In fact, the free-state constitution proposed in Topeka during the fall of 1855 initially barred free African Americans from settling in the state. Moreover, the 1861 state constitution denied blacks voting rights and segregated the school system. A large minority of constitutional delegates even supported total "negro exclusion."[76]

Although the abolitionist wing of the free-state movement effectively combated slavery in the region, it was not as successful in challenging white supremacy. Proslavery and antislavery settlers entered the Union together as Kansans in 1861, and the first Kansans agreed that whiteness would reign supreme in their new state. Their common use of racialized rhetoric to attack each other ironically brought them together in defense of whiteness.

Kansans proved to be sensitive to a variety of threats to white racial purity, which included the presence of both blacks and Indians, and they developed ideologies and public policies designed to minimize the impact of blackness and redness. In the case of the Indians, missionaries, Indian agents, and settlers agreed that removal to reservations and/or "civilization" and total assimilation via intermarriage with whites would best serve both Indian and Anglo needs. Because some Indians refused to change on their own, they would have to be exterminated, moved, or physically infused with white blood. Those tribes who insisted on cultural and political sovereignty would simply be killed or placed on reservations. Those who embraced "civilized" white culture, on the other hand, could join the ranks of whiteness through intermarriage and prosper in the expanding Republic.

As for African Americans, they would not be enslaved in the new state of Kansas but would be denied citizenship and the suffrage and would be destined to occupy the lowest social and economic rungs of "free" Kansas society. Slavery, an institution that epitomized the southern expression of white supremacy, died in Kansas, but the victory of antislavery forces was marred by racism. Furthermore, whites in Kansas, whether northern or southern, disdained interracial sex with blacks and worked in different ways toward creating a society in Kansas that prohibited such unions. The northern faction may have "won" the battle in Bleeding Kansas, but ultimately, whiteness won the war.

CONCLUSION

After attending an antislavery meeting held to protest the Kansas-Ne-braska Act, Samuel N. Wood and his wife, Margaret, left their Ohio home in May 1854 to settle in Kansas Territory. In part because of their efforts and the hardships they and other free-state settlers endured during the territorial era, Sam and Margaret found themselves living in a free Kansas just seven years later. The Woods arrived in Kansas bringing only their passionate commitment to abolitionism and the possessions they could pack into their covered wagon. By the 1860s, however, the Wood family had acquired land south of Lawrence, a modest home that Sam and his father-in-law had built, and a printing press. While the Woods's biography is compelling because it chronicles the struggle over slavery between abolitionists like themselves, their antislavery counterparts, and proslavery men and women, it is their printing press that tells the larger story of Bleeding Kansas.[1]

Jotham Meeker, one of the first Baptist missionaries among the Shawnee Indians in Kansas, first purchased the printing press in Cincinnati, Ohio, in the early 1830s and began printing the *Shawnee Sun* in 1834. The *Sun,* or the "Shau-wau-nowe Ke-sauth-wau," was the first newspaper ever published exclusively in an Indian language and eventually became a popular bilingual paper in the region. After Meeker died in January 1854, the missionary board sold the press to George W. Brown, who began publishing the antislavery paper, the *Herald of Freedom.* After the press's tenure at the *Herald of Freedom* and another like-minded paper, the *Freedom's Champion,* Sam Wood acquired it and used it to publish several different papers that touted various social causes from impartial suffrage to spiritualism.[2] The press, traveling from Ohio to Kansas, published stories that covered the lives of Indians and missionaries, antislavery and proslavery settlers, and, undoubtedly, the Civil War. The press and the men and women who used it, witnessed the bleeding borders among gender, race, and region before the Civil War.

Jotham Meeker used the press at the Baptist Mission to publish stories pertaining to Indian life in eastern Kansas Territory after the Shawnee and Delaware migration from the Ohio Valley and Great Lakes region in the 1820s and 1830s. The Shawnee and the Delaware had already experienced life among white missionaries and fur traders and were accustomed to dealing with the Great Father by the time they arrived on the banks of the lower Missouri. They had also endured conflicts with resident Indian tribes who jockeyed with emigrant tribes for land and hunting grounds. In addition, a good number of Indians intermarried with other tribes and with French and Anglo fur traders; together they produced a growing population of mixed-race children who were neither wholly Indian nor French nor Anglo. Indians and whites struggled to coexist peacefully in a region that would soon be characterized by overt conflict.

Emigrant tribes fared better among white settlers in Kansas Territory than the resident Kaw, Kickapoo, and Osage tribes, in part because tribes such as the Shawnee and Delaware appeared more "civilized" and willing to adopt white social and cultural norms. Some practiced Christianity or a syncretic blend of native and Christian spiritual forms, and some had intermarried with white traders or settlers and produced mixed-race children. Mixed-blood Indian couples such as Abelard and Quindaro Guthrie utilized their knowledge of multiple languages and cultures, trading and doing business with various Indian tribes and white settlers. Their ability to understand native and white ways enabled them to traverse the bleeding border successfully but would ultimately foreshadow how mixed-race Kansans, like other mixed-race people in the region, facilitated the wholesale displacement and dispossession of Indian land and culture by whites.[3]

Unlike the Shawnee and Delaware, the resident Kansas Indians received the brunt of white criticism and became the targets of various civilization and extermination efforts advocated by white settlers and the federal government. Refusing to relinquish their language and culture, the Kaw, Kickapoo, and Osage battled with government troops and local white militias over land and definitions of civilization. Because they resisted white encroachment and often defended their tribal sovereignty with violence, these resident Indians gained reputations as savage beasts destined for removal or extermination. These Indians refused to allow white to bleed into red, and they consequently lost their right to remain in Kansas and live among the white settlers.

Understanding how the Anglo and Indian worlds merged through economic, religious, and sexual exchange helps explain how white racial identity formed at midcentury. The Indian presence in Kansas enabled Anglo settlers to see themselves as civilized, moral, white beings in opposition to the savage, degraded, red "other." In addition, most northern and southern settlers in Kansas tabled their differences over slavery and united on the ground of white supremacy in reference to Indians. Whiteness created a tenuous bond among the first white settlers in the region that facilitated the wholesale dispossession of Indians' land and derided Indian culture. Few voices objected when the federal officials and missionaries urged the complete conversion of Indians to white ways or the removal and/or extermination of those tribes who refused to adopt white social and cultural norms. Although "Bleeding Kansas" typically refers to the blood spilled by proslavery and antislavery settlers, the bleeding actually began as white bled into red and as red struggled to maintain its sovereignty.

Jotham Meeker's press chronicled the convergence of the Indian and Anglo worlds in Kansas, and the same press, under George W. Brown's ownership, would print stories recording the collision of North and South on the bleeding border. While politics and demographics explain a great deal about why Kansas entered the Union as a free state, one can only understand how that happened by thoroughly examining the people who articulated, both verbally and physically, the conflict between slavery and free labor. When one explores Bleeding Kansas at the grass-roots level, black and white faces emerge, as do female and male actors.

African American slaves and white abolitionists worked tirelessly to prevent the implantation of slavery in Kansas. Slaves resisted their masters' attempts to set up plantations in the region by running away to Iowa and Nebraska, and abolitionists facilitated slaves' successful northern departures by booking them tickets on the Underground Railroad. Women were crucial to the success of the antislavery movement in Kansas; they provided food and housing for runaway slaves in the area, and they actively contributed to the proliferation of antislavery literature in Kansas and throughout the country. Ignoring the impact of black slave resistance and female antislavery activism, conceals the breadth, depth, and strength of a movement that was, at its core, fueled by the people.

Free-state forces would have been considerably weaker had they not redefined women's gender roles to include their participation in the politics and warfare of Kansas.[4] These assertive antislavery women rarely shied away from judging their fellow male settlers on a variety of issues, in particular, on their manhood. Women such as Julia Louisa Lovejoy joined newspaper editors such as George W. Brown and other cultural critics in their evaluation of southern and northern manhood. Northerners argued that the southern "myrmidons of border ruffianism" exceeded the proper boundaries of manhood by raping and pillaging innocent free-state settlers. They claimed that southern men in Kansas betrayed the southern code of chivalry and transgressed the proper boundaries between men and women; by raiding women's closets and shooting at them with guns, southern honor's "gloss" had indeed "become dim."[5] In addition, northern critics accused southern men of acting more like animals than men.

Southerners responded to these critiques by questioning northern manhood. In the eyes of proslavery Kansans, northern men paled in comparison to their southern counterparts because they lacked the virility, courage, and willingness to use violence to defend northern principles. Northern men might excel at manufacturing and skilled trades, but the essence of manhood resided in a man's ability to use firearms quickly and effectively in defense of honor. Because the duel epitomized southern manhood, northern men's reluctance to engage in violent duels proved to the South that southerners were more manly. In the end, some northerners began to agree with these southern critiques, especially after the Sack of Lawrence in 1856, and northern definitions of manhood began incorporating the need for aggressive, proactive violence in pursuit of antislavery goals. What both factions shared from the beginning, however, was a belief that true manhood was white manhood, and that casting doubt on racial identity could simultaneously question gender identity.

Indeed, a belief in white supremacy often knitted the North and South together in their ideologies about race. In addition to uniting on the grounds of white supremacy in reference to Indians, northern and southern settlers in Kansas agreed that miscegenation between whites and blacks should be prevented at all costs. Indian-white amalgamation rarely received the intense negative attention that black-white sexual relations did, and both North and South appeared extremely concerned that events in Kansas would increase miscegenation. "Don't you see old Buck coming?" asked the *Weston Argus*, and many northerners and southerners alike were deeply troubled by the prospect of his arrival.

Variant definitions of whiteness and different programs for achieving and maintaining white supremacy split the two groups into proslavery and antislavery camps, however. Northerners and southerners disagreed about how best to prevent miscegenation. The North argued that slavery facilitated miscegenation because it enabled slave masters to have sexual relations with their female slaves. The South, on the other hand, claimed that slavery kept the races separate and, more important, maintained a racial hierarchy that kept all whites firmly above blacks on the social and economic ladder. Furthermore, southerners argued, abolitionism would certainly result in amalgamation, because the abolitionists' love for the slave encouraged whites to engage in social and sexual relations with African Americans. Thus a common fear of miscegenation stoked both antislavery and proslavery fires, and Kansas provided a central arena for the articulation of that fear.

Examining the bleeding border between Missouri and Kansas illustrates how tensions within ideologies of gender, race, and sexuality pushed the North and the South further apart politically while uniting the two regions on the grounds of white supremacy. Free labor meant free *white* labor, according to men such as Andrew J. Francis, who settled in Kansas Territory after emigrating from his native Ohio. Francis helped organize the "free white State party" in Kansas Territory, the motto of which was "Slavery before free negroes." Francis represented many Kansans when he said, "I would prefer to have Kansas as a free State, provided there were no negroes allowed to live in the Territory. If they were to be here, I preferred that they should be under masters."[6] Though free-state forces triumphed in using popular sovereignty to save Kansas from slavery, theirs was a victory for whiteness and white supremacy, not racial equality.

The discourse on Bleeding Kansas articulated ideas about race, gender, and miscegenation that also mimicked a national discussion about the formation of a national identity rooted in white male supremacy. As white, male suffrage expanded during the Jacksonian era and as the possibilities of female and black suffrage surfaced in the mid-nineteenth century, lawmakers struggled to define citizenship and national identity in ways that honored the pursuit of democracy but limited the rights of citizenship to white men.[7] By carefully and narrowly determining the boundaries of "citizen," the male voting public defined itself by excluding women, blacks, Indians, and immigrants from the formal body politic.

The instructions given in 1855 by federal authorities to census takers in territorial Kansas illustrate this phenomenon of selective "citizen making." The government directed the census takers to count as citizens all white males, specifically excluding women, slaves, and "any Indians or persons of Indian blood." Territorial governor Andrew Reeder issued the order as follows: "A qualified voter must be free, of white blood, twenty-one years of age, an actual resident of the Territory, dwelling here with the *bona fide* intention of making it his home, and a native or naturalized citizen of the United States."[8] The census recorded white women and children's names below those of their male relatives, and females were accorded some public recognition through their association with these men. Most African Americans' names, however, were not recorded; they shared the same status as hogs and cattle by being enumerated with an *X*, and Indians were not counted at all. Thus as the government quantified its territories, it also qualified what kind of person would enjoy citizenship and nurtured a national identity defined by whiteness and maleness.

But the ascension of a racially exclusionary definition of citizenship did not gain complete hold on political life in Kansas. In 1854 the Kansas correspondent for the *New York Daily Tribune* urged his readers to note the appalling suggestion made by the proslavery *Squatter Sovereign* that free blacks be barred from entering Kansas and Nebraska. The *Sovereign*'s actions demonstrated "the importance of prompt counteracting movements by the friends of freedom," and in fact, in 1861 free blacks were not barred from entering the new state and African Americans moved to Kansas in droves after the Civil War.[9] Known as the "land of old John Brown," Kansas attracted a stream of Exodusters, black sharecroppers who escaped the poverty and violent racism of the Deep South, and several all-black colonies formed in rural Kansas in the 1870s and 1880s.[10] Although blacks did not find the land of Canaan they hoped existed on the Kansas prairie, they did benefit from a small population of whites and blacks who honored the state's abolitionist legacy and worked toward racial justice and equality in Kansas.

The "land of old John Brown" may have been a destination point for former slaves after the Civil War, but it was mainly a departure point for its Indian residents. By the turn of the twentieth century the largest bands of Indian and half-breed tribes had been removed to small reservations within the state or, more likely, to larger reservations in Oklahoma. Even though many tribes attempted to adopt white ways in post–Civil War Kansas, their possession of rich farm land often negated any claims they made on the privileges of whiteness, such as citizenship or land ownership.[11] In his *Standard History of Kansas and Kansans,* published in 1918, William E. Connelly chronicled the migration of dozens of tribes in and out of Kansas over the course of the nineteenth century. "The land-shark stood by to despoil the Indian" at every turn, he concluded.[12] Furthermore, according to the U.S. government in 1876, "an Indian [was] not a person within the meaning of the law" and thus had no citizenship rights in Kansas or elsewhere.[13] As Bleeding Kansas receded into the state's historical past, so did its Indian population.

The borders in Kansas merged in ways that allowed increased participation for white women in politics and provided African Americans limited, racially segregated educational and economic opportunities, but they also eliminated the chances for Indians or Indianness to survive in the state. The situation at the national level paralleled Kansas: Women politicked for suffrage and won that right in many western states (though they would have to wait until 1920 for federal elections), black men gained the suffrage in 1870 and were able to own property, especially in the North, but most Indians in the country were relegated to reservations, poverty, and alcoholism. During and after the Civil War the nation bled as Kansas had; although slavery was abolished, white supremacy would reign supreme for decades to come.

Sexism and racism persisted throughout the twentieth century, and Kansas would remain a flashpoint in the nation's negotiation with its racist past. One hundred years after the Kansas-Nebraska Act passed, the Supreme Court handed down a decision against the Topeka, Kansas, Board of Education, forcing it to allow black children to attend integrated schools. One can be sure that if Samuel Wood's press had survived until 1954, it would have recorded the momentous events of the 1950s, as the borders in Kansas and elsewhere continued to bleed.

EPILOGUE

In 2004, pundit Thomas Frank asked, "What's the matter with Kansas?" in his best-selling book by the same name. Frank uses Kansas, his home state, as a representative example of a national political phenomenon: the political shift to the right of "ordinary," working-class Americans. Frank wonders why and how "conservatives won the heart of America," particularly when conservative political policies often undermine their constituents' economic self-interest. Although Frank focuses mainly on class and culture to answer his question, he considers race and gender in his analysis of Kansas's political identity, and his commentary provides a fruitful opportunity to reflect on his conclusions in light of my work on Kansas's historical roots.[1]

In chapter 9, "Kansas Bleeds for Your Sins," Frank boldly asserts, "One thing [Kansas] doesn't do is racism," and he harkens back to the territorial era and its abolitionist founders as the source of the state's "mythic identity" and its history of anti-racism. He notes that even radical "Cons" (conservatives) such as Sen. Sam Brownback honor the state's proud abolitionist past by refusing to "play the race card" to convert voters to his party and his causes. He also reports that the NAACP chose Kansas as a prime location for their landmark *Brown v. Board of Education* case precisely because of the state's reputable history of race relations. According to Topeka journalist David Aubrey, "Kansas, with its free state past was selected to show that racial discrimination wasn't just a Southern problem, but a national shame. If Kansas treated blacks as second-class citizens, the rest of the country had to take special notice."[2] To be fair, Frank acknowledges that Kansas's record on race is not perfect, and he cites the state's 1920s flirtations with the KKK and 1970s white flight to the suburbs of Kansas City in his footnotes. But he seems to reify the state's mythic identity by assuming that most Kansans reject racism in part because they honor its noble, free-state heritage. Conversely, its racist, KKK-spawning history stems not from these hallowed New England mothers and fathers but from those damned Missourians who crossed the border and brought slavery and its accompanying racism to the virgin soil of Kansas.

Bleeding Borders fundamentally challenges this interpretation and will undoubtedly raise the ire of many Kansans who cherish a mythologized, antiracist account of the state's origins. It also should push Frank and others to consider racism as one answer to "What's the matter with Kansas?" As a native Kansan myself, I approached this project, and especially its conclusions, with a fair amount of hesitation. After all, my education, at the public high school just across town from the one Frank attended, was steeped in free-state mythology, as we studied the magnificent mural of John Brown in the state capitol building and lauded his legacy. I grew up hating the state of Missouri, and only recently did I realize that this hatred had been nurtured by historical roots, not merely college basketball rivalries. Kansas City natives are careful to distinguish on which side of the border they reside, and when asked the proverbial question, I remember answering, with conceit, "The right side."

Discovering the reality that the right side, the side that resisted the establishment of slavery in the region, was also the wrong side, the side that allowed segregated schools, that disenfranchised black voters, and that spawned social and political institutions that discriminated against blacks *and* Native Americans, was a rude awakening. For in addition to harboring pride in my free-state heritage, I also counted myself a northerner, someone wholly different from those prejudiced, backward southerners I had learned about in the civil rights unit of my American history class. Finding myself now firmly established in the Deep South, I look back on this naïveté with humor and irony; this John Brown admirer now teaches students who wear Confederate uniforms to fraternity balls! But what has been so liberating and enlightening about this project is the realization that the seeds of racism in our nation's history planted themselves throughout the country, in the cottonfields of Mississippi and, yes, even in the wheat fields of Kansas. I hope *Bleeding Borders* conveys this message without detracting from the bravery and honest commitment to racial equality touted by Kansas's abolitionist vanguard, John Brown among them.

But what about the women who played such an integral role in Kansas's first generation? What's the matter with Kansas women and how has gender shaped Kansas politics? Frank notes that "Kansas was traditionally ahead of the crowd on women's rights," citing the early suffrage battles in the 1860s and laws that protected abortion rights in the 1970s to illustrate its political tilt to the left on women's issues. But hot-button topics such as abortion and gay rights pulled many Kansas women to the conservative side in the 1980s and 1990s. Frank highlights these conservative women in his book, but the remarkable thing about them is that for the most part, they're strong, confident, and politically active. Take antisuffrage darling Kay O'Connor, who in the process of running for state senator in 2001, ironically claimed that maybe women's suffrage wasn't such a good idea after all.[3]

O'Connor's case is instructive because she embodies a legacy of female political activism that originated in Kansas's territorial era and characterizes the state's history to the present. Kansas women were the first in the country to be able to vote in school board elections in 1861, they were some of the first to vote in municipal elections in 1886, and the state boasted the country's first female mayor the following year. The nation's first all-woman city council took office in Oskaloosa, Kansas, in 1888, and Kansas women earned the suffrage in tax and bond issues in 1903. They did not receive full suffrage rights until 1912, but they were one of only eight states at the time who granted women the vote. Finally, Kansas was the first state in the country to elect outright a female U.S. senator, Nancy Landon Kassebaum, who took office in 1978 and was the only female member of the Senate at the time.[4] Thus it appears that Kansas's "strong-minded women," such as Sara Robinson, Margaret Wood, and Clarina Nichols, carved out a space for women in Kansas politics that has been remarkably resilient, regardless of party affiliation.

O'Connor's critique of women's suffrage, however, would make Clarina Nichols roll in her grave. So what is the matter with these Kansas women? Have they betrayed their foremothers' heritage by aligning themselves with conservative politics? The short answer is no. What has happened, I think, is that conservative women, who typically stayed out of the public sphere during the nineteenth and twentieth centuries, are now trumpeting their political voice by embracing conservative causes. Nineteenth-century women might have touted radical ideas while safely ensconced in their lace petticoats and broadcasting professions of true womanhood, but twenty-first-century women have stepped outside the private sphere with the protection of conservative causes to shield them from accusations of improper womanhood. They are following in Clarina Nichols's footsteps, albeit while wearing very different shoes.

These women, like their more liberal foremothers, enjoy support from the men in their worlds. Free-state men recognized that their cause could be strengthened by enlisting their wives and daughters in the fight for a free Kansas, and they shifted their gender identities accordingly. *Both* masculine men and feminine women could write political editorials in the nation's newspapers and even use guns to defend themselves from the barbarian ruffians who crossed the border. Now the "Cons" realize a similar advantage; put the housewives to work against the godless liberals who want to legalize abortion and gay marriage. Who better to fight these battles than conservative women, who by their very natures can claim authority over pregnancy and marriage, the birthright of "all" women? At a recent abortion rights rally in Jackson, Mississippi, the most outspoken protestor from the prolife camp was a pregnant woman with her three younger children in tow. Although her speech and her graphic signs marked her as a political being, her cause, her maternity, and the children by her side reminded everyone that she remained at her core a traditional, conservative woman.

So perhaps we can begin to answer Frank's question in a number of new ways: First, conservative women, historically inactive politically (like many of the southern women who moved to Kansas in the 1850s), are now playing an integral role in certain political causes, even running for office because of them. And Kansas (and the nation?) has moved to the Right because of their activism. Second, Kansans "do racism" and always have. As historian Rusty Monhollon and I recently noted, "From its earliest days Kansas was something of a paradox for blacks; seeking to escape Jim Crow and racism in the South they often confronted both—albeit less virulent and in different forms—in the land of John Brown."[5] One trip to the former location of Quindaro, a hotbed of abolitionism in the 1850s that is now an urban slum in Kansas City, Kansas, will illustrate Kansas's ugly underbelly of racism; boarded up shops, trash-ridden crack houses, and the sullen faces of black poverty will remind you that Kansas continues to struggle with racial equality. If a stroll down Quindaro Avenue is not enough to convince you, then read the recent stories in the Topeka paper about water and land battles between the Kickapoo Indians and the state and federal governments. Their small reservation is home to several hundred surviving Kansas Kickapoo, but their water supply is contaminated and they cannot gain the legal right to fix the problem.[6] And finally, the last fullblooded Kaw Indian, the tribe for which the state of Kansas was named, died in 2000.[7] Now only those Indians who intermarry with whites or who run successful casinos can survive. It seems as if white Kansans continue to devalue Indian rights, a practice so painfully initiated in the 1840s and 1850s.

If we acknowledge Kansas's history, with its triumphs *and* challenges, instead of lauding a mythical past, answering Frank's question is easy. Kansas's roots have produced rather predictable branches: A consistent strain of conservatism and a reluctance to change has persisted among the state's citizens, even while bursts of spectacular radicalism continue to push the populace in new directions. The recent election of a female, Democratic governor and the rejection of intelligent design by the state school board indicate that the ghosts of Sam Wood and the free-state radicals may be rising again. But it is equally likely that Kansas conservatives will find willing converts among the metaphorical descendants of the free-staters and the Border Ruffians, for both groups have qualities that reside in all Kansans and, indeed, all Americans.

NOTES

INTRODUCTION

1. Papers concerning Susannah (Yoacham) Dillon, Adrienne Christopher Folder, Miscellaneous Collection, Library and Archives Division, Kansas State Historical Society, Topeka (hereafter cited as KSHS). Christopher was Yoacham's great-granddaughter.

2. Michael Fellman, "Rehearsal for the Civil War: Antislavery and Proslavery at the Fighting Point in Kansas, 1854–1856," in *Antislavery Reconsidered: New Perspectives on the Abolitionists,* ed. Lewis Perry and Michael Fellman (Baton Rouge: Louisiana State Press, 1979), 288. See also Michael Fellman, *Inside War: The Guerrilla Conflict in Missouri During the American Civil War* (New York: Oxford University Press, 1989), 13. Throughout this book I will use the terms "Free-Soil" and "antislavery" interchangeably; both terms denote opposition to slavery in the territories only, which distinguishes this view from abolitionism, whose proponents advocated immediate abolition throughout the country. The term "free state" connotes those Kansas settlers who embraced the antislavery view and thus argued against slavery in Kansas, but some "free staters" were also abolitionists.

3. For an excellent historiographical review essay, see Gunja SenGupta, "Bleeding Kansas," *Kansas History: A Journal of the Central Plains* 24 (Winter 2001–2002): 318–341. See also Nicole Etcheson, *Bleeding Kansas: Contested Liberty in the Civil War Era* (Lawrence: University Press of Kansas, 2004); Michael Morrison, *Slavery and the American West: The Eclipse of Manifest Destiny and the Coming of the Civil War* (Chapel Hill: University of North Carolina Press, 1997), 126–188; James McPherson, *Battle Cry of Freedom: The Era of the Civil War* (New York: Oxford University Press, 1988), 145–169; William Freehling, *The Road to Disunion: Secessionists at Bay, 1776–1854* (New York: Oxford University Press, 1990), 536–566; James A. Rawley, *Race and Politics: "Bleeding Kansas" and the Coming of the Civil War* (Philadelphia: Lippincott, 1969); and Kenneth Stampp, *America in 1857: A Nation on the Brink* (New York: Oxford University Press, 1990), 144–181. These scholars chart the political history of Bleeding Kansas beginning with the passage of the Kansas-Nebraska Act in May 1854 and ending with either the passage of the antislavery Wyandot Constitution in 1859 or the entrance of Kansas to the Union as a free state in 1861. Freehling in particular does an excellent job of navigating the complicated waters of the disintegrating two-party system in the context of the national debate between Whigs and Democrats over popular sovereignty and the expansion of slavery. For a primarily demographic interpretation,

see William O. Lynch, "Population Movements in Relation to the Struggle for Kansas," in *Studies in American History, Inscribed to James Albert Woodburn*, by James Albert Woodburn (Bloomington: Indiana University, 1926), 383–404.

4. In a similar vein, Margaret S. Creighton recasts the Battle of Gettysburg by examining what she calls the "outsiders" of the battle in *Colors of Courage: Gettysburg's Forgotten History, Immigrants, Women, and African Americans in the Civil War's Defining Battle* (New York: Basic Books, 2005).

5. Drew Gilpin Faust writes, "Male prerogative and male responsibility thus served as the organizing principle of southern households and southern society; white men stood at the apex of a domestic pyramid of power and obligation that represented a microcosm of the southern social order." See Faust, *Mothers of Invention: Women of the Slaveholding South in the American Civil War* (Chapel Hill: University of North Carolina Press, 1996), 32, 4.

6. On southern honor, see Bertram Wyatt-Brown, *The Shaping of Southern Culture: Honor, Grace, and War, 1760s–1880s* (Chapel Hill: University of North Carolina Press, 2001); Bertram Wyatt-Brown, *The House of Percy: Honor, Melancholy and Imagination in a Southern Family* (New York: Oxford University Press, 1994); Betram Wyatt-Brown, *Southern Honor: Ethics and Behavior in the Old South* (New York: Oxford University Press, 1982); and Kenneth Greenberg, *Honor and Slavery: Lies, Duels, Noses, Masks, Dressing as a Woman, Gifts, Strangers, Humanitarianism, Death, Slave Rebellions, the Proslavery Argument, Baseball, Hunting, and Gambling in the Old South* (Princeton: Princeton University Press, 1996).

7. On womanhood in the nineteenth century, see Kathryn Kish Sklar, *Catharine Beecher: A Study in American Domesticity* (New Haven: Yale University Press, 1973); Nancy Cott, *The Bonds of Womanhood: Woman's Sphere in New England, 1780–1835* (New Haven: Yale University Press, 1977); Joan Jensen, *Loosening the Bonds: Mid-Atlantic Farm Women, 1750–1850* (New Haven: Yale University Press, 1986); and Mary Poovey, *Uneven Development: The Ideological Work of Gender in Mid-Victorian England* (Chicago: University of Chicago Press, 1988). On manhood, see J. A. Mangan and James Walvin, eds., *Manliness and Morality: Middle-Class Masculinity in Britain and America, 1800–1940* (New York: St. Martin's Press, 1987); Mark Carnes and Clyde Griffen, eds., *Meanings for Manhood: Constructions of Masculinity in Victorian America* (Chicago: University of Chicago Press, 1990); E. Anthony Rotundo, *American Manhood: Transformations in Masculinity from the Revolution to the Modern Era* (New York: Basic Books, 1993); Michael Kimmel, *Manhood in America: A Cultural History* (New York: Free Press, 1996); and Gail Bederman, *Manliness and Civilization: A Cultural History of Gender and Race in the United States, 1880–1917* (Chicago: University of Chicago Press, 1995). On gender in the mid-nineteenth-century American West, see Susan Lee Johnson, *Roaring Camp: The Social World of the California Gold Rush* (New York: W. W. Norton, 2000).

8. On the Kansas-Nebraska Act, see Morrison, *Slavery and the American West*, 126–156; Freehling, *Road to Disunion*, 536–565; McPherson, *Battle Cry*, 121–123; Rawley, *Race and Politics*, 26–38; Gerald Wolff, *The Kansas-Nebraska Bill: Party, Section, and the Coming of the Civil War* (New York: Revisionist Press, 1977); James Malin, *The Nebraska Question* (Lawrence: University Press of Kansas, 1953); and Roy F. Nichols, "The Kansas-Nebraska Act: A Century of Historiography," *Mississippi Valley Historical Review* 43 (September 1956): 187–212.

9. McPherson, *Battle Cry*, 58, 123–124.

10. On Indians in nineteenth-century Kansas, see Joseph B. Herring, *The Enduring Indians of Kansas: A Century and a Half of Acculturation* (Lawrence: University Press of Kansas, 1990); H. Craig Miner and William Unrau, *The End of Indian Kansas: A Study of Cultural Revolution, 1854–1871* (Lawrence: Regents Press of Kansas, 1978); William Unrau, *The Kansa Indians: A History of the Wind People, 1673–1873* (Norman: University of Oklahoma Press, 1971); and Paul Gates, *Fifty Million Acres: Conflicts over Kansas Land Policy* (New York: Atherton Press, 1966). On conflict among Indian missionaries in Kansas, see Kevin Abing, "A Holy Battleground: Methodist, Baptist, and Quaker Missionaries among Shawnee Indians, 1830–1844," *Kansas History* 21 (Summer 1998): 118–137.

11. For studies of Anglo-Indian contact, see Richard White, *The Middle Ground: Indians, Empires, and Republics in the Great Lakes Region, 1650–1815* (Cambridge: Cambridge University Press, 1991); Daniel Usner, *Indians, Settlers, and Slaves in a Frontier Exchange Economy* (Chapel Hill: University of North Carolina Press, 1992); Philip Deloria, *Playing Indian* (New Haven: Yale University Press, 1998); James Axtell, *The Invasion Within: The Contest of Cultures in Colonial North America* (New York: Oxford University Press, 1985); James Merrell, *The Indians' New World: Catawbas and Their Neighbors from European Contact through the Era of Removal* (Chapel Hill: University of North Carolina Press, 1989); Daniel Richter, *The Ordeal of the Longhouse: The Peoples of the Iroquois League in the Era of European Colonization* (Chapel Hill: University of North Carolina Press, 1992); Peter C. Mancall, *Deadly Medicine: Indians and Alcohol in Early America* (Ithaca, N.Y.: Cornell University Press, 1995); and Glenda Riley, *Confronting Race: Women and Indians on the Frontier, 1815–1915* (Albuquerque: University of New Mexico Press, 2004).

12. Gunja SenGupta, *For God and Mammon: Evangelicals and Entrepreneurs, Masters and Slaves in Territorial Kansas, 1854–1860* (Athens: University of Georgia Press, 1996), 5.

13. Etcheson, *Bleeding Kansas*, 4.

14. David Roediger, *Colored White: Transcending the Racial Past* (Berkeley and Los Angeles: University of California Press, 2002), 130, 122. Though Roediger briefly considers "white settlers and red indians" in his pathbreaking study, *The Wages of Whiteness: Race and the Making of the American Working Class* (New York: Verso, 1991), he quickly dismisses the influence of redness on whiteness because of Indians' diminished presence in the East (where white workers were concentrated) and because of their perceived "independence" (22). For other studies that "move beyond the Black-white binary," see Elliott West, "Reconstructing Race," *Western Historical Quarterly* 34 (Spring 2003): 7–26; Matthew Frye Jacobson, *Whiteness of a Different Color: European Immigrants and the Alchemy of Race* (Cambridge: Harvard University Press, 1998); Theodore Allen, *The Invention of the White Race*, vol. 1, *Racial Oppression and Social Control* (London: Verso, 1994); Cheryl Harris, "Whiteness as Property," *Harvard Law Review* 106 (June 1993): 1709–91; Alexander Saxton, *The Rise and Fall of the White Republic: Class Politics and Mass Culture in Nineteenth-Century America* (London: Verso, 1990); Ronald Takaki, *Iron Cages: Race and Culture in Nineteenth-Century America* (New York: Oxford University Press, 1990); and Reginald Horsman, *Race and Manifest Destiny: The Origins of American Racial Anglo-Saxonism* (Cambridge: Harvard University Press, 1981).

15. For similar discussions of variegated whiteness among white populations, see Ja-

cobson, *Whiteness of a Different Color,* and Neil Foley, *The White Scourge: Mexicans, Blacks, and Poor Whites in Texas Cotton Culture* (Berkeley and Los Angeles: University of California Press, 1998).

16. Sara Tappan Robinson, *Kansas: Its Interior and Exterior Life* (Boston: Crosby, Nichols, 1856), 42.

17. Amy S. Greenberg, *Manifest Manhood and the Antebellum American Empire* (Cambridge and New York: Cambridge University Press, 2005), 14, 11; Melanie Susan Gustafson, *Women and the Republican Party, 1854–1924* (Urbana: University of Illinois Press, 2001), 1–33; and Michael Pierson, *Free Hearts and Free Homes: Gender and American Antislavery Politics* (Chapel Hill: University of North Carolina Press, 2003). See also Kristin Hoganson, "Garrisonian Abolitionists and the Rhetoric of Gender, 1850–1860," *American Quarterly* 45 (December 1993): 558–595. For one of the few studies that focuses on southern women in antebellum politics, see Elizabeth Varon, *We Mean to Be Counted: White Women and Politics in Antebellum Virginia* (Chapel Hill: University of North Carolina Press, 1998).

CHAPTER 1.

1. Clara Gowing to George Martin, May 7, 1908, Delaware Indians, History, Box 590, Library and Archives Division, KSHS (hereafter cited as Delaware Indians, History, KSHS); Clara Gowing, "A Wedding Among the Indians," in Delaware Indians, History, KSHS.

2. For a discussion of several mixed-race couples in Kansas Territory, see Allen M. Coville, "Incidents relative to the early history and border wars of Kansas as seen and heard by one who was there (in 1854)," original manuscript, Library and Archives Division, KSHS. Several historians have considered Indian-Anglo and Indian-French sexual and marriage relationships in Missouri and eastern Kansas. See Tanis C. Thorne, *The Many Hands of My Relations: French and Indians on the Lower Missouri* (Columbia: University of Missouri Press, 1996); John Ewers, "Mothers of Mixed-Bloods: The Marginal Woman in the History of the Upper Missouri," in *Probing the American West,* ed. K. Ross Toole (Santa Fe: Museum of New Mexico, 1962), 26–70; and William E. Unrau, *Mixed-Bloods and Tribal Dissolution: Charles Curtis and the Quest for Indian Identity* (Lawrence: University Press of Kansas, 1989). For two studies that examine mixed-bloods in several locations, see Robert Bieder, "Scientific Attitudes toward Indian Mixed-Bloods in Early Nineteenth Century America," *Journal of Ethnic Studies* 8 (Summer 1980): 17–30, and Jacqueline Peterson, "The People in Between: Indian-White Marriage and the Genesis of a Metis Society and Culture in the Great Lakes Region, 1680–1830" (Ph.D. diss., University of Illinois at Chicago, 1981).

3. For the middle-ground concept, see White, *Middle Ground,* 187–188. Paul Gates astutely noted over a generation ago that Bleeding Kansas involved more than the controversy over slavery; he argued that conflicts with Indians characterized as much or more of the early settlers' daily lives as did the struggle over slavery. See Gates, *Fifty Million Acres,* 3–10. See also Kevin Abing, "Before Bleeding Kansas: Christian Missionaries, Slavery, and the Shawnee Indians in Pre-Territorial Kansas, 1844–1854," *Kansas History* 24 (Spring 2001): 54–71.

4. Edmund Morgan first suggested the importance of racism toward Indians to the establishment of race-based slavery in colonial Virginia. See Morgan, *American Slavery, American Freedom: The Ordeal of Colonial Virginia* (New York: W. W. Norton, 1975), especially 232–234. More recently, Kathleen Brown has examined the intersection of racialized ideas about Indians and blacks in *Good Wives, Nasty Wenches, and Anxious Patriarchs: Race, Gender, and Power in Colonial Virginia* (Chapel Hill: University of North Carolina Press, 1996). However, few authors have carefully examined the continuing importance of white contact with Indians in the formation of white racial identity during the nineteenth century. For some notable exceptions, see Saxton, *Rise and Fall of the White Republic*, 183–205, 269–293, and 321–349; Takaki, *Iron Cages;* Harris, "Whiteness as Property," 1721–1736; Dana Nelson, *National Manhood: Capitalist Citizenship and the Imagined Fraternity of White Men* (Durham, N.C.: Duke University Press, 1998); and Riley, *Confronting Race*, 8, 61, 212–239. See also Elliott West, "Reconstructing Whiteness," for a consideration of Indians' and Mexicans' affect on white racial identity at midcentury.

5. White, *Middle Ground*, 187–188. For case studies that examine the transformation of Indian society after European colonization, see Anthony Wallace, *The Death and Rebirth of the Seneca* (New York: Vintage, 1969); James Axtell, *The European and the Indian: Essays in the Ethnohistory of Colonial North America* (New York: Oxford University Press, 1981) and *The Invasion Within: The Contest of Cultures in Colonial North America* (New York: Oxford University Press, 1985); Merrell, *Indians' New World;* Richter, *Ordeal of the Longhouse;* Mancall, *Deadly Medicine;* and Neal Salisbury, "The Indians' Old World: Native Americans and the Coming of Europeans," *William and Mary Quarterly* 53 (July 1996): 435–458.

6. Herring, *Enduring Indians of Kansas*, 2. For other studies of Indians in Kansas, see Miner and Unrau, *End of Indian Kansas*, and Unrau, *Kansa Indians*.

7. Herring, *Enduring Indians of Kansas*, 13–18, and Jeremy Neely, *The Border Between Them: Violence and Reconciliation on the Kansas-Missouri Line* (Columbia: University of Missouri Press, 2007), 7–23. See also Tony R. Mullis, *Peacekeeping on the Plains: Army Operations in Bleeding Kansas* (Columbia: University of Missouri Press, 2004) for a study of the army's role in removing, resettling, and policing the emigrant tribes in Kansas.

8. Herring, *Enduring Indians of Kansas*, 13.

9. Portions of the Shawnee and Delaware tribes migrated from the Ohio River Valley to Missouri during the late eighteenth and early nineteenth centuries. See Daniel H. Usner, "An American Indian Gateway: Some Thoughts on the Migration and Settlement of Eastern Indians around Early St. Louis," *Gateway Heritage* 11 (Winter 1990–91): 42–51.

10. Alfred Cumming to George Manypenny, January 2, 1855, Letters Received by the Office of Indian Affairs, Bureau of Indian Affairs, MF 234, Roll 55, NARA (hereafter cited as Letters Received–Office).

11. For a general history of the Delaware, see Clinton Weslager, *The Delaware Indians: A History* (New Brunswick: Rutgers University Press, 1972). See also Earl P. Olmstead, *Blackcoats among the Delaware: David Zeisberger on the Ohio Frontier* (Kent, Ohio: Kent State University Press, 1991), which examines the Moravian Delaware missions in Ohio.

12. Alfred Cumming to George Manypenny, January 2, 1855, Letters Received–Office, MF 234, Roll 56.

13. See Alfred Cumming to George Manypenny, February 24, 1857.

14. Thomas Johnson to the Hon. O. Brown, Commissioner of Indian Affairs, October 12, 1849, Kansa Indians, History, Box 2, Library and Archives Division, KSHS (hereafter cited as Kansa Indians, History, KSHS).

15. See Jerry Clark, *The Shawnee* (Lexington: University Press of Kentucky, 1993) and David Edmunds, *Tecumseh and the Quest for Indian Leadership* (Boston: Little, Brown, 1984).

16. Alfred Cumming to George Manypenny, February 24, 1857.

17. Ibid.

18. Joseph Jablow, *Illinois, Kickapoo, and Potawatomi Indians* (New York: Garland, 1974).

19. John Joseph Mathews, *The Osages: Children of the Middle Waters* (Norman: University of Oklahoma Press, 1961), 615.

20. Charles Monroe Chase to the *True Republican and Sentinel* (Sycamore, Ill.), August 7, 1863, Charles Chase Papers, Miscellaneous Collections, Library and Archives Division, KSHS (hereafter cited as Chase Papers).

21. John W. Whitfield, Committee Report, Kaws, 1853, Kansa Indians, History, KSHS.

22. George Manypenny to Hon. R. McClelland, Secretary of the Interior, May 3, 1856, Letters Received–Office, 1851–1856, MF 234, Roll 55.

23. Alfred Cumming to George Manypenny, February 24, 1857.

24. Ibid.

25. Ibid.

26. Thorne, *Many Hands of My Relations*, 149.

27. See Patricia Seed, *Ceremonies of Possession in Europe's Conquest of the New World, 1492–1640* (New York: Cambridge University Press, 1995), for a comparison of early colonial efforts at Indian conversion among the Spanish, French, Dutch, and English colonists and missionaries. James Axtell's *Invasion Within* also compares Catholic and Protestant missions. For several studies that consider Catholic missions during the colonial era, see Jerald Milanich, *Laboring in the Fields of the Lord: Spanish Missions and Southeastern Indians* (Washington, D.C.: Smithsonian Institution Press, 1999); Christopher Vecsey, *On the Padre's Trail* (South Bend, Ind.: University of Notre Dame Press, 1996); and Karen Anderson, *Chain Her by One Foot: The Subjugation of Women in Seventeenth-Century New France* (London: Routledge, 1991). See also Abing, "Before Bleeding Kansas," for a discussion of Protestant missionaries among the Shawnee in Kansas.

28. Herring, *Enduring Indians of Kansas*, 5.

29. George Schultz, *An Indian Canaan: Isaac McCoy and the Vision of an Indian State* (Norman: University of Oklahoma Press, 1972).

30. Alfred Gray to George H. Patterson, June 12, 1860, Alfred Gray Correspondence, 1855–1879, Box 361, Library and Archives Division, KSHS.

31. Committee Report, Shawnees, submitted by J. C. Berryman, 1842, Kansa Indians, History, KSHS.

32. Coville, "Incidents," 5.

33. Elizabeth Morse to J. G. Pratt, September 2, 1861, Delaware Indians, History, KSHS.

34. Francis W. Lea, Committee Report, 1852, Kansa Indians, History, KSHS.

35. Thomas Mosely Jr., Committee Report, Delaware, 1851, Kansa Indians, History, KSHS.

36. Elizabeth Morse to J. G. Pratt, September 2, 1861.

37. Committee Report, Shawnees, submitted by J. C. Berryman.

38. Jordan Euphrates Journeycake, "All must stand before the Judgement seat of Christ," Delaware Indians, History, KSHS.

39. For several comprehensive studies of the relationship between abolitionism and Christianity, see Lewis Perry, *Radical Abolitionism: Anarchy and the Government of God in Antislavery Thought* (Ithaca: Cornell University Press, 1973); John R. McKivigan, *War Against Proslavery Religion: Abolitionism and the Northern Churches, 1830–1865* (Ithaca: Cornell University Press, 1984); and John R. McKivigan and Mitchell Snay, eds., *Religion and the Antebellum Debate over Slavery* (Athens: University of Georgia Press, 1998).

40. Two of the largest Catholic missions in the area served the Kickapoo and Pottawatomie, two groups who repeatedly lacked "civilized" behavior, according to Protestants such as Sara Robinson. See William Whites Graves, *History of the Kickapoo Mission and Parish: The First Catholic Church in Kansas* (St. Paul, Kans.: Journal Press, 1938), and Thomas H. Kinsella, *A Centenary of Catholicity in Kansas, 1822–1922* (Kansas City, Mo.: Casey Printing, 1921).

41. Joseph Gambone, "The Forgotten Feminist: The Papers of Clarina I. H. Nichols," *Kansas Historical Quarterly* 39 (Spring 1973): 54; Robinson, *Kansas,* 30, 57. Glenda Riley argues that most Anglo women in the West "helped perpetuate racial problems" even though many of them were able to connect with and understand Indians in a more "intimate" way than Anglo men. See Riley, *Confronting Race,* 7–10.

42. For example, many of the Delawares in the region had moved from Moravian missions in Ohio and became associated with the Moravians in Kansas. Similarly, the majority of the Shawnee Indians that white settlers had contact with in Kansas lived or had lived at the Methodist mission just west of Kansas City. See Olmstead, *Blackcoats among the Delaware,* and Lois Nettleship, "Mission to the Indians," in *The Shawnee Indians in Johnson County* (Shawnee Mission, Kans.: Johnson County Center for Local History, 1985).

43. Robinson, *Kansas,* 30.

44. B. F. Van Horn to George W. Martin, January 4, 1909, Benjamin F. Van Horn Papers, Miscellaneous Collections, Library and Archives Division, KSHS (hereafter cited as Van Horn Papers).

45. J. W. Mosher, "French Frank, The Indian Trader," Frank La Loge Papers, Miscellaneous Collections, Library and Archives Division, KSHS.

46. Sylvester H. Clarke to his wife, June 23, 1855, Sylvester H. Clarke Papers, Miscellaneous Collections, Library and Archives Division, KSHS (hereafter cited as Clarke Papers).

47. Mancall, *Deadly Medicine.* See also Usner, "American Indian Gateway," 48.

48. Alfred Cumming to George Manypenny, January 2, 1855.

49. Burton A. James to George Manypenny, January 31, 1855, Letters Received–Office, 1851–1856, MF 234, Roll 55.

50. Alfred Cumming to George Manypenny, January 2, 1855.

51. "Statement of Losses Interview, Mrs. Fannie Kelly Claim," 1864, Fanny Kelly Papers, Miscellaneous Collections, Library and Archives Division, KSHS. See also T. J. Stiles,

ed., *In Their Own Words: Warriors and Pioneers* (New York: Perigee Books, 1996), 55–69.

52. "Mary and Hayden D. McMeekin, Natives of Kentucky and 'Pioneer Settlers' of Leavenworth," Hayden D. McMeekin Papers, Miscellaneous Collections, Library and Archives Division, KSHS (hereafter cited as McMeekin Papers). See also the *United States Biographical Dictionary and Portrait Gallery of Eminent and Self-Made Men* (New York: U.S. Biographical Publishing, 1878), 685.

53. Mary Lawrence McMeekin Morton, "Some Incidents in My Life in Kansas During the Early Days," McMeekin Papers.

54. Clara Harding Jordan, "In My Hundred and Second Year," *Museum Graphics* (Winter 1953), cited in Jane B. Frick, "Women Writers Along the Rivers, 1850–1950: The Roles and Images of Women in Northwestern Missouri and Northeastern Kansas as Evidenced by Their Writings" (Ph.D. diss., University of Missouri–Kansas City, 1982).

55. W. B. Royall to Brig. Gen. R. Jones, June 21, 1848, W. B. Royall Papers, Miscellaneous Collections, Library and Archives Division, KSHS.

56. "Letters relative to squatters on Delaware land near Fort Leavenworth," extract from the Report of the Commissioner of Indian Affairs, Delaware Agency, 1855–57, MF 234, Roll 274, NARA.

57. Ibid.

58. W. B. Royall to Brig. Gen. Robert Jones, June 21, 1848. A berdache is an Indian who is thought to possess the male and female sexes in one body. Berdache Indians were often revered by their communities because they possessed double the spiritual power of a single-sexed being. See Sara Evans, "The First American Woman," in *Women's America: Refocusing America's Past,* ed. Linda Kerber and Jane DeHart (New York: Oxford University Press, 1982), 31–41. See also Walter Williams, *The Spirit and the Flesh: Sexual Diversity in American Indian Culture* (Boston: Beacon Press, 1986).

59. Wilcomb Washburn, cited in Allen, *Invention of the White Race* 1:38. On Native American gender roles, see Joan M. Jensen, "Native American Women and Agriculture: A Seneca Case Study," in *Women and Power in American History: A Reader,* 2 vols., ed. Kathryn Kish Sklar and Tom Dublin (Englewood Cliffs, N.J.: Prentice Hall, 1991), 1:8–23. Jensen argues that Indian women "dominated agricultural production in the tribes of the eastern half of the United States. In many of these tribes the work of the women provided over half of the subsistence and secured for them not only high status but also public power" (8). See also Laura F. Klein and Lillian A. Ackerman, eds., *Women and Power in Native North America* (Norman: University of Oklahoma Press, 1995); Nancy Shoemaker, ed., *Negotiators of Change: Historical Perspectives on Native American Women* (New York: Routledge, 1995); and Riley, *Confronting Race.*

60. Gowing, "Wedding Among the Indians."

61. John W. Whitfield, Committee Report, Kaws.

62. For several studies that examine the middle-class family in the nineteenth century, see Cott, *Bonds of Womanhood;* Sklar, *Catharine Beecher;* and especially Mary P. Ryan, *Cradle of the Middle Class: The Family in Oneida county, New York, 1790–1865* (Cambridge: Cambridge University Press, 1981).

63. John W. Whitfield, Committee Report, Kaws.

64. Thomas Johnson to Major B. F. Robinson, August 29, 1853, Kansa Indians, History, KSHS.

65. Rep. John Sherman cited in Wilcomb E. Washburn, *The American Indian and the United States: A Documentary History* (New York: Random House, 1973), 1:1521.

66. Richard Slotkin notes the same process of recognition of humanity through attempts at dehumanization and otherness in *The Fatal Environment: The Myth of the Frontier in the Age of Industrialization, 1800–1890* (New York: HarperCollins, 1985), 78–80.

67. The growing literature on whiteness studies includes Horsman, *Race and Manifest Destiny;* David Roediger, *Toward the Abolition of Whiteness: Essays on Race, Politics, and Working Class History* (London: Verso, 1994); Roediger, *Wages of Whiteness;* Allen, *Invention of the White Race;* Saxton, *Rise and Fall of the White Republic;* and Foley, *White Scourge.*

68. Washburn, *American Indian* 1:1393.

69. Cheryl Harris connects whiteness with the privilege of citizenship and the right to seize Indian lands for white ownership. See Harris, "Whiteness as Property," 1721. See also Morgan, *American Slavery, American Freedom,* where he notes that colonial Virginians "learned their first lessons in racial hatred by putting down the Indians" (328).

70. James Hindman Diary, March 1857, James Hindman Papers, Miscellaneous Collections, Library and Archives Division, KSHS (hereafter cited as Hindman Papers).

71. Martha Chenault to "mother," February 16, 1851, Sac and Fox Indians, History, Library and Archives Division, KSHS (hereafter cited as Sac and Fox Indians, History, KSHS).

72. Clemmie Boon to Victoria Boon, May 22, 1851, Sac and Fox Indians, History, KSHS.

73. See Thorne, *Many Hands of My Relations;* Ewers, "Mothers of Mixed-Bloods"; Unrau, *Mixed-Bloods and Tribal Dissolution;* and Bieder, "Scientific Attitudes toward Indian Mixed-Bloods."

74. John Montgomery, Committee Report, Kaws, 1856–56, Kansa Indians, History, KSHS.

75. Ibid.

76. Alfred Cumming to George Manypenny, February 24, 1857. Cumming included this story in his report precisely because the Pottawatomie council was meeting and trying to apportion Le Clerc's children's annuity payments when Cumming visited the reservation.

77. Sylvester Clarke Journal, August 25, 1855, Clarke Papers.

78. William Connelley, "Biographical Sketch of Abelard Guthrie," 1898, Abelard Guthrie Journal, Library and Archives Division, KSHS (hereafter cited as Guthrie Journal).

79. December 16, 1858, Guthrie Journal.

80. April 15, 1858, Guthrie Journal.

81. Ibid.

82. March 31, April 9, 1858, Guthrie Journal.

83. See October 6, December 15, 16, 1858, Guthrie Journal.

84. Guthrie complained about his hired hand's drinking problem on numerous occasions. He traveled to town several times to find "George" at the saloon when he was supposed to be at work. See August 22, September 9, 10, 12, and 13, 1858, Guthrie Journal.

85. April 5, 1858, Guthrie Journal.

86. John M. Coward, *The Newspaper Indian: Native American Identity in the Press, 1820–*

1890 (Urbana: University of Illinois Press, 1999), 3. One of the most extreme examples of white settlers putting these ideas into practice is the 1864 Sand Creek massacre of hundreds of Sioux and Osage men, women, and children by a volunteer army in eastern Colorado and western Kansas. See David Svaldi, *Sand Creek and the Rhetoric of Extermination: A Case Study in Indian-White Relations* (Lanham, Md.: University Press of America, 1989), and Saxton, *Rise and Fall of the White Republic*, 269–288.

87. October 4, 1858, Guthrie Journal.

CHAPTER 2.

1. *Kansas Weekly Herald*, March 24, 1855, reprinted in the *Lawrence (Kans.) Herald of Freedom*, May 25, 1855; *Kansas Weekly Herald*, May 25, 1855. The *Weekly Herald* used the phrase "nigger stealer" in this story to describe an abolitionist, and the related term, "negro stealer," also gained some currency in the proslavery papers. Lawrence, Kansas, served as a focal point for the Underground Railroad in the area, and many proslavery Kansans loathed the town and its citizens. See Richard B. Sheridan, *Freedom's Crucible: The Underground Railroad in Lawrence and Douglas County, Kansas, 1854–1865* (Lawrence: University of Kansas, 1998), and Todd Mildfelt, *The Secret Danites: Kansas' First Jayhawkers* (Richmond, Kans.: Todd Mildfelt, 2003).

2. Fellman, *Inside War*, 19.

3. Morrison, *Slavery and the American West*, 10.

4. Etcheson, *Bleeding Kansas*, 219.

5. Stanley Harrold, *Subversives: Antislavery Community in Washington, D.C., 1828–1865* (Baton Rouge: Louisiana State University Press, 2003), 12. The biracial antislavery community formed in Washington to combat slavery and the slave trade shares many commonalities with the antislavery community in Kansas Territory.

6. Etcheson concludes, "Just as proslavery Missourians had always feared, free Kansas created a free Missouri and a free nation" (*Bleeding Kansas*, 245). I assert that this process of "freeing Kansas," led by abolitionists and slaves, began prior to the wartime events that she narrates in her final chapter. My argument is similar to William Link's in *Roots of Secession: Slavery and Politics in Antebellum Virginia* (Chapel Hill: University of North Carolina Press, 2003). Link examines how Virginia's "subversive emissaries," like abolitionists, free blacks and rebellious slaves, shaped the political debate and pushed the state toward secession.

7. Michael Magliari finds that Indian labor in California prior to the Civil War was inherently unfree. Even though the state rejected black slavery in its 1850 Constitution, the "1850 Act for the Government and Protection of Indians," legalized various forms of virtual slavery for Indians. See Michael Magliari, "Free Soil, Unfree Labor: Cave Johnson Couts and the Binding of Indian Workers in California, 1850–1867," *Pacific Historical Review* 73, no. 3 (2004): 349–389.

8. The literature on free labor is too vast to survey here. For a selection of the most prominent studies, see Eric Foner, *Free Soil, Free Labor, Free Men: The Ideology of the Republican Party before the Civil War* (New York: Oxford University Press, 1970); Jonathan A. Glickstein, *Concepts of Free Labor in Antebellum America* (New Haven: Yale University Press, 1991); Robert J. Steinfeld, *The Invention of Free Labor: The Employment Relation in*

English and American Law and Culture, 1350–1870 (Chapel Hill: University of North Carolina Press, 1991); and Gunther Peck, *Reinventing Free Labor: Padrone and Immigrant Workers in the North American West, 1880–1930* (Cambridge: Cambridge University Press, 2000). For a study of free labor families on the frontier, see John Mack Faragher, *Sugar Creek: Life on the Illinois Prairie, 1819–1865* (New Haven: Yale University Press, 1986).

9. David D. Smits, "The 'Squaw Drudge': A Prime Index of Savagism," *Ethnohistory* 29, no. 4 (1982): 301. On Indian women, gender, and agriculture, see Theda Perdue, *Cherokee Women: Gender and Culture Change* (Lincoln: University of Nebraska Press, 1998), 17–40; Klein and Ackerman, *Women and Power in Native North America;* Shoemaker, *Negotiators of Change;* and Riley, *Confronting Race.* For colonial examples of this perception of Indian women by white settlers, see Brown, *Good Wives, Nasty Wenches, and Anxious Patriarchs,* 42–75, and Smits, "Squaw Drudge," 281–297. See William Cronon, *Changes in the Land: Indians, Colonists, and the Ecology of New England* (New York: Hill and Wang, 1983) for the origins of differences in Anglo-Indian land use in the Northeast.

10. Berryman quoted in Abing, "Before Bleeding Kansas," 58; E. V. Sumner to Major D. C. Buell, January 30, 1851, Letters Sent from Ft. Leavenworth, January 24, 1844–December 7, 1852, Bureau of Indian Affairs Manuscripts, NARA, Kansas City, Mo.

11. West, "Reconstructing Race," 11. Douglass quote from Linda K. Kerber, "The Abolitionist Perception of the Indian," *Journal of American History* 62 (September 1975): 294. See also Coward, *Newspaper Indian,* 2–3.

12. Randall B. Woods, "Integration, Exclusion, or Segregation? The 'Color Line' in Kansas, 1878–1900," *Western Historical Quarterly* 14, no. 2 (April 1983): 181–198.

13. Etcheson, *Bleeding Kansas,* 31. See also R. Douglas Hurt, *Agriculture and Slavery in Missouri's Little Dixie* (Columbia: University of Missouri Press, 1992).

14. Henry Clay, "An Address Delivered to the Colonization Society of Kentucky," December 17, 1829, full text available at http://www.kyvl.org/kentuckiana/cgi-bin/Ebind3html/3/ac0405?seq=3;trans/ (accessed May 28, 2007); also cited in Alisse Portnoy, *Their Right to Speak: Women's Activism in the Indian and Slave Debates* (Cambridge: Harvard University Press, 2005), 88.

15. Charles Monroe Chase Scrapbook, letter dated August 21, 1863, Chase Papers.

16. Col. Alexander Johnson, "Slaves in Kansas Territory," Biography, Miscellaneous Thomas Johnson Papers, Box M44, Library and Archives Division, KSHS (hereafter cited as Johnson Papers).

17. Horsman, *Race and Manifest Destiny,* 190. Horsman notes a shift in the government's thoughts on Indians' potential as a race between 1830 and 1850. The burgeoning scientific literature on the origins and hierarchy of the various "distinct" races and the protracted conflicts between Indians and white settlers on the expanding western frontier contributed to the idea that Indians were fundamentally racially inferior. See Horsman, *Race and Manifest Destiny,* 191.

18. September 15, 1858, Guthrie Journal.

19. Abing, "Before Bleeding Kansas," 58.

20. Zu Adams, "Slaves in Kansas," typescript, Slavery Collection, 1, Library and Archives Division, KSHS; Johnson, "Slaves in Kansas Territory." See also Charles Cory, "Slavery in Kansas," 12, 15, and Nettleship, "Mission to the Indians," for corroborative accounts of Maj. R. W. Cummins and his slaves. Henry Shindler, "When Slaves Were Owned

in Kansas by Army Officers," *Leavenworth Times,* October 13, 1912, cited in SenGupta, *For God and Mammon,* 118. SenGupta's factual account of slavery in Kansas Territory mirrors my own in many ways, although I place more emphasis on the impact of slavery's presence in Kansas.

21. Abing, "Before Bleeding Kansas," 58.

22. Cummins quoted in ibid., 60.

23. Thomas Mosely, Committee Report, Wyandot, 1849, Kansa Indians, History, KSHS.

24. For several accounts of southern political "victories" and proslavery ideology in Kansas, see Bill Cecil-Fronsman, "'Death to All Yankees and Traitors in Kansas': The *Squatter Sovereign* and the Defense of Slavery in Kansas," *Kansas History* 16 (Spring 1993): 22–33; Floyd C. Shoemaker, "Missouri's Proslavery Fight for Kansas," *Missouri Historical Review* 48 (April 1954): 231; William Stanley Hoole, ed., "A Southerner's Viewpoint of the Kansas Situation, 1856–1857: The Letters of Lieut. Col. A. J. Hoole, C.S.A.," *Kansas Historical Quarterly* 3 (February 1934): 43; and SenGupta, *For God and Mammon,* 28–40, 116–130.

25. *Weekly Southern Democrat,* July 21, 1855. Although the Republican Party was officially founded in 1854 and its precursor, the Free-Soil Party, had all but dissolved, many Missourians referred to Republicans as Free-Soilers or, more disparagingly (and inaccurately), abolitionists. I use the terms "antislavery" and "free state" interchangeably, because the beliefs of the Free State party were more antislavery than abolitionist.

26. *Democratic Platform,* September 21, 1854.

27. "Slaves and Slavery," History of Slaves, Manuscript Collection 640, Library and Archives Division, KSHS (hereafter cited as History of Slaves); and SenGupta, *For God and Mammon,* 41. See also "Kansas Territorial Census of March 1855," reprinted in *1855 Territory of Kansas Census,* 2 vols. (Overland Park: Kansas Statistical Publications, 1985). According to SenGupta's research, 186 slaves resided in Kansas, not 193. I accept the 193 figure because that is the number most often cited in Manuscript Collection 640; also, the census takers did not include slaves owned by Indians or military personnel, so a lower number would, I think, be even less representative of the actual number of slaves who lived in the territory. See SenGupta, *For God and Mammon,*192n15.

28. Charles E. Cory, "Slavery in Kansas," *Collections of the Kansas State Historical Society* 7 (Louisville, Ky.: Lost Cause Press, 1977), 9. Cory notes that the first official census of the territory, taken in February 1855, counted 193 slaves and 151 free blacks, but he questions that enumeration and argues that slaves were undercounted.

29. John James Ingalls to "Father," June 10, 1859, John J. Ingalls Papers, Collection #177, Box 1, Family Correspondence, 1858–1889, Library and Archives Division, KSHS.

30. SenGupta, *For God and Mammon,* 127. SenGupta cites several accounts that claim the slave population "more than doubled" between 1855 and 1857.

31. "Kansas Territorial Census of March 1855." See also table in SenGupta, *For God and Mammon,* 122.

32. Sen. Davy Atchison argued that making Kansas a slave state was crucial to maintaining the security of the institution in his home state, Missouri. See Freehling, *Road to Disunion,* 545–553. Other southern states argued that making Kansas a slave state was necessary for slavery's survival throughout the border South. The *Charleston Mercury* worried

that the loss of Kansas would lead to abolition in Missouri, Kentucky, and, finally, Virginia. See Stampp, *America in 1857*, 144–145.

33. *Weekly Southern Democrat*, July 21, 1855.

34. "An appeal to the South from the Kansas Emigration Society of Missouri, published in the Southern newspapers," cited in W. L. Fleming, "The Buford Expedition to Kansas," *American Historical Review* 6 (October 1900): 38. The *Montgomery (Ala.) Advertiser and Gazette* was one of "several" southern papers that published Missouri's appeal.

35. See James C. Malin, "The Proslavery Background of the Kansas Struggle," *Mississippi Valley Historical Review* 10, no. 3 (December 1923): 289; Freehling, *Road to Disunion*, 550–551; and McPherson, *Battle Cry*, 145–147.

36. Quoted in Etcheson, *Bleeding Kansas*, 148.

37. *Westport (Mo.) Frontier News*, October 6, 1855.

38. Territorial governor Wilson Shannon announced Buford's arrival to the area on June 27, 1856. See Wilson Shannon to President Franklin Pierce, June 27, 1856, Territorial Troubles File, Kansas Territory Executive Department Correspondence, Library and Archives Division, KSHS.

39. "Col. Buford's Propositions," *Eufala (Ala.) Spirit of the South*, copied on request in other southern newspapers, reprinted in Fleming, "Buford Expedition," 40. See also Etcheson, *Bleeding Kansas*, 42.

40. Letter to President Franklin Pierce, July 17, 1856, Letters Received by the Central Superintendency, Bureau of Indian Affairs, NARA, Kansas City, Mo (hereafter cited as Letters Received–Central Superintendency). See also letter from G. W. Clarke to George H. Manypenny, December 26, 1856, Letters Received–Central Superintendency, for a corroborative account of this incident.

41. B. Harding to Zu Adams, September 9, 1895, "Slaves and Slavery," History of Slaves.

42. B. F. Stringfellow to *Montgomery Advertiser*, quoted in D. W. Wilder, *Annals of Kansas, 1541–1885* (Topeka: T. Dwight Thacher, 1885), 73. See also Lester B. Baltimore, "Benjamin F. Stringfellow: The Fight for Slavery on the Missouri Border," *Missouri Historical Review* 62, no. 1 (1967): 14–29.

43. "The Laws of the Territory of Kansas," reprinted in *The Border Ruffian Code in Kansas* (New York: Tribune Office, 1856), Snyder Collection, University of Missouri, Kansas City (hereafter cited as *Border Ruffian Code*).

44. *Free South*, August 1860, P. P. Wilcox Scrapbook, vol. 1, Library and Archives Division, KSHS (hereafter cited as Wilcox Scrapbook). See also "Negro Insurrection," *Kansas City (Mo.) Enterprise*, November 11, 1856, and "Negro Excitement," *Independence (Mo.) Occidental Messenger*, September 3, 1859.

45. "Horrible Murder," *Weekly Southern Democrat*, October 22, 1855.

46. *Star of Empire*, January 1, 1857.

47. *Border Ruffian Code*, 2; "Statutes of 1855," chap. 151, reprinted in Cory, "Slavery in Kansas," 4.

48. *Western Dispatch* (Independence, Mo.), June 8, 1855, cited in Sylvester H. Clarke, "Recollections of Territorial Kansas," Clarke Papers.

49. *Border Ruffian Code*, 2; "Statutes of 1855," chap. 151, reprinted in Cory, "Slavery in Kansas," 4.

50. Stringfellow quoted in Wilder, *Annals of Kansas*, 74–75.

51. "Pro-slavery Resolutions," June 10, 1854, History–Proslavery Miscellaneous, Library and Archives Division, KSHS (hereafter cited as History–Proslavery Miscellaneous).

52. "Missouri Emigration," report of a meeting, June 3, 1854, History–Proslavery Miscellaneous.

53. Although the Dred Scott decision in 1857 appeared to reinforce this idea and essentially endorsed the constitutionality of the Kansas-Nebraska Act, Republicans continued to battle with southern Democrats about the legitimacy of slavery west of Missouri. See Morrison, *Slavery in the American West*, 198.

54. *Independence Dispatch* cited in the *Democratic Platform*, September 14, 1854.

55. John McNamara, *Three Years on the Kansas Border by a Clergyman of the Episcopal Church* (New York: Miller, Orton, & Mulligan, 1856), 51–54.

56. *Squatter Sovereign*, August 21, 1855, Wilcox Scrapbook. For an additional account of this incident, see "Observations and Experiences of Charles W. Rust in Atchison Co., 1855," History Atchison County, C. W. Rust Manuscript, Library and Archives Division, KSHS.

57. *Star of Empire*, January 1, 1857. Proslavery advocates used vigilante tactics to combat abolitionists throughout the country, but the prevalence of violence in Kansas perhaps suggests that slaveholders suffered from a more acute sense of insecurity in Kansas than elsewhere in the South. For a few of the numerous studies that examine violence against abolitionists, see Julie Roy Jeffrey, *The Great Silent Army of Abolitionism: Ordinary Women in the Antislavery Movement* (Chapel Hill: University of North Carolina Press, 1998), 49–52; Merton L. Dillon, *Slavery Attacked: Southern Slaves and Their Allies, 1619–1865* (Baton Rouge: Louisiana State University Press, 1990); Perry, *Radical Abolitionism*, 231–261; and Aileen Kraditor, *Means and Ends in American Abolitionism: Garrison and His Critics on Strategy and Tactics, 1834–1850* (New York: Pantheon, 1969).

58. "Watch the Abolitionists," *Squatter Sovereign*, August 7, 1855, Wilcox Scrapbook, vol. 1, p. 9.

59. Slaves sometimes drowned themselves during the Middle Passage to avoid slavery in the New World. For a few of the studies on slave resistance that consider slave suicide in multiple contexts, see Michael Mullin, *Africa in America: Slave Acculturation and Resistance in the American South and the British Caribbean, 1736–1831* (Urbana: University of Illinois Press, 1992); Deborah Gray White, *Ar'n't I a Woman: Female Slaves in the Plantation South* (New York: Norton, 1985); and Gerald Mullin, *Flight and Rebellion: Slave Resistance in Eighteenth-Century Virginia* (New York: Oxford University Press, 1972).

60. "Watch the Abolitionists" and "An Abolitionist Badly Whipped," *Squatter Sovereign*, August 7, 1855, Wilcox Scrapbook, vol. 1, pp. 9–17.

61. *Squatter Sovereign*, August 7, 1855, Wilcox Scrapbook, 17.

62. Benjamin F. Stringfellow, "Negro-Slavery, No Evil, OR the North and the South; the Effects of Negro-Slavery as exhibited in the census, by a comparison of the condition of the slaveholding and non-slaveholding states," in *Report Made to the Platte County Self-Defensive Association* (St. Louis: M. Niedner, 1854), 1.

63. *Kansas Weekly Herald*, May 11, 1855.

64. John Hope Franklin and Loren Schweninger, *Runaway Slaves: Rebels on the Plantation* (New York: Oxford University Press, 1999), 10, 1–6.

65. W. H. Mackey to George Adams, March 26, 1902, "Slaves and Slavery," History of Slaves. See also Cory, "Slavery in Kansas," 14. Cory asserts the slave women were owned at Fort Riley.

66. *Lecompton (Kans.) Union*, December 2, 1856.

67. Cory, "Slavery in Kansas," 14. For an extensive study and map of the Kansas Underground Railroad, see Sheridan, *Freedom's Crucible*.

68. *Missouri Republican*, May 25, 1856.

69. Hurt, *Agriculture and Slavery*, 258–259; Harriet C. Frazier, *Runaway and Freed Missouri Slaves and Those Who Helped Them, 1763–1865* (Jefferson, N.C.: McFarland, 2004), 101.

70. *Glasgow Weekly Times*, November 17, 1859; *Saturday Morning Visitor* (Waverly and St. Thomas), July 30, 1859, both cited in Hurt, *Agriculture and Slavery*, 258–259.

71. Hurt, *Agriculture and Slavery*, 259.

72. John Bowles to Franklin B. Sanbourne, April 4, 1859, cited in Sheridan, *Freedom's Crucible*, 8.

73. Adams, "Slaves in Kansas," 7.

74. See ibid., 10. See also John Armstrong, "Reminiscences of Slave Days in Kansas," History of Slaves. Armstrong assisted Ann Clarke during one of the legs of her trip through Kansas Territory.

75. See ibid., 11.

76. Mrs. J. B. Abbott, "Some Underground Railway Stations," *Club Member* 6 (April 1908): 30–32, cited in Sheridan, *Freedom's Crucible*, 39.

77. "Reminiscences of Mrs. J. B. Abbott, September 1, 1895," in "Slaves and Slavery," History of Slaves.

78. Ibid.

79. James Montgomery to George Stearns, November 24, 1860, March 11, 1861, and October 6, 1860, George and Mary Stearns Correspondence and Miscellaneous Papers, 1857–1864, Collection 507, Library and Archives Division, KSHS (hereafter cited as Stearns Correspondence). For a probing study of Montgomery's antislavery activism, see Brian R. Dirck, "By the Hand of God: James Montgomery and Redemptive Violence," *Kansas History: A Journal of the Central Plains* 27 (Spring–Summer 2004): 100–15.

80. Jonas Colburn to Peggy Colburn, December 8, 1856, Jonas Colburn Papers, Miscellaneous Collections, Library and Archives Division, KSHS (hereafter cited as Colburn Papers).

81. See Jonas Colburn to Peggy Colburn, December 8, 1856.

82. John E. Stewart to Thaddeus Hyatt, December 20, 1859, cited in Sheridan, *Freedom's Crucible*, 45–47.

83. For one of the many accounts of Brown's conflicts in Kansas, see Stephen B. Oates, *To Purge This Land with Blood: A Biography of John Brown* (Amherst: University of Massachusetts Press, 1984).

84. Olive Owen, "The Underground Railroad," in "Slaves and Slavery," History of Slaves.

85. Ibid., 7. For additional accounts of this "Battle of the Spurs," see Sheridan, *Freedom's Crucible*, 77–87.

86. James Montgomery to George Stearns, December 12, 1860, Stearns Correspondence.

87. Benjamin F. Van Horn to George W. Martin, January 3, 1909, Van Horn Papers.

88. Daniel R. Anthony to James Montgomery, December 3, 1860, James Montgomery Collection, Military Papers, 1859–1905, Collection 446, Library and Archives Division, KSHS (hereafter cited as Montgomery Collection).

89. See Anthony to Montgomery, December 3, 1860. For a study that analyzes the army's role in Bleeding Kansas, see Mullis, *Peacekeeping on the Plains*, 153–233.

90. James Montgomery to George Stearns, December 12, 1860, Montgomery Collection.

91. W. W. Thayer to James Montgomery, April 16, 1861, Montgomery Collection.

92. Though Missouri did not, of course, secede from the Union, proslavery Missourians' loyalty to the Union was at best tenuous and at worst nonexistent (Quantrill's Confederate raid on Lawrence, Kansas, in August 1863 is the best example of some Missourians' repudiation of Union loyalty). See McPherson, *Battle Cry*, 290–294, 786.

93. Thomas H. Gladstone, *The Englishman in Kansas* (New York: Miller, 1857), 120–121. Gladstone recorded this interaction with the proslavery man in May 1856 after spending an afternoon with him on a riverboat headed down the Missouri. It's unlikely that Gladstone recorded the quote verbatim, but the sentiment is understood.

94. For the reasons why Lecompton failed, see Etcheson, *Bleeding Kansas*, 170–184.

95. Adams, "Slaves in Kansas," 2.

96. Although the vast majority of slaves left the territory or were freed, roughly a dozen slaves continued to be held in bondage until 1861, even though the Kansas territorial legislature passed an antislavery statute in February 1860. See Gary L. Cheatham, "'Kansas Shall Not Have the Right to Legislate Slavery Out': Slavery and the 1860 Antislavery Law," *Kansas History* 23, no. 3 (Autumn 2000): 154–171.

97. James Montgomery to George Stearns, December 14, 1860, Montgomery Collection.

98. Frazier, *Runaway and Freed Missouri Slaves*, 1.

99. "Bitter Fruits: The Suicide of Slavery," *St. Louis Intelligencer*, n.d., Kansas Territorial Clippings, vol. 3, KSHS.

100. Jeffrey, *Great Silent Army*, 171–174.

CHAPTER 3.

1. Joseph A. Cody to Mrs. Cody, April 19, 1858, and May 27, 1859, Miscellaneous Collection, Cody File, Library and Archives Division, KSHS.

2. I refer to "traditional" and "Victorian" gender norms as ideals or models of social behavior that originated in England and influenced American gender relations during the nineteenth century. Mary Poovey claims that men and women "were subject . . . to the constraints imposed by the binary organization of difference and the foregrounding of sexual nature" (*Uneven Development*, 22). Linda Gordon argues persuasively that

the perpetuation of the belief in inherent differences between the sexes sustained a variety of corresponding dichotomous categories in the United States, like "public:private, warlike:peaceful, and active:passive." See Linda Gordon, "On 'Difference,'" *Genders* 10 (Spring 1991): 91–111.

3. Very few women embodied this essentially middle-class, urban ideal, but many women attempted to mimic the ideal or were influenced by its proliferation in nineteenth-century public culture and literature. For studies that focus on true womanhood and the ideology of domesticity, see Sklar, *Catherine Beecher*; Cott, *Bonds of Womanhood*; Ryan, *Cradle of the Middle Class*; and Barbara Epstein, *The Politics of Domesticity: Women, Evangelism and Temperance in Nineteenth-Century America* (Middletown, Conn., Wesleyan University Press, 1981). Some historians argue that pioneer women, who lived in environments similar to early Kansas, also aspired to Victorian gender norms. See Joan E. Cashin, *A Family Venture: Men and Women on the Southern Frontier* (New York: Oxford University Press, 1991); Julie Roy Jeffrey, *Frontier Women: The Trans-Mississippi West, 1840–1880* (New York: Hill and Wang, 1979); John Mack Faragher, *Women and Men on the Overland Trail* (New Haven: Yale University Press, 1979); Glenda Riley, *The Female Frontier: A Comparative View of Women on the Prairie and the Plains* (Lawrence: University Press of Kansas, 1988); and Riley, *Confronting Race*.

4. Julie Roy Jeffrey and Susan Zaeske note similar contributions made by women to the success of the national antislavery movement, although the subjects of their studies rarely combated proslavery forces face to face. See Jeffrey, *Great Silent Army*, and Zaeske, *Signatures of Citizenship: Petitioning, Antislavery and Women's Political Identity* (Chapel Hill: University of North Carolina Press, 2003). Nicole Etcheson examines women's political activity in Kansas in her article "'Laboring for the Freedom of This Territory': Free-State Kansas Women in the 1850s," *Kansas History* (Summer 1998): 68–87.

5. Major Jefferson Buford cited in Douglas Brewerton, *The War in Kansas* (New York: Derby and Jackson, 1856), 211.

6. One of the few studies that considers antebellum southern women's political culture is Varon, *We Mean to Be Counted*. Approximately 15 percent of all southern women were illiterate in 1860, but illiteracy was higher in rural areas. See Varon, *We Mean to be Counted*, 80fn8. See also LeeAnn Whites, "The Tale of Two Minors: Women's Rights on the Border," in *Women in Missouri History: In Search of Power and Influence*, ed. LeeAnn Whites, Mary C. Neth, and Gary R. Kremer (Columbia: University of Missouri Press, 2004), 101–118, for a discussion of Missouri women during and after the war.

7. *Weekly Southern Democrat*, August 30, 1855.

8. Most historians of women and the family in the antebellum South argue that patriarchy remained firmly intact during the 1850s and governed women's lives in both the public and private spheres. The historiography suggests that southern women were denied access to public forms of social and political expression. See Cashin, *Family Venture*; Catherine Clinton and Nina Silber, eds., *Divided Houses: Gender and the Civil War* (New York: Oxford University Press, 1992); and George Rable, *Civil Wars: Women and the Crisis of Southern Nationalism* (Urbana: University of Illinois Press, 1991) for discussions of southern women's political and social lives. All four authors generally agree that the antebellum South was rigidly patriarchal. Consequently, they claim that southern women,

regardless of class, adhered to their prescribed social roles and remained essentially politically passive. Two glaring exceptions to this rule regarding southern women are the Grimké sisters, who traveled throughout the North publicly denouncing the evils of slavery. See Gerda Lerner, *The Grimké Sisters from South Carolina: Rebels against Slavery* (Boston: Houghton Mifflin, 1967). Victoria Bynum demonstrates that some southern women challenged patriarchal control in the Old South, but she agrees that southern women were more constrained then their northern sisters by southern patriarchy. See Bynum, *Unruly Women: The Politics of Social and Sexual Control in the Old South* (Chapel Hill: University of North Carolina Press, 1992). During the Civil War itself, some southern women began to experience challenges to traditional gender roles because of the absence of southern men. See LeeAnn Whites, "The Civil War as a Crisis in Gender," in Clinton and Silber, *Divided Houses*, 3–21, and Faust, *Mothers of Invention*. See also Michael Fellman, *Inside War*, 193–230, for an analysis of Missouri women in the context of guerrilla warfare, but Fellman focuses almost exclusively on the war itself, not on the antebellum conflict.

9. The ability of free-state women to defy gender conventions may also relate to the presence of Indian women in the region who did not adhere to white, middle-class notions of femininity. One Kansas settler, Fannie Kelly, was captured by local Indians and maintained her feminine identity by frequently comparing herself favorably with her female captors. She wrote, "I was compelled to live with the Squaws, painted and dressed as one of their number, had to work and help them with their drudgery." See "Statement of Losses Interview, Mrs. Fannie Kelly Claim."

10. In 1846 William Lloyd Garrison defined his view of woman's rights as follows: "What are the Rights of Woman? Define what are the Rights of Man, and thou has answered the question." See Christopher Dixon, "'A True Manly Life': Abolitionism and the Masculine Ideal," *Mid-America: An Historical Review* 77 (Fall 1995): 217. See also Hoganson, "Garrisonian Abolitionists," 292–293.

11. Margaret Wood, speech reprinted in the *Lawrence (Kans.) Herald of Freedom*, January 13, 1855.

12. Julia Louisa Lovejoy Diary, December 31, 1829, Library and Archives Division, KSHS (hereafter cited as Lovejoy Diary). For a discussion of Lovejoy's activism in Kansas, see Michael Pierson, "'In Our Own History': Julia Louisa Lovejoy and the Politics of Benevolence in Bleeding Kansas," *Heritage of the Great Plains* 37 (2004): 48–56, and Pierson, *Free Hearts and Free Homes*, 148–150.

13. Michael Pierson, "'A War of Extermination': A Newly Uncovered Letter by Julia Louisa Lovejoy, 1856," *Kansas History* 16 (Summer 1993): 120–122; Jeffrey, *Great Silent Army*, 147–48. For a brief account of Elijah Lovejoy's murder, see Perry, *Radical Abolitionism*, 75.

14. Margaret L. Wood, *Memorial of Samuel N. Wood* (Kansas City: Hudson-Kimberly, 1892), 21; William Connelley, "Biographical Sketch," Samuel and Margaret Wood Papers, Miscellaneous File, Library and Archives Division, KSHS.

15. The Wood marriage withstood a variety of stresses due to their involvement in politics. They married amid the controversy over the Compromise of 1850 and quickly left for Kansas because of the "horrid" Kansas-Nebraska Act. In Kansas they endured long separations because of Sam's involvement in the free-state forces and land speculation. Their

marriage came to an abrupt end when Sam Wood was assassinated in Hugoton, Kansas, in 1891 after a political quarrel with a county-seat judge. Margaret witnessed the entire event and fought (unsuccessfully) for the prosecution of her husband's murderer for years after his death.

16. Clarina Irene Howard Nichols to Susan Wattles, March 27, May 2, and July 14, 1859, Augustus and Susan Wattles Papers, Library and Archives Division, KSHS (hereafter cited as Wattles Papers).

17. Robinson, *Kansas*. Robinson's novel went through seven editions by 1857, thus indicating its popularity.

18. Charles Robinson to Sara Robinson, September 29, 1856, Charles and Sara T. D. Robinson Papers, Library and Archives Division, KSHS (hereafter cited as Robinson Papers). The Robinson home had been destroyed by proslavery Missourians during the "Sack of Lawrence" in May 1856.

19. Pierson, *Free Hearts and Free Homes*, 141, 140.

20. Julia Louisa Lovejoy, "Letters from Kanzas," reprinted in the *Kansas Historical Quarterly* 11 (February 1942): 29–44.

21. Julia Louisa Lovejoy to the *Independent Democrat*, August 25, 1856, cited in Pierson, "War of Extermination," 122.

22. Wood, *Memorial of Samuel N. Wood*, 70. The events Margaret Wood recounts in this letter refer to the "Sack of Lawrence" on May 21, 1856, when an estimated eight hundred proslavery men attacked Lawrence. See William Connelley, *Standard History of Kansas*, 498–500, for details of the conflict.

23. Lydia Maria Child, "The Kansas Emigrants," *New York Daily Tribune*, October 23, 1856. Greeley scheduled Child's column to run for a week before the 1856 presidential election, which pitted Republican candidate John Charles Frémont against Democrat Franklin Pierce. For a more detailed analysis of Child's involvement with Kansas, see Carolyn L. Karcher, "From Pacifism to Armed Struggle: L. M. Child's 'The Kansas Emigrants' and Antislavery Ideology in the 1850s," *ESQ* 34 (3rd Quarter 1988): 140–158, and Margaret Kellow, "'For the Sake of Suffering Kansas': Lydia Maria Child, Gender and the Politics of the 1850s," *Journal of Women's History* 5 (Fall 1993): 32–49.

24. Elisabeth Shove to Thaddeus Hyatt, October 16, 1856, Thaddeus Hyatt Papers, 1843–1898, Library and Archives Division, KSHS (hereafter cited as Hyatt Papers).

25. Jeffrey, *Great Silent Army*, 189–190.

26. Helen Bushman to Thaddeus Hyatt, October 8, 1856, Hyatt Papers.

27. Mrs. Major W. Mitchell to Thaddeus Hyatt, October 17, 1856, and Rachel C. Denison to Horace Greeley, November 24, 1856, Hyatt Papers.

28. Mrs. J. H. Corwin to Thaddeus Hyatt, October 24, 1856, Hyatt Papers.

29. Jeffrey, *Great Silent Army*, 177. Jeffrey acknowledges that the increased attention to Kansas attracted many antislavery advocates who were "no friends of the southern slave" and instead were only concerned with preserving western soil for white free labor.

30. Receipt and "schedule of goods" found in Stearns Correspondence.

31. S. Cabot Jr. to James Blood, December 28, 1856, James Blood Papers, Collection 281, Library and Archives Division, KSHS (hereafter cited as Blood Papers).

32. W. J. Potter to Thomas H. Webb, February 12, 1861, Stearns Correspondence.

33. Sheridan, *Freedom's Crucible*, 142–143.

34. Harrison Hannahs to Harvey D. Rice, July 27, 1896, Johnson Papers. See chapter 2 of this work for more on women's work on the UGRR.

35. Richard Cordley, "Lizzie and the Underground Railroad," *Pioneer Days in Kansas* (New York: Pilgrim Press, 1903), cited in Sheridan, *Freedom's Crucible*, 72–73.

36. Jeffrey, *Great Silent Army*, 87–93, and Zaeske, *Signatures of Citizenship*, 1–5.

37. Sarah Robinson, "Kansas Emigrant Farewell," January 1856, Robinson Papers.

38. Sylvester H. Clarke to F. G. Adams, June 5, 1893, Clarke Papers. Clarke was an original Kansas settler who "found among [his] papers a copy" of Winchell's song and sent it to Adams, then secretary of the Kansas State Historical Society.

39. "Petition of Ladies" to Territorial Governor, Territorial Troubles File, Kansas Territory Executive Department Correspondence, Library and Archives Division, KSHS.

40. "Kansas Aid" petition, Blood Papers. The petition was signed by twenty-five people, including four women: Rebecca S. Smith, Sarah Dungan, Elizabeth Blackford and Rachel Eastburn.

41. Harrison Hannahs to Harvey D. Rice, July 27, 1896, Biography, Box M35, KSHS.

42. Jonas Colburn to Peggy Colburn, July 7, 1856, Colburn Papers.

43. Jonas Colburn to Peggy Colburn, December 8, 1856, Colburn Papers.

44. See Nancy Isenberg, *Sex and Citizenship in Antebellum America* (Chapel Hill: University of North Carolina Press, 1998), especially chapter 3, for a discussion of how antislavery women's political behavior was interpreted by the antebellum public.

45. Charles Robinson to Sara Robinson, September 29, 1856, Robinson Papers.

46. Clarina Nichols to Thaddeus Hyatt, October 15, 4, 1856, Hyatt Papers.

47. Elizabeth Cady Stanton, Susan B. Anthony, and Matilda Joslyn Gage, ed., *History of Woman Suffrage*, vol.1 (New York: Fowler & Wells, 1881), 187.

48. *Kansas Republican,* June 11, 1857.

49. Hannah Anderson Ropes, *Six Months in Kansas, by a Lady* (Boston: J. P. Jewett, 1856), 118–119. Ropes returned East and worked as a nurse during the Civil War at Union Hotel Hospital in Washington, D.C., where she served as Louisa May Alcott's supervisor. Ropes died in 1863 after contracting typhoid pneumonia at the hospital. See Hannah Anderson Ropes, *Civil War Nurse: The Diary and Letters of Hannah Ropes*, ed. John R. Brumgardt (Knoxville: University of Tennessee Press, 1980) and Louisa May Alcott, *The Selected Letters of Louisa May Alcott*, ed. Joel Myerson and Daniel Shealy (Athens: University of Georgia Press, 1995), 339.

50. *Democratic Platform,* April 6, May 11, 1854.

51. *Star of Empire,* January 17, September 5, 1857.

52. Frick, "Women Writers Along the Rivers," 69, 48.

53. Robinson, *Kansas,* 328. For additional comments concerning the general anxiety about Border Ruffian attacks, see Ropes, *Six Months in Kansas;* "Life in Kansas," *New York Daily Tribune,* May 23, October 23, 1856; and "Effects of Border Ruffianism," April 12, 1856, and "Testimony of a Woman," June 21, 1856, *National Anti-Slavery Standard.*

54. One newspaper account also implied that free-state women were victims of ruffian sexual abuse. See J. M. Washburne, "'Border Ruffians': How Abolitionists and Negroes Were Killed and Persecuted," *Philadelphia Times,* March 13, 1884. Washburne wrote, "Many cases of personal cruelty committed on women and young girls might be related,

but the deeds were so horrid that . . . words of delicacy would blush to be used in telling [them]."

55. Robinson, *Kansas*, 256.

56. Mary A. Killam to Nahum A. Child, November 29, 1859, Miscellaneous Collection, Mary Killam File, KSHS.

57. Sylvester H. Clarke Diary, August 24, 1855, in Clarke, "Recollections of Territorial Kansas."

58. Elvira Cody to "Father and Mother," July 16, 1857, Miscellaneous Collection, Co-Com, KSHS.

59. *Kansas Republican*, June 25, 1857.

60. Women's political involvement in the free-state fight gave them the experience and credibility necessary to lobby for women's rights during the territorial and early statehood era. Their male peers recognized their political importance by granting them suffrage rights in school elections and by advancing their property rights. Clarina Nichols wrote that she found "the woman's rights cause is being carried forward by men even." See C. I. H. Nichols to Susan Wattles, March 27, 1859, Wattles Papers.

61. Charles M. Chase to the Editor of the *True Republican and Sentinel*, August 10, 1863, Chase Papers. Rebekah Weber Bowen uncovers the same trend in one county in Missouri during the Civil War. She writes, "As women became recognized protectors, men became the protected—a significant shift in gender roles." See Bowen, "The Changing Role of Protection on the Border: Gender and the Civil War in Saline County," in *Women in Missouri History: In Search of Power and Influence*, ed. LeeAnn Whites, Mary C. Neth, and Gary R. Kremer (Columbia: University of Missouri Press, 2004), 124. See also Bynum, *Unruly Women*, 130–150.

62. Both Union and Confederate forces used female spies during the Civil War. See Lyde Cullen Sizer, "Acting Her Part: Narratives of Union Women Spies," in Clinton and Silber, *Divided Houses*, 114–133.

63. Connelley, "Biographical Sketch."

64. George W. Martin, "Kansas Fifty Years Ago," *Emporia Gazette*, July 4, 1907, Kansas History Clippings, vol. 5, Library and Archives Division, KSHS.

65. A. G. Patrick, "Early Kansas Recollections," *New Era* (Valley Falls, Kans.), April 20, 1878, Kansas History Clippings, vol. 3, KSHS.

66. Ropes, *Six Months in Kansas*, 327. For an additional account of a similar incident, see George H. Coe, "Making Kansas a Free State," *New Haven Leader*, May 9, 1909, Kansas Reminiscences Clippings, vol. 3, KSHS.

67. I use Bertram Wyatt-Brown's definition of southern honor, which he defines as "a masculine ideal—aggressive, possibly rash, jealous of the family name, and protective of its women." In addition to delineating the code of southern honor, Wyatt-Brown also finds that southern men followed a "chivalric code," which included treating women with respect and observing a kind of "Roman Stoicism," a toughness of mind and body. See Wyatt-Brown, *House of Percy*, 7, 9–12. See also Wyatt-Brown's *Southern Honor* and *Shaping of Southern Culture*.

68. The only refutation of this opinion I found was Atchison's own assertions that he had followed a strict code of honor during the "Sack." In a speech he gave three months before the raid, he affirmed his commitment to the "code of laws" in place in the terri-

tory: "I would not advise you to burn houses, I would not advise you to shoot a man—If you burn a house you turn a family out of doors, if you shoot a man you shoot a father, a husband—do nothing dishonorable. No man is worthy of a border ruffian who would do a dishonorable act." See Malin, "Proslavery Background," 301.

69. Robinson, *Kansas*, 243. See also Malin, "Proslavery Background," 300–303, for a discussion of Atchison's speech and the attack on Lawrence. Michael Fellman asserts that few women suffered bodily harm or sexual abuse as a result of guerrilla warfare in Missouri, but he documents the prevalence of "symbolic rape," which consisted of verbal sexual assault and intrusion into women's bedrooms and personal belongings. According to this definition, Sara Robinson and other free-state women experienced "symbolic rape" during the Sack of Lawrence and other proslavery attacks. See Fellman, *Inside War*, 206–211.

70. Erastus D. Ladd to the *Marshall Statesman* (Milwaukee, Wisc.), October 1, 1856, Miscellaneous Collection, Kem-Kim, KSHS.

71. *St. Louis Intelligencer*, quoted in the *New York Daily Tribune*, May 25, 1865.

72. Wood, *Memorial of Samuel N. Wood*, 52.

73. Susannah Marshall Weymouth, "Mrs. S. M. Weymouth's History," Old Settlers' Association, October 9, 1899, History, Shawnee County, no. 3, KSHS.

74. Ropes, *Six Months in Kansas*, 117.

75. "Statement of William Crutchfield," n.d., William Elsey Connelley Collection, Box 43, Library and Archives Division, KSHS (hereafter cited as Connelley Collection). Crutchfield observed firsthand the event he described to Connelley.

76. Joanna Stratton, *Pioneer Women: Voices from the Kansas Frontier* (New York: Simon and Schuster, 1981), 111.

77. Mrs. W. H. Corning, *Western Border Life; or What Fanny Hunter Saw and Heard in Kanzas [sic] and Missouri* (New York: Derby, 1856), 55–56, cited in Laura McCall, "Armed and 'More or Less Dangerous': Women and Violence in American Frontier Literature, 1820–1860," in *Lethal Imagination: Violence and Brutality in American History*, ed. Michael Bellesiles (New York: New York University Press, 1990), 172.

78. Robinson, *Kansas*, 207.

79. "Observations and Experiences of Charles W. Rust." Rust was one of the Speck's neighbors and recorded the incident in his personal papers.

80. Philo Tower, *Slavery Unmasked: Being a Truthful Narrative of a Three Year's Residence and Journeying in Eleven Southern States* (Rochester, N.Y.: E. Barrow, 1856), 422.

81. Statement of C. W. Cherry in "Narratives on Quantrill and the Border War," Connelley Collection.

82. Charles Monroe Chase to the *True Republican and Sentinel*, August 22, 1863, Chase Papers.

83. Ibid.

84. Martin, "Kansas Fifty Years Ago." Martin was then secretary of the Kansas State Historical Society.

85. I am not arguing here that northern women helped win the Civil War but that women provided crucial support in Kansas and throughout the nation for the antislavery movement, which many would argue played an important role in precipitating the war. Bleeding Kansas certainly stimulated interest in and support for the Republican Party,

whose presidential candidate's election in 1860 caused the first wave of secession. See Morrison, *Slavery and the American West*, 10, 126–156.

86. Martin, "Kansas Fifty Years Ago."

87. Margaret McCarter, "The Foundation of the Woman's Kansas Day Club," Kansas Scrap Book, Biography-Women, 107–110, KSHS. See also Michael Goldberg, *An Army of Women: Gender and Politics in Gilded Age Kansas* (Baltimore: Johns Hopkins University Press, 1997), 10–17.

88. Charles Robinson quoted in "Grand Celebration," *Kansas Free State*, July 9, 1855.

CHAPTER 4.

1. For a brief account of Brooks's attack on Sumner, see McPherson, *Battle Cry*, 149–153, and T. Lloyd Benson, *The Caning of Senator Sumner* (New York: Wadsworth, 2004).

2. *New York Daily Tribune*, May 26, May 23, 1856. A myrmidon is defined by the Oxford English Dictionary as an "unscrupulously faithful follower or hireling; a hired ruffian; a base attendant."

3. *Western Dispatch*, quoted in *New York Daily Tribune*, June 2, 1856.

4. For an analysis of the post–Civil War "true man" and his relationship to retaliatory violence, see Richard Maxwell Brown, *No Duty to Retreat: Violence and Values in American History and Society* (New York: Oxford University Press, 1991), 9–11

5. Anthony Rotundo, "Learning about Manhood: Gender Ideals and the Middle-class Family in Nineteenth-century America," in Mangan and Walvin, *Manliness and Morality;* 35–51. Rotundo shows that the Masculine Achiever, an individualist, "encouraged accomplishment, autonomy and aggression—all in the service of an intense competition for success in the market-place"; the Christian Gentleman, on the other hand, emerged as "an evangelical response to the competitive impulse that was turned loose" by capitalism and its Masculine Achievers (37). See also Rotundo, *American Manhood;* Carnes and Griffin, *Meanings for Manhood;* Kimmel, *Manhood in America;* Mangan and Walvin, *Manliness and Morality;* Dixon, "True Manly Life," 213–236; and Stephen Kantrowitz, "Fighting Like Men: Civil War Dilemmas of Abolitionist Manhood," in *Battle Scars: Gender and Sexuality in the American Civil War*, ed. Catherine Clinton and Nina Silber (New York: Oxford University Press, 2006), 19–40; John Stauffer, "Embattled Manhood and New England Writers, 1860–1870," in *Battle Scars: Gender and Sexuality in the American Civil War*, ed. Catherine Clinton and Nina Silber (New York: Oxford University Press, 2006), 120–139; and Greenberg, *Manifest Manhood*, 14, 11.

6. Nina Silber, "Intemperate Men, Spiteful Women, and Jefferson Davis," in Clinton and Silber, *Divided Houses*, 286.

7. Wyatt-Brown, *House of Percy*, 9. For discussions of southern honor, see Wyatt-Brown, *House of Percy* and *Southern Honor;* Greenberg, *Honor and Slavery;* and David G. Pugh, *Sons of Liberty: The Masculine Mind in Nineteenth-Century America* (Westport, Conn.: Greenwood Press, 1983), 3–44.

8. Richard Slotkin is one scholar who examines the relationship between frontier lawlessness and violence in his books, *Regeneration through Violence: The Mythology of the American Frontier, 1600–1860* (New York: HarperCollins, 1973) and *The Fatal Environment: The Myth of the Frontier in the Age of Industrialization, 1800–1860* (New York: HarperCol-

lins, 1985), 3–48. On manhood and gender in the American West, see Peck, *Reinventing Free Labor,* especially 117–157; Johnson, *Roaring Camp;* Susan L. Johnson, "'A Memory Sweet to Soldiers': The Significance of Gender in the History of the American West," *Western Historical Quarterly* 24, no. 4 (November 1993): 495–517; Elizabeth Jameson, *All that Glitters: Class, Conflict, and Community in Cripple Creek* (Urbana: University of Illinois Press, 1998); Katherine Morrissey, "Engendering the West," in *Under an Open Sky: Rethinking America's Western Past,* ed. William Cronon, George Miles, and Jay Gitlin (New York: W. W. Norton, 1992); Faragher, *Women and Men on the Overland Trail;* Faragher, *Sugar Creek;* and Kristen Tegtmeier, "'The Ladies of Lawrence are Arming!'" in *Antislavery Violence: Sectional, Racial, and Cultural Conflict in Antebellum America,* ed. John R. McKivigan and Stanley Harrold (Knoxville: University of Tennessee Press, 1999), 215–235.

9. Cited in the sworn testimony of Charles Robinson, in House, *Report of the Special Committee Appointed to Investigate the Troubles in Kansas; With the Views of the Minority of Said Committee,* 34th Cong., 1st sess. (Washington, D.C.: Cornelius Wendell, 1856), 1069, NARA, Washington, D.C. (hereafter cited as *Report of the Special Committee*).

10. Nicole Etcheson, "Good Men and Notorious Rogues: Vigilantism in Massac County, Illinois, 1846–1850," in *Lethal Imagination: Violence and Brutality in American History,* ed. Michael Bellesiles (New York: New York University Press, 1990), 149.

11. Kantrowitz, "Fighting Like Men," 19.

12. Lucy Larcom, "Call to Kansas," 1855, reprinted in Wilder, *Annals of Kansas,* 57.

13. SenGupta, *For God and Mammon,* and Etcheson, "Labouring for the Freedom," 68–87.

14. Larcom, "Call to Kansas."

15. On the formation of free labor ideology and its proliferation at midcentury, see Foner, *Free Soil, Free Labor, Free Men;* Glickstein, *Concepts of Free Labor;* and Steinfeld, *Invention of Free Labor.* On the whiteness of free labor ideology, see Roediger, *Wages of Whiteness,* and Saxton, *Rise and Fall of the White Republic.*

16. Robinson, *Kansas,* 60, iii–iv.

17. Samuel C. Pomeroy to George S. Parks, April 24, 1855, Samuel Clarke Pomeroy Papers, Collection 476, Library and Archives Division, KSHS.

18. Robinson, *Kansas,* 13.

19. In reality, many northern men were just as violent as southern men, as the popularity of "Beecher's Bibles" demonstrates. However, many northerners remained committed to the ideal of nonviolence even if the reality only sometimes matched this ideal.

20. *Missouri Democrat,* October 29, 1856. The importance of settling the frontier with Free-Soil families is fully explored in Pierson, *Free Hearts and Free Homes,* and Michael Pierson, "'Free Hearts and Free Homes': Representations of Family in the American Antislavery Movement" (Ph.D. diss., State University of New York at Binghamton, 1993), especially 48–55.

21. *New York Daily Tribune,* May 23, 1856.

22. Charles Robinson quoted in SenGupta, *For God and Mammon,* 108.

23. Free labor ideology was not, of course, a monolithic concept, and the transfer of ideology into practice was imperfect. Differing definitions of the "ideal" free labor family and the varied environments in which free laborers lived and worked, all shaped the ways

in which free labor ideology played out on the ground. For two studies that examine the tensions within free labor ideology and how these tensions contributed to differing definitions of manhood see Peck, *Reinventing Free Labor*, and Johnson, *Roaring Camp*.

24. George W. Hunt and Charles Stearns to James Blood, September 29, 1856, Blood Papers.

25. *Missouri Democrat*, October 25, 1856.

26. Amos Lawrence to Giles Richards, December 10, 1855 (emphasis added), Amos Adams Lawrence Correspondence, Library and Archives Division, KSHS.

27. *Missouri Republican*, October 16, 1856.

28. *Doniphan (Kansas) Constitutionalist*, May 23, 1856.

29. Phillip S. Paludan, "The American Civil War Considered as a Crisis in Law and Order," *American Historical Review* 77, no. 4 (October 1972): 1028. See also William Carrigan, *The Making of a Lynching Culture: Violence and Vigilantism in Central Texas, 1836–1916* (Urbana: University of Illinois Press, 2004).

30. Fellman, *Inside War*, 18.

31. Statement of Matthew R. Walker to Mr. Anderson, May 22, 1856, *Report of the Special Committee*.

32. Nicole Etcheson notes a similar phenomenon in 1840s southern Illinois: "Each side [of the vigilante conflict] asserted that the other acted lawlessly, and both sides used violence in the name of the law." See Etcheson, "Good Men and Notorious Rogues," 151.

33. Speech of Hon. Mordecai Oliver of Missouri, March 7, 1856, *Appendix to the Congressional Globe*, 34th Cong., 1st sess., 169, NARA (hereafter cited as *Appendix to the Congressional Globe*).

34. *Richmond Enquirer* reprinted in the *National Anti-Slavery Standard*, April 26, 1856.

35. Bertram Wyatt-Brown also notes this correlation between southern masculinity, honor and classical Greek values. See Wyatt-Brown, *House of Percy*, 11–12. Walker Percy told an interviewer, "Behave like a gentleman, the Southern honor code, chivalry, grace about doing right, treating women with respect. If somebody insults you then fight. Aren't these the Roman stoic virtues? [A] tough, Roman, chivalric code was much more military than Christian" (12).

36. *Kansas Weekly Herald*, December 15, 1854. I do not want to suggest that southern honor and southern manhood were interchangeable concepts, but I do want to emphasize how closely they were interconnected. A proper southern man would not be considered manly unless he was also considered honorable, but his honor was not solely dependent upon maintaining a proper code of manhood; a man's honor also related to his female dependents' adherence to proper gender codes and his family's reputation. See Wyatt-Brown, *House of Percy*, 9.

37. Greenberg, *Honor and Slavery*, 17. Bertram Wyatt-Brown was not the first to suggest that the code of southern honor and hence southern manhood was linked to slavery and racism, but he has explored the relationship most extensively in his work. He argued in *Southern Honor* that "white man's honor and black man's slavery became in the public mind of the South practically indistinguishable" (16). While Wyatt-Brown acknowledged that a concept of honor existed before slavery became racialized, slavery's growth and expansion in the South coexisted with southern honor's entrenchment in southern society.

In *Honor and Slavery*, Kenneth Greenberg has gone even further than Wyatt-Brown by arguing that "since Southern gentlemen defined a slave as a person without honor, all issues of honor relate to slavery" (xiii).

38. Stephanie McCurry, *Masters of Small Worlds: Yeoman Households, Gender Relations, and The Political Culture of the Antebellum South Carolina Low Country* (New York: Oxford University Press, 1995).

39. See James Oliver Horton and Lois E. Horton, "Violence, Protest, and Identity: Black Manhood in Antebellum America" and "Freedom's Yoke: Gender Conventions Among Antebellum Free Blacks," in *Free People of Color*, ed. James Oliver Horton (New York: Oxford University Press, 1993), 80–122.

40. See Foner, *Free Soil, Free Labor, Free Men*, for the classic analysis of free labor ideology. For the racist foundations of free labor ideology, see Eugene Berwanger, *The Frontier Against Slavery: Western Anti-Negro Prejudice and the Slavery Extension Controversy* (Urbana: University of Illinois Press, 1971); Horsman, *Race and Manifest Destiny*; and Takaki, *Iron Cages*.

41. See Peck, *Reinventing Free Labor*, 136–139, and Johnson, *Roaring Camp*, 99–140.

42. *New York Daily Tribune*, October 23, 1856.

43. *New York Daily Tribune*, October 24, 1856.

44. General Thomas Ewing, "The Struggle for Freedom in Kansas," *Cosmopolitan Magazine*, May 1894.

45. Testimony of Charles Robinson taken at Lecompton, June 6, 1856, *Report of the Special Committee*. The official passenger list for the first NEEAC party, issued by Thomas H. Webb, secretary of the NEEAC, counted a total of 182 passengers, 45 of whom were women and children, thus challenging Robinson's report that 70 women joined the first party. The second NEEAC party included 50 women and children, out of a total of 144 passengers, while the third party included 22 women out of a total of 90 emigrants. These figures challenge Robinson's statistics, but they do not discount his overall assertion that the NEEAC encouraged family migration. In fact, if one includes the number of emigrants who traveled with family members, most likely brother-brother pairs, the percentage of families traveling in the second emigration party reaches 56 percent. See *Report of the Special Committee*, 887–892.

46. I'm using the term "coequal" in the sense that Nancy Isenberg uses it in her book, *Sex and Citizenship in Antebellum America*, xviii. Isenberg uses the term to resolve the binary opposition between "equal" and "different," for she believes early feminists conceived the term to claim difference and equality with men simultaneously.

47. Thomas H. Webb, *Information for Kanzas Immigrants* (Boston: Alfred Mudge and Son, 1855), 15, cited in Etcheson, "Laboring for the Freedom," 283. For examples of free-state men who approved of women stepping outside the domestic sphere, see chapter 3 of this work.

48. Maj. Jefferson Buford cited in Brewerton, *War in Kansas*, 211; Kansas special correspondent, "Governor Geary and his 'Peace,'" October 13, 1856, reprinted in *New York Daily Tribune*, October 23, 1856.

49. Greenberg, *Honor and Slavery*, xii.

50. For one study that examines the gendered expectations between men and women

in the South, see Brenda Stevenson, *Life in Black and White: Family and Community in the Slave South* (New York: Oxford University Press, 1996), 37–62. Some abolitionists began questioning the legitimacy of chivalry in the 1830s and 1840s. Lydia Maria Child claimed that chivalry should "pass away with barbarism," and William Lloyd Garrison argued that chivalry "practically crushes and degrades woman." Quoted in Dixon, "True Manly Life," 228.

51. Robinson, *Kansas*, 248.

52. Ropes, *Six Months in Kansas*, 151, 208–209.

53. *New York Daily Tribune*, June 21, May 23, 1856.

54. *Chicago Tribune*, April 20, 1857, cited in Fellman, *Inside War*, 14.

55. Ropes, *Six Months in Kansas*, 111, 217. The language Ropes employs suggests that she exhibited a certain kind of attraction for these "brawny," southern men. Although northern manhood may have been more refined and proper, it also may have lost a sense of sexual virility. Ropes's opinions not only reflected her belief in the inherent savageness of western, "uncivilized" men but undoubtedly related to her class values as well. Ropes's upper-middle-class roots shaped her opinions about the Missourians, and her derogatory statements resonated with a condescending attitude toward lower-class people in general. Ropes's comments also might reflect an awareness of the Indian population in western Missouri and eastern Kansas, whom settlers commonly referred to as "savage."

56. This othering process has recently been termed "pseudospeciation," the process by which humans dehumanize their enemies in order to make it easier to disparage and even kill them. See Robert S. McElvaine, *Eve's Seed: Biology, the Sexes, and the Course of History* (New York: McGraw-Hill, 2001), 50. Michael Fellman refers to a related process called "savage-baiting" in which "northern antislavery writers represented the cultural conflict as all civilized Northerners versus all Missourians—all of whom were defined as atavistic primitives." See Fellman, *Inside War*, 15.

57. July 8, August 20, 1856, Lovejoy Diary.

58. *Kansas City Star*, January 16, 1916.

59. "Testimony of a Woman," June 21, 1856, *National Antislavery Standard*.

60. *Baltimore Patriot*, reprinted in the *Liberator*, June 2, 1854, cited in Dixon, "True and Manly Life," 228.

61. *Washington Union*, March 31, 1858.

62. Speech of Hon. W. R. Smith, March 10, 1856, *Appendix to the Congressional Globe*, 158.

63. *Journal of Commerce* reprinted in *New York Daily Tribune*, May 28, 1856.

64. See Greenberg, *Honor and Slavery*, xii.

65. Speech of Hon. Mordecai Oliver, March 7, 1856, *Appendix to the Congressional Globe*, 169. See also Dale E. Watts, "Plows and Bibles, Rifles and Revolvers: Guns in Kansas Territory," *Kansas History: A Journal of the Central Plains* 21 (1998): 30–45.

66. *Western Dispatch*, May 23, 1856, reprinted in *New York Daily Tribune*, June 2, 1856.

67. *Kansas Weekly Herald*, March 9, 1855. The "Aid" folks this settler observed were undoubtedly members of the New England Emigrant Aid Company.

68. The most enduring proponent of this proslavery defense was George Fitzhugh, who argued in favor of southern "domestic slavery" and against the slavery of northern

"Free Society" in *Sociology for the South or the Failure of Free Society* (Richmond, Va.: A. Morris, 1854) and *Cannibals All! Or Slaves without Masters* (Richmond, Va.: A. Morris, 1857).

69. *Kansas Weekly Herald*, April 20, 1855. The *Squatter Sovereign* was published in Atchison, another proslavery community, whereas the *Herald* was published in Leavenworth.

70. The language employed by the *Herald* and the *Squatter* may indicate class and educational differences between certain groups of proslavery settlers. The editors of the *Herald* tried to project an educated, thus wealthier image of themselves and their paper; however, I do not have any data regarding the class background of each of the papers' readerships in Leavenworth and Atchison.

71. *New York Daily Tribune*, May 24, May 22, 1856.

72. *New York Daily Tribune*, May 23, 1856.

73. *Lexington (Mo.) Express*, reprinted in *New York Daily Tribune*, May 30, 1856.

74. However, many abolitionists who argued against violence during the initial settlement of Kansas gradually changed their course and supported military action after peaceful negotiations proved ineffective in combating proslavery forces. See Tegtmeier, "Ladies of Lawrence are Arming!" 215. See also Perry, *Radical Abolitionism*, 260. In addition to Brown, James H. Lane often stood ready to respond with violence when engaged in conflicts with proslavery men. See W. E. B. Du Bois, *John Brown: A Biography* (New York: M. E. Sharpe, 1997), 83–85.

75. After the Sack of Lawrence, Brown was "indignant that there had been no resistance; . . . [he] denounced the members of the committee and leading free state men as cowards, or worse," and said that "something must be done to show these barbarians that we too have rights!" See Du Bois, *John Brown*, 74.

76. See affidavits of Mahala Doyle, James Harris, Louisa Jane Wilkinson, and Morton Bourn, *Report of the Special Committee*, 1193–1200, to confirm Brown's involvement in the crimes. Only James Redpath, Brown's friend and biographer, denied that Brown committed the Pottawatomie murders. See James Malin, *John Brown and the Legend of Fifty-Six* (New York: Haskell House, 1971).

77. George W. Brown, *The Rescue of Kansas from Slavery with False Claims Corrected* (Rockford, Ill.: George W. Brown, 1902), 150–151.

78. Most Christian "nonresistant abolitionists" were committed to nonviolence, but even Garrison, the most popular nonresistant, was moved by Brown's actions to consider violent action as a legitimate response to proslavery aggression. See Perry, *Radical Abolitionism*, 57, 259.

79. *Liberty (Mo.) Tribune*, May 30, 1856. See also a letter from D. R. Atchison to the *Boonville (Mo.) Weekly Observer*, August 23, 1856. Brown continued his violent attacks in Kansas throughout the summer of 1856.

80. Peter Wallenstein, "Incendiaries All: Southern Politics and the Harpers Ferry Raid," in *His Soul Goes Marching On: Responses to John Brown and the Harpers Ferry Raid*, ed. Paul Finkelman (Charlottesville: University Press of Virginia, 1995), 158.

81. See ibid., 149. See also James McPherson, *Ordeal by Fire: Civil War and Reconstruction* (New York: McGraw Hill, 2001), 128–129. While Ruffin's quotation may seem at odds with earlier southern accounts of northerners' unwillingness to use violence, I believe

the two forms of verbal attacks lead to the same conclusion: Southerners feared northern abolitionists and demeaned their capabilities as men in order to discount and deflect this fear. Perhaps the shift in language in relation to Brown indicates a desire to "rally the troops" and acknowledge the very real threat that abolitionists like Brown posed to southern slavery.

82. Lydia Maria Child to James Montgomery, December 26, 1861, Montgomery Collection. Child wrote earlier that same year, "Much as I deprecate civil war, I deliberately say even *that* is better than compromises of principle." See Stauffer, "Embattled Manhood," 133. For more on Montgomery's violent antislavery activism, see chapter 2 of this volume and Brian Dirck, "By the Hand of God," 105–115.

83. Joel Porte, ed., *Emerson and His Journals* (Cambridge, Mass.: Belknap Press, 1982), 474. Emerson wrote in early 1858, "All the children born in the last three years or 8 years should be charged with love of liberty, for their parents have been filled with Kansas & antislavery" (481).

84. *Practical Christian*, November 26, 1859, cited in Perry, *Radical Abolitionism*, 259. Amy Greenberg finds a similar split in ideas about manhood in her study of filibustering at midcentury. See Greenberg, *Manifest Manhood*, 11.

85. Ralph Waldo Emerson, "From Moral Sense to Universal Man," in *Apostle of Culture: Emerson as Preacher and Lecturer*, by David Robinson (Philadelphia: University of Pennsylvania Press, 1982), 50–55; Fellman, *Inside War*, 17.

86. *New York Daily Tribune*, May 20, 1856; *Cleveland Herald*, reprinted in the *New York Daily Tribune*, May 26, 1856; *National Anti-Slavery Standard*, June 21, 1856.

87. See "The Connecticut Kansas Colony," *Kansas Historical Quarterly* 12 (Spring 1956): 1–7.

88. Beecher quoted in Clifford E. Clark, *Henry Ward Beecher: Spokesman for a Middle-Class America* (Urbana: University of Illinois Press, 1978), 123, 125.

89. *National Anti-Slavery Standard*, January 5, 1856. Michael Fellman similarly notes that Stearns, "perhaps the only pacifist Garrisonian in the whole Kansas territory, could justify killing Pukes as subhumans sunk in a pit below the realm of humanity." See Fellman, *Inside War*, 15.

90. *Liberator*, reprinted in the *National Anti-Slavery Standard*, April 12, 1856; *Topeka Tribune*, August 25, 1856, cited in Fellman, *Inside War*, 21.

CHAPTER 5.

1. The *Weston (Mo.) Argus*, November 21, 1856, Wilcox Scrapbook. Democrats coined the term "miscegenation" to attack Lincoln's presidency in 1864, but I've chosen to use it interchangeably with "amalgamation" (a term that contemporaries used before and after 1864) to connote interracial sex. See Elise Lemire, *"Miscegenation": Making Race in America* (Philadelphia: University of Pennsylvania Press, 2002), 4.

2. Leslie A. Schwalm argues that midwesterners' "understanding of white supremacy had been premised on the right and ability to exclude first Indian people and then African Americans from the region." See Schwalm, "'Overrun with Free Negroes': Emancipation and Wartime Migration in the Upper Midwest," *Civil War History* (June 2004): 148. See also Horsman, *Race and Manifest Destiny*, 189–248, and Slotkin, *Fatal Environment*. While

Horsman doesn't consider Kansas directly and Slotkin does so only tangentially (he focuses on John Brown in Kansas), their observations regarding the national attitudes about and violence toward racial others on the frontier and in the context of westward expansion can apply to this particular border region as well.

3. West, "Reconstructing Race," 9.

4. Quoted in Jean Fagan Yellin, ed., *Incidents in the Life of a Slave Girl*, by Harriet A. Jacobs (Cambridge: Harvard University Press, 1987), 4.

5. Statement of Charles Robinson taken at Lecompton, June 6, 1856, *Report of the Special Committee*.

6. See Bill Cecil-Fronsman, *Common Whites: Class and Culture in Antebellum North Carolina* (Lexington: University Press of Kentucky, 1992), and McCurry, *Masters of Small Worlds*.

7. Statement of Matthew R. Walker taken at Leavenworth, May 22, 1856, *Report of the Special Committee*.

8. See Jacobson, *Whiteness of a Different Color*, for a thorough overview of how immigration and race affected nineteenth-century ideas about citizenship and whiteness. In fact, the nation would define U.S. citizenship in the decade following Kansas's entry into the Union. With the passage of the Fourteenth and Fifteenth Amendments (1868 and 1870), the nation defined citizenship by race and gender, first leaving all black and white women out of the definition de jure and later by excluding all blacks through de facto segregation and racial intimidation.

9. On interracial sex, see Lemire, *"Miscegenation"*; Ann Laura Stoler, *Carnal Knowledge and Imperial Power: Race and the Intimate in Colonial Rule* (Berkeley and Los Angeles: University of California Press, 2002); Martha Hodes, *Sex, Love, Race: Crossing Boundaries in North American History* (New York: New York University Press, 1999); Martha Hodes, *White Women, Black Men: Illicit Sex in the Nineteenth-Century South* (New Haven: Yale University Press, 1997); and Susan Courtney, *Hollywood Fantasies of Miscegenation* (New York: Princeton University Press, 2004). For a comprehensive overview of whiteness studies, see Shelley Fisher Fishkin, "Interrogating Whiteness, Complicating Blackness: Remapping American Culture," *American Quarterly* 47 (September 1995): 428–466. Fishkin focuses almost exclusively on black/white issues but acknowledges that scholars such as Gloria Anzaldua and Neil Foley include a multiplicity of races and ethnicities in their work on race and identity formation in the United States. See Gloria Anzaldua, *Borderlands: La Frontera/The New Mestiza* (San Francisco: Aunt Lute Books, 1987); Foley, *White Scourge*; and Antonia Castaneda, "Women of Color and the Rewriting of Western History: The Discourse, Politics and Decolonization of History," *Pacific Historical Review* 61 (November 1992): 501–533. See also West, "Reconstructing Race."

10. Foley, *White Scourge*, 7.

11. Ibid., 35.

12. *Kansas Weekly Herald*, March 30, 1855, cited in Fellman, *Inside War*, 19.

13. Hodes, *White Women, Black Men*, 7.

14. Martha Hodes, "Wartime Dialogues on Illicit Sex," in Clinton and Silber, *Divided Houses*, 235, 234.

15. Hodes compiles a variety of articles on the subject of interracial sex that include Indian-Anglo and Indian-black encounters in her anthology, *Sex, Love, Race*. See especially chapters 1, 2, 4, and 5.

16. For a selection of the growing scholarly literature on whiteness, see Roediger, *Colored White*; Roediger, *Toward the Abolition of Whiteness*; Roediger, *Wages of Whiteness*; Allen, *Invention of the White Race*; Saxton, *Rise and Fall of the White Republic*; Horsman, *Race and Manifest Destiny*; Jacobson, *Whiteness of a Different Color*; Toni Morrison, *Playing in the Dark: Whiteness and the Literary Imagination* (Cambridge: Harvard University Press, 1992); Eric Lott, *Love and Theft: Blackface Minstrelsy and the American Working Class* (New York: Oxford University Press, 1993); and Karyn D. McKinney, *Being White: Everyday Whiteness and the Meaning of Race and Racism* (New York: Routledge, 2004). Horsman and Saxton are the only two authors cited here who dedicate a significant portion of their analyses to how white racial identity was formed in relation to Indians.

17. Deloria, *Playing Indian*, 1–9. For other studies that examine the influence of "indianness" on white identity, see Michael Paul Rogin, *Fathers and Children: Andrew Jackson and the Subjugation of the American Indian* (New York: Knopf, 1975); Robert Berkhofer, *The White Man's Indian: Images of the American Indian from Columbus to the Present* (New York: Knopf, 1978); Takaki, *Iron Cages*; and Slotkin, *Regeneration through Violence.*

18. West, "Reconstructing Race," 9, 12.

19. Washburn, *American Indian* 1:62.

20. Roediger, *Toward the Abolition of Whiteness*, 12–14; 75–77. Roediger acknowledges that whiteness and the formation of white racial identity varied according to class and gender position, and argues that these potential conflicts among populations of white people weakened their ability to use whiteness as a tool of racial unification. He ultimately calls for a "withering away of whiteness" because it is "the empty and terrifying attempt to build an identity based on what one isn't and on whom one can hold back" (13). See chapter 1 of this work for a more extensive discussion of Indian-white relations in Kansas Territory. See also Riley, *Confronting Race,* 212–239. Riley finds that white colonialist and racist ideas endured even as some Anglo women gained sympathy and understanding for American Indians on the frontier.

21. Charles Bluejacket, Paschal Fish, and John Silverheels, all Shawnee "half-breeds," were educated at the Shawnee Indian Mission and lived near the school. See Mrs. C. C. Ely, "Some of Our Experiences with Indians in Johnson County, Kansas, and Surrounding Counties," original manuscript, 1932, Library and Archives Division, KSHS.

22. Samuel C. Pomeroy to James Blood, February 3, 1855, Blood Papers.

23. James Hindman Diary, March 1857, Hindman Papers.

24. Mary Lawrence McMeekin, "Some Incidents in My Life in Kansas during the Early Days," original manuscript, McMeekin Papers.

25. *New York Daily Tribune*, May 29, 1856. It's possible that this "Pennsylvania Dutchman" was actually a German because Germans were often referred to as Dutch (an Americanization of Deutsch). If this is the case, my interpretation of the reporter's observation would differ only slightly in that the "Dutchman," though more closely connected to an Anglo-Saxon heritage as a German, would still have tainted this heritage by marrying an Indian woman and producing mixed-race children.

26. Charles M. Chase to the *True Republican and Sentinel,* August 19, 1863, Chase Papers.

27. Thomas Johnson to the Hon. O. Brown, Commissioner of Indian Affairs, October 12, 1849.

28. Thomas Johnson to Major Benjamin F. Robinson, August 29, 1853. Johnson's civ-

ilization rhetoric here is similar to Thomas Jefferson's. See Anthony F. Wallace, *Jefferson and the Indians: The Tragic Fate of the First Americans* (Cambridge, Mass.: Belknap Press, 1999).

29. John Montgomery, Committee Report, Kaws, 1855–56, Letters Received–Central Superintendency.

30. Ely, "Some of Our Experiences." Mrs. Ely's grandparents adopted the Indian girl and Ely lived with them for a time during her youth.

31. *Kansas Weekly Herald,* July 7, 1855.

32. While no quantitative data exists, the general consensus among historians who study cross-racial sexuality is that the vast majority of these unions were between white men and Indian women. See Gary Nash, "The Hidden History of Mestizo America," Jennifer M. Spear, "'They Need Wives': Metissage and the Regulation of Sexuality in French Louisiana, 1699–1730," and Richard Godbeer, "Eroticizing the Middle Ground: Anglo-Indian Sexual Relations along the Eighteenth-Century Frontier," all in Hodes, *Sex, Love, Race,* 10–59, 91–111.

33. My argument here is similar to what Susan Courtney finds in her research on representations of interracial sex on the big screen. She argues that "such destabilizations of race are partly grounded by the rigid conventions of gender identity . . . [the] temporary transgression of one register of difference is negotiated or stabilized through the reassertion of another." See Courtney, *Hollywood Fantasies of Miscegenation,* 4.

34. See Brown, *Good Wives, Nasty Wenches, and Anxious Patriarchs,* especially chapter 4, "Engendering Racial Difference," 107–136. She writes, "These early laws were among the most important of all slave statutes in Virginia. They created a legal discourse of slavery rooted in the sexual, social and economic lives of African laborers and effectively naturalized the condition of slavery by connecting it to a concept of race," 136.

35. For a discussion of the origins of and the unique American phenomenon called the "one drop rule," see F. James Davis, *Who Is Black? One Nation's Definition* (University Park: Pennsylvania State University Press, 1991).

36. September 2, 1858, Guthrie Journal.

37. Benjamin F. Stringfellow, "An Abolition Trick Exposed!" broadside from the *Weston Reporter,* August 7, 1854, housed in the Western Historical Manuscript Collection, Columbia, Mo.

38. Johnson, "Slaves in Kansas Territory," Johnson Papers.

39. Riley, *Confronting Race,* 24–25. See 11–94 for a discussion of what she calls the "frontier philosophy," which underscored Anglo women's approach to civilizing the West. See also Henry Nash Smith, *Virgin Land: The American West as Symbol and Myth* (New York: Vintage, 1950), and Slotkin, *Fatal Environment.* Senator Charles Sumner, "The Crime against Kansas; The Apologies for the Crime; The True Remedy," May 20, 1856, http://facweb.furman.edu/~benson/docs/sumnerksh2.htm/ (accessed May 24, 2007).

40. Carolyn Merchant is one current scholar who analyzes the gendering of nature and the land. See Merchant, *Ecological Revolutions: Nature, Gender, and Science in New England* (Chapel Hill: University of North Carolina Press, 1989), and Carolyn Merchant, *The Death of Nature: Women, Ecology and the Scientific Revolution* (San Francisco: Harper and Row, 1980).

41. Abraham Lincoln to Joshua Speed, August 24, 1855, in *This Fiery Trial: The Speeches*

and Writings of Abraham Lincoln, ed. William E. Gienapp (New York: Oxford University Press, 2002), 35.

42. Abraham Lincoln, "Speech on the Kansas-Nebraska Act," October 16, 1854, in *Complete Works of Abraham Lincoln*, ed. John G. Nicolay (New York: Tandy-Thomas, 1894), 190–262.

43. *New York Daily Tribune*, May 22, 1856.

44. *New York Daily Tribune*, May 23, 1856.

45. *New York Daily Tribune*, May 26, 1856.

46. Ibid.

47. *New York Daily Tribune*, May 23, November 4, 1856.

48. *New York Daily Tribune*, November 5, 1856.

49. *Kansas Republican*, June 10, 1858.

50. Ropes, *Six Months in Kansas*, 224.

51. *Kansas Republican*, June 10, 1858.

52. Anonymous, "A Song for the Time," *New York Daily Tribune*, May 27, 1856.

53. July 18, 1860, Lovejoy Diary.

54. March 20, 1860, Lovejoy Diary.

55. *National Anti-Slavery Standard*, January 5, 1856. For other examples, see 98–100 of this work.

56. Letter from Pardee Butler to James Redpath, May 7, 1856, reprinted in *National Anti-Slavery Standard*, May 31, 1856.

57. See Horsman, *Race and Manifest Destiny*, 281–284; and Eric Lowery Love, "Race over Empire" (Ph.D. diss., Princeton University, 1996).

58. *National Anti-Slavery Standard*, May 31, 1856.

59. Johnston Lykins to Sylvester Clarke, December 22, 1857, Clarke Papers.

60. *Richmond Enquirer*, quoted in *National Anti-Slavery Standard*, April 26, 1856.

61. *Kansas Weekly Herald*, July 19, 1856, cited in Fellman, *Inside War*, 19.

62. Robinson, *Kansas*, 256.

63. Rep. T. L. Harris, March 13, 1856, *Appendix to the Congressional Globe*, 156.

64. See Rep. M. Oliver, March 7, 1856, *Appendix to the Congressional Globe*, and *Missouri Republican*, May 12, 1856, quoted in the *New York Daily Tribune*, May 20, 1856.

65. *Washington Union*, March 31, 1858.

66. *Report of the Special Committee*, 1193–1195.

67. *Kansas Weekly Herald*, April 27, 1855. This poem uses John Milton's *Paradise Lost* for its narrative guide. See book 9, especially line 455 onward, for the section of the epic poem that the *Herald* writer mimics.

68. Perhaps tarring and feathering in the mid-nineteenth century functioned in much the same way that blackface did in the late nineteenth and early twentieth centuries. On blackface and white racial identity, see Eric Lott, *Love and Theft*; Roediger, *Wages of Whiteness*; and Michael Rogin, "Blackface, White Noise: The Jewish Jazz Singer Finds his Voice," *Critical Inquiry* 18 (Spring 1992): 417–453.

69. *Report of the Special Committee*, 65, 972.

70. *Squatter Sovereign*, n.d., Wilcox Scrapbook, 9.

71. *Kansas Republican*, June 8, 1857.

72. Robinson, *Kansas*, 8.

73. Thomas H. Webb to James Montgomery, December 21, 1860, Montgomery Collection.

74. Erastus D. Ladd to the *Statesman* (Marshall, Wisc.), December 20, 1854.

75. Allen, *Invention of the White Race*, 139. The final constitution that ushered Kansas into the union in 1861 maintained segregation. However, the state's reputation as the "land of John Brown" attracted thousands of blacks to its borders in the 1870s. See Nell Irvin Painter, *Exodusters: Black Migration to Kansas after Reconstruction* (New York: Knopf, 1977) for a thorough overview and analysis of this migration.

76. See Berwanger, *Frontier Against Slavery*, 97–122.

CONCLUSION

1. Wood, *Memorial of Samuel N. Wood.*

2. "Biography of Jotham Meeker," printed source material, Ottawa Indians manuscript file, Library and Archives Division, KSHS.

3. See Unrau, *Mixed-Bloods and Tribal Dissolution.* Here I am only referring to Indian-Anglo mixed-race peoples.

4. The same women who spearheaded the antislavery movement in Kansas would lead the fight for black and women's suffrage in the state. See Goldberg, *Army of Women.* Antislavery activist Clarina Nichols, for example, introduced a motion to strike the word "male" from the first state constitution in Kansas. Her motion did not pass, but women did gain the right to vote in school elections in 1861 and in municipal elections in 1887.

5. Ellen C. DuBois, *Feminism and Suffrage: The Emergence of an Independent Women's Movement in America* (Ithaca: Cornell University Press, 1999).

6. "Testimony of Andrew J. Francis," June 4, 1856, *Report of the Special Committee.*

7. See Isenberg, *Sex and Citizenship in Antebellum America,* xi–xvi.

8. Andrew Reeder, Precept, *1855 Kansas Territorial Census.*

9. *New York Daily Tribune,* May 22, 1854.

10. See Painter, *Exodusters.*

11. Even the Osage, who had so stubbornly resisted white ways prior to the Civil War, changed their habits in the 1870s in an attempt to assimilate and maintain their land rights. See Thorne, *Many Hands of My Relations,* 209–244.

12. William E. Connelley, *A Standard History of Kansas and Kansans,* vol. 1 (New York: Lewis Publishing, 1918), 271.

13. Thorne, *Many Hands of My Relations,* 238.

EPILOGUE

1. Thomas Frank, *What's the Matter With Kansas: How Conservatives Won the Heart of America* (New York: Metropolitan Books, 2004).

2. *Topeka Capital-Journal,* February 28, 2000, cited in Frank, *What's the Matter,* 284fn4.

3. Frank, *What's the Matter with Kansas,* 90. Kay O'Connor said, "I think the 19th Amendment, while it's not an evil in and of itself, is a symptom of something I don't approve of. . . . The 19th Amendment is around because men weren't doing their jobs, and I

think that's sad. I believe the man should be the head of the family. The woman should be the heart of the family." See the *Kansas City Star,* September 29, 2001. O'Connor currently serves as a state senator for the Ninth District of Kansas.

4. Dianne Bystrom, "From Voting to Running for Political Office: The Role of Women in Midwestern Politics," Carrie Chapman Catt Center for Women and Politics, Iowa State University, 2002, http://www.iastate.edu/~cccatt/midwestwomen.htm/ (accessed May 23, 2007).

5. Rusty Monhollon and Kristen Tegtmeier Oertel, "From Brown to Brown: A Century of Struggle for Equality," *Kansas History* 27 (Spring–Summer 2004): 118.

6. See, for example, an editorial written by Kickapoo Tribal Council member Steve Cadue in the *Topeka Capital-Journal,* May 31, 2006. See also "Kickapoos Hope Lawsuit will Bring about Reservoir," June 16, 2006.

7. See obituary of William Mehojah, *Kansas City Star,* April 28, 2000.

BIBLIOGRAPHY

MANUSCRIPT COLLECTIONS

Kansas State Historical Society, Topeka

James Blood Papers, Collection 281
Charles Chase Papers, Miscellaneous Collections
Sylvester H. Clarke Papers, Miscellaneous Collections
Jonas Colburn Papers, Miscellaneous Collections
William Elsey Connelley Collection
Delaware Indians, History
Susan and Rush Elmore Papers
Alfred Gray Correspondence
Abelard Guthrie Journal
James Hindman Papers, Miscellaneous Collections
History of Slaves, Manuscript Collection 640
Thaddeus Hyatt Papers
John J. Ingalls Papers, Collection 177
Thomas Johnson Papers
Kansa Indians, History
Kansas History Clippings, Vols. 1–5
Kansas Territory Executive Department Correspondence
Fanny Kelly Papers, Miscellaneous Collections
Frank La Loge Papers, Miscellaneous Collections
Hayden D. McMeekin Papers, Miscellaneous Collections
James Montgomery Collection
Samuel Clarke Pomeroy Papers, Collection 476
Charles and Sara T. D. Robinson Papers
W. B. Royall Papers, Miscellaneous Collections
Sac and Fox Indians, History

George and Mary Stearns Correspondence and Miscellaneous Papers, Collection 507
Benjamin F. Van Horn Papers, Miscellaneous Collections
Augustus and Susan Wattles Papers
P. P. Wilcox Scrapbook
Samuel and Margaret Wood Papers

Missouri Historical Society, Columbia

Thomas Hart Benton Papers
George Caleb Bingham Papers
Isaac Campbell Papers
Charles Monroe Chase Papers
James S. Rollins Papers
Frederick Starr Papers

Western Historical Manuscript Collection, Kansas City, Mo.

Martha Lykins Bingham and Johnston Lykins Papers
William Elsey Connelley Letters

Western Historical Manuscript Collection, St. Louis, Mo.

Dyson–Bell–Sans Souci Papers

GOVERNMENT DOCUMENTS

1855 Territory of Kansas Census. 2 vols. Overland Park: Kansas Statistical Publications, 1985.
Letters Received by the Central Superintendency. Records of the Bureau of Indian Affairs, 1793–1989. M234, RG 75. NARA, Central Plains Region, Kansas City, Mo.
Letters Received by the Office of Indian Affairs. Records of the Bureau of Indian Affairs, 1793–1989. Rolls 55–56, M234, RG 75. NARA, Washington, D.C.
U.S. Congress. House. *Report of the Special Committee Appointed to Investigate the Troubles in Kansas; With the Views of the Minority of Said Committee.* Rept. 200. 34th Cong., 1st sess. (Washington, D.C.: Cornelius Wendell, 1856). NARA, Washington, D.C.

PUBLISHED PRIMARY SOURCES

Brewerton, Douglas. *The War in Kansas.* New York: Derby and Jackson, 1856.
Brown, George W. *The Rescue of Kansas from Slavery with False Claims Corrected.*

Rockford, Ill.: George W. Brown, 1902.

Gladstone, Thomas H. *The Englishman in Kansas.* New York: Miller, 1857.

McNamara, John. *Three Years on the Kansas Border by a Clergyman of the Episcopal Church.* New York: Miller, Orton, & Mulligan, 1856.

Robinson, Sara Tappan. *Kansas: Its Interior and Exterior Life.* Boston: Crosby, Nichols, 1856.

Ropes, Hannah A. *Six Months in Kansas, by a Lady.* Boston: J. P. Jewett, 1856.

Tower, Philo. *Slavery Unmasked: Being a Truthful Narrative of a Three Year's Residence and Journeying in Eleven Southern States.* Rochester: E. Barrow, 1856.

Wilder, D. W. *The Border Ruffian Code in Kansas.* New York: Tribune Office, 1856.

Williams, R. H. *With the Border Ruffians: Memories of the Far West, 1852–1868.* London: J. Murray, 1907.

Wood, Margaret L. *Memorial of Samuel N. Wood.* Kansas City, Mo.: Hudson-Kimberly, 1892.

NEWSPAPERS AND MAGAZINES

Atlantic Monthly (Boston)

Boonville (Mo.) Weekly Observer

Chicago Tribune

Democratic Platform (Liberty, Mo.)

Harper's Weekly (New York)

Industrial Luminary (Parkville, Mo.)

Jefferson City (Mo.) Inquirer

Kansas City Star

Kansas Free State (Lawrence)

Kansas Republican

Kansas Weekly Herald (Leavenworth)

Lawrence (Kans.) Herald of Freedom

Lecompton (Kans.) Union

Liberator (Boston)

Liberty (Mo.) Tribune

Missouri Republican (St. Louis)

National Anti-slavery Standard (New York)

New Haven (Conn.) Leader

New York Daily Tribune

Republican (Lawrence, Kans.)

Squatter Sovereign (Atchison, Kans.)

Star of Empire (Weston, Mo.)

St. Louis Intelligencer

Washington Union (Lecompton, Kans.)

Weekly Southern Democrat (Parkville, Mo.)

Weston (Mo.) Argus

SECONDARY SOURCES

Abing, Kevin. "A Holy Battleground: Methodist, Baptist, and Quaker Missionaries among Shawnee Indians, 1830–1844." *Kansas History: A Journal of the Central Plains* 21 (Summer 1998): 118–137.

Allen, Theodore. *The Invention of the White Race*. Vol. 1, *Racial Oppression and Social Control*. London: Verso, 1994.

Axtell, James. *The European and the Indian: Essays in the Ethnohistory of Colonial North America*. New York: Oxford University Press, 1981.

——. *The Invasion Within: The Contest of Cultures in Colonial North America*. New York: Oxford University Press, 1985.

Bederman, Gail. *Manliness and Civilization: A Cultural History of Gender and Race in the United States, 1880–1917*. Chicago: University of Chicago Press, 1995.

Bellesiles, Michael A. *Lethal Imagination: Violence and Brutality in American History*. New York: New York University Press, 1999.

Benson, T. Lloyd. *The Caning of Senator Sumner*. New York: Wadsworth, 2004.

Berwanger, Eugene. *The Frontier Against Slavery: Western Anti-Negro Prejudice and the Slavery Extension Controversy*. Urbana: University of Illinois Press, 1967.

Bieder, Robert. "Scientific Attitudes toward Indian Mixed-Bloods in Early Nineteenth Century America." *Journal of Ethnic Studies* 8 (Summer 1980): 17–30.

Billington, Monroe Lee, and Roger D. Hardaway, eds. *African Americans on the Western Frontier*. Boulder: University Press of Colorado, 1998.

Brown, Kathleen. *Good Wives, Nasty Wenches, and Anxious Patriarchs: Race, Gender, and Power in Colonial Virginia*. Chapel Hill: University of North Carolina Press, 1996.

Brown, Richard Maxwell. *No Duty to Retreat: Violence and Values in American History and Society*. New York: Oxford University Press, 1991.

Carnes, Mark, and Clyde Griffen, eds. *Meanings for Manhood: Constructions of Masculinity in Victorian America*. Chicago: University of Chicago Press, 1990.

Carrigan, William. *The Making of a Lynching Culture: Violence and Vigilantism in Central Texas, 1836–1916*. Urbana: University of Illinois Press, 2004.

Cashin, Joan. *A Family Venture: Men and Women on the Southern Frontier*. New York: Oxford University Press, 1991.

Castañeda, Antonia. "Women of Color and the Rewriting of Western History: The Discourse, Politics, and Decolonization of History." *Pacific Historical Review* 61 (November 1992): 501–533.

Cecil-Fronsman, Bill. "'Advocate the Freedom of White Men, as Well as that of

Negroes': The Kansas Free State and Antislavery Westerners in Territorial Kansas." *Kansas History: A Journal of the Central Plains* 20 (Summer 1997): 102–115.

———. *Common Whites: Class and Culture in Antebellum North Carolina.* Lexington: University Press of Kentucky, 1992.

———. "'Death to All Yankees and Traitors in Kansas': The *Squatter Sovereign* and the Defense of Slavery in Kansas." *Kansas History: A Journal of the Central Plains* 16 (Spring 1993): 22–33.

Clark, Jerry. *The Shawnee.* Lexington: University Press of Kentucky, 1993.

Clinton, Catherine. *The Plantation Mistress: Woman's World in the Old South.* New York: Pantheon, 1982.

Clinton, Catherine, and Nina Silber, eds. *Battle Scars: Gender and Sexuality in the American Civil War.* New York: Oxford University Press, 2007.

———. *Divided Houses: Gender and the Civil War.* New York: Oxford University Press, 1992.

Cott, Nancy. *The Bonds of Womanhood: "Woman's Sphere" in New England, 1780–1835.* New Haven: Yale University Press, 1977.

Deloria, Philip. *Playing Indian.* New Haven: Yale University Press, 1998.

Dillon, Merton. *Slavery Attacked: Southern Slaves and Their Allies, 1619–1865.* Baton Rouge: Louisiana State University Press, 1990.

Dirck, Brian R. "By the Hand of God: James Montgomery and Redemptive Violence." *Kansas History: A Journal of the Central Plains* 27 (Spring–Summer 2004): 100–115.

DuBois, Ellen C. *Feminism and Suffrage: The Emergence of an Independent Woman's Movement in America.* Ithaca: Cornell University Press, 1978.

Earle, Jonathan H. *Jacksonian Antislavery and the Politics of Free Soil, 1824–1854.* Chapel Hill: University of North Carolina Press, 2004.

Etcheson, Nicole. *Bleeding Kansas: Contested Liberty in the Civil War Era.* Lawrence: University Press of Kansas, 2004.

———. "'Laboring for the Freedom of This Territory': Free-State Kansas Women in the 1850s." *Kansas History: A Journal of the Central Plains* 21 (Summer 1998): 68–87.

Faragher, John Mack. *Sugar Creek: Life on the Illinois Prairie, 1819–1865.* New Haven: Yale University Press, 1986.

———. *Women and Men on the Overland Trail.* New Haven: Yale University Press, 1979.

Faust, Drew Gilpin. *Mothers of Invention: Women of the Slaveholding South in the American Civil War.* Chapel Hill: University of North Carolina Press, 1996.

Fellman, Michael. "At the Nihilist Edge: Reflections on Guerrilla Warfare during the American Civil War." In *On the Road to Total War: The American Civil War and the German Wars of Unification, 1861–1871,* ed. Stig Forster and Jorg

Nagler, 519–540. Cambridge: Cambridge University Press, 1997.

———. *Inside War: The Guerrilla Conflict in Missouri during the American Civil War.* New York: Oxford University Press, 1989.

———. "Rehearsal for the Civil War: Antislavery and Proslavery at the Fighting Point in Kansas, 1854–1856." In *Antislavery Reconsidered: New Perspectives on the Abolitionists,* ed. Lewis Perry and Michael Fellman, 287–307. Baton Rouge: Louisiana State Press, 1979.

Fishkin, Shelley Fisher. "Interrogating Whiteness, Complicating Blackness: Remapping American Culture." *American Quarterly* 47 (September 1995): 428–466.

Foley, Neil. *The White Scourge: Mexicans, Blacks, and Poor Whites in Texas Cotton Culture.* Berkeley and Los Angeles: University of California Press, 1998.

Foner, Eric. *Free Soil, Free Labor, Free Men: The Ideology of the Republican Party Before the Civil War.* New York: Oxford University Press, 1970.

Fredrickson, George. *The Black Image in the White Mind.* Hanover, N.H.: Wesleyan University Press,1971.

Freehling, William. *The Road to Disunion: Secessionists at Bay, 1776–1854.* New York: Oxford University Press, 1990.

Gates, Paul. *Fifty Million Acres: Conflicts over Kansas Land Policy.* New York: Atherton Press, 1966.

Glickstein, Jonathan A. *Concepts of Free Labor in Antebellum America.* New Haven: Yale University Press, 1991.

Goldberg, Michael. *An Army of Women: Gender and Politics in Gilded Age Kansas.* Baltimore: Johns Hopkins University Press, 1997.

Goodrich, Thomas. *War to the Knife: Bleeding Kansas, 1854–1861.* Mechanicsburg, Pa.: Stackpole Books, 1998.

Gordon, Linda. "On 'Difference.'" *Genders* 10 (Spring 1991): 91–111.

Greenberg, Kenneth. *Honor and Slavery: Lies, Duels, Noses, Masks, Dressing as a Woman, Gifts, Strangers, Humanitarianism, Death, Slave Rebellions, the Proslavery Argument, Baseball, Hunting, and Gambling in the Old South.* Princeton: Princeton University Press, 1996.

Griffin, Clyde, and Mark Carnes. *Meanings for Manhood: Constructions of Masculinity in Victorian America.* Chicago: University of Chicago Press, 1990.

Gustafson, Melanie. *Women and the Republican Party, 1854–1924.* Urbana: University of Illinois Press, 2001.

Herring, Joseph B. *The Enduring Indians of Kansas: A Century and a Half of Acculturation.* Lawrence: University Press of Kansas, 1990.

Hodes, Martha, ed. *Sex, Love, Race: Crossing Boundaries in North American History.* New York: New York University Press, 1999.

Horsman, Reginald. *Manifest Destiny: The Origins of American Racial Anglo-Saxonism.* Cambridge: Harvard University Press, 1981.

Horton, James, ed. *Free People of Color.* New York: Oxford University Press, 1993.

Hurt, R. Douglas. *Agriculture and Slavery in Missouri's Little Dixie*. Columbia: University of Missouri Press, 1992.

Isenberg, Nancy. *Sex and Citizenship in Antebellum America*. Chapel Hill: University of North Carolina Press, 1998.

Jacobson, Matthew Frye. *Whiteness of a Different Color: European Immigrants and the Alchemy of Race*. Cambridge: Harvard University Press, 1998.

Jeffrey, Julie Roy. *Frontier Women: The Trans-Mississippi West, 1840–1880*. New York: Hill and Wang, 1979.

———. *The Great Silent Army of Abolitionism: Ordinary Women in the Antislavery Movement*. Chapel Hill: University of North Carolina Press, 1998.

Jensen, Joan. *Loosening the Bonds: Mid-Atlantic Farm Women, 1750–1850*. New Haven: Yale University Press, 1986.

Johnson, Susan Lee. "'A Memory Sweet to Soldiers': The Significance of Gender in the History of the American West." *Western Historical Quarterly* 24 (November 1993): 495–517.

———. *Roaring Camp: The Social World of the California Gold Rush*. New York: W. W. Norton, 2000.

Kellow, Margaret. "'For the Sake of Suffering Kansas': Lydia Maria Child, Gender and the Politics of the 1850s." *Journal of Women's History* 5 (Fall 1993): 32–49.

Kimmel, Michael. *Manhood in America: A Cultural History*. New York: Free Press, 1996.

Klein, Laura F., and Lillian A. Ackerman, eds. *Women and Power in Native North America*. Norman: University of Oklahoma Press, 1995.

Kraditor, Aileen. *Means and Ends in American Abolitionism: Garrison and His Critics on Strategy and Tactics, 1834–1850*. New York: Pantheon, 1969.

Lerner, Gerda. *The Grimké Sisters from South Carolina: Rebels against Slavery*. Boston: Houghton Mifflin, 1967.

Lott, Eric. *Love and Theft: Blackface Minstrelsy and the American Working Class*. New York: Oxford University Press, 1993.

Lynch, William O. "Population Movements in Relation to the Struggle for Kansas." *Studies in American History, Inscribed to James Albert Woodburn*. Bloomington: Indiana University Press, 1926.

Malin, James. *The Nebraska Question*. Lawrence: University Press of Kansas, 1953.

Mancall, Peter C. *Deadly Medicine: Indians and Alcohol in Early America*. Ithaca, N.Y.: Cornell University Press, 1995.

Mangan, J. A., and James Walvin, eds., *Manliness and Morality: Middle-Class Masculinity in Britain and America, 1800–1940*. New York: St. Martin's Press, 1987.

Marsh, Margaret. *Suburban Lives*. New Brunswick: Rutgers University Press, 1990.

————. "Suburban Men and Masculine Domesticity." *American Quarterly* 40 (June 1988): 165–186.

McCurry, Stephanie. *Masters of Small Worlds: Yeoman Households, Gender Relations, and the Political Culture of the Antebellum South Carolina Low Country.* New York: Oxford University Press, 1995.

McElvaine, Robert. *Eve's Seed: Biology, the Sexes, and the Course of History.* New York: McGraw-Hill, 2001.

McKivigan, John R. *Abolitionism and Issues of Race and Gender.* New York: Garland, 1999.

————. *War Against Proslavery Religion: Abolitionism and the Northern Churches, 1830–1865.* Ithaca: Cornell University Press, 1984.

McKivigan, John R., and Stanley Harrold, eds. *Antislavery Violence: Sectional, Racial, and Cultural Conflict in Antebellum America.* Knoxville: University of Tennessee Press, 1999.

McKivigan, John R., and Mitchell Snay, eds. *Religion and the Antebellum Debate over Slavery.* Athens: University of Georgia Press, 1998.

McPherson, James. *Battle Cry of Freedom: The Era of the Civil War.* New York: Oxford University Press, 1988.

Merrell, James. *The Indians' New World: Catawbas and Their Neighbors from European Contact through the Era of Removal.* Chapel Hill: University of North Carolina Press, 1989.

Mildfelt, Todd. *The Secret Danites: Kansas' First Jayhawkers.* Richmond, Kans.: Todd Mildfelt, 2003.

Miner, Craig H., and William Unrau. *The End of Indian Kansas: A Study of Cultural Revolution, 1854–1871.* Lawrence: Regents Press of Kansas, 1978.

Monhollon, Rusty, and Kristen Tegtmeier Oertel. "From Brown to Brown: A Century of Struggle for Equality." *Kansas History* 27 (Spring–Summer 2004): 118.

Moore, Winfred B., Jr., Kyle S. Sinisi, and David H. White, eds. *Warm Ashes: Issues in Southern History at the Dawn of the Twenty-First Century.* Columbia: University of South Carolina Press, 2003.

Morgan, Edmund. *American Slavery, American Freedom: The Ordeal of Colonial Virginia.* New York: Norton, 1975.

Morrison, Michael A. *Slavery and the American West: The Eclipse of Manifest Destiny and the Coming of the Civil War.* Chapel Hill: University of North Carolina Press, 1997.

Mullin, Gerald. *Flight and Rebellion: Slave Resistance in Eighteenth-Century Virginia.* New York: Oxford University Press, 1972.

Mullin, Michael. *Africa in America: Slave Acculturation and Resistance in the American South and the British Caribbean, 1736–1831.* Urbana: University of Illinois Press, 1992.

Mullis, Tony R. *Peacekeeping on the Plains: Army Operations in Bleeding Kansas*. Columbia: University of Missouri Press, 2004.

Nelson, Dana D. *National Manhood: Capitalist Citizenship and the Imagined Fraternity of White Men*. Durham, N.C.: Duke University Press, 1998.

Nevins, Allan. *The Ordeal of the Union*. Vol. 2. New York: Scribner, 1947.

Nichols, Roy F. "The Kansas-Nebraska Act: A Century of Historiography." *Mississippi Valley Historical Review* 43 (September 1956): 187–212.

Oates, Stephen B. *To Purge This Land with Blood: A Biography of John Brown*. Amherst: University of Massachusetts Press, 1984.

Oertel, Kristen Tegtmeier. "'The Free Sons of the North' versus 'The Myrmidons of Border Ruffianism': What Makes a Man in Bleeding Kansas?" *Kansas History: A Journal of the Central Plains* 25 (Autumn 2002): 174–189.

Olmstead, Earl P. *Blackcoats among the Delaware: David Zeisberger on the Ohio Frontier*. Kent, Ohio: Kent State University Press, 1991.

Omi, Michael, and Howard Winant. *Racial Formation in the United States*. New York: Routledge, 1986.

Painter, Nell Irvin. *Exodusters: Black Migration to Kansas after Reconstruction*. New York: Knopf, 1977.

Paludan, Philip S. "The American Civil War Considered as a Crisis in Law and Order." *American Historical Review* 77 (1972): 1013–1034.

Peavey, Linda. *Women in Waiting in the Westward Movement: Life on the Home Frontier*. Norman: University of Oklahoma Press, 1994.

Peck, Gunther. *Reinventing Free Labor: Padrone and Immigrant Workers in the North American West, 1880–1930*. Cambridge: Cambridge University Press, 2000.

Perry, Lewis. *Radical Abolitionism: Anarchy and the Government of God in Anti-Slavery Thought*. Ithaca: Cornell University Press, 1973.

Phillips, Christopher. "'The Crime against Missouri': Slavery, Kansas, and the Cant of Southernness in the Border West." *Civil War History* 48 (2002): 60–81.

———. *Missouri's Confederate: Claiborne Fox Jackson and the Creation of Southern Identity in the Border West*. Columbia: University of Missouri Press, 2000.

Pierson, Michael. *Free Hearts and Free Homes: Gender and American Antislavery Politics*. Chapel Hill: University of North Carolina Press, 2003.

———. "'In Our Own History': Julia Louisa Lovejoy and the Politics of Benevolence in Bleeding Kansas." *Heritage of the Great Plains* 37 (2004): 48–56.

———. "'A War of Extermination': A Newly Uncovered Letter by Julia Louisa Lovejoy, 1856." *Kansas History* 16 (Summer 1993): 120–122.

Poovey, Mary. *Uneven Development: The Ideological Work of Gender in Mid-Victorian England*. Chicago: University of Chicago Press, 1988.

Pugh, David G. *Sons of Liberty: The Masculine Mind in Nineteenth-Century America*. Westport, Conn.: Greenwood Press, 1983.

Rable, George. *Civil Wars: Women and the Crisis of Southern Nationalism*. Urbana: University of Illinois Press, 1991.

Rawley, James A. *Race and Politics: "Bleeding Kansas" and the Coming of the Civil War*. Philadelphia: Lippincott, 1969.

Richter, Daniel. *The Ordeal of the Longhouse: The Peoples of the Iroquois League in the Era of European Colonization*. Chapel Hill: University of North Carolina Press, 1992.

Roediger, David. *Colored White: Transcending the Racial Past*. Berkeley and Los Angeles: University of California Press, 2002.

———. *Towards the Abolition of Whiteness: Essays on Race, Politics, and Working-Class History*. New York: Verso, 1994.

———. *The Wages of Whiteness: Race and the Making of the American Working Class*. New York: Verso, 1991.

Rogin, Michael Paul. *Fathers and Children: Andrew Jackson and the Subjugation of the American Indian*. New York: Knopf, 1975.

Rotundo, E. Anthony. *American Manhood: Transformations in Masculinity from the Revolution to the Modern Era*. New York: Basic Books, 1993.

Ryan, Mary P. *Cradle of the Middle Class: The Family in Oneida County, New York, 1790–1865*. Cambridge: Cambridge University Press, 1981.

Saxton, Alexander. *The Rise and Fall of the White Republic: Class Politics and Mass Culture in Nineteenth-Century America*. London: Verso, 1990.

Schultz, George. *An Indian Canaan: Isaac McCoy and the Vision of an Indian State*. Norman: University of Oklahoma Press, 1972.

Schwalm, Leslie A. "'Overrun with Free Negroes': Emancipation and Wartime Migration in the Upper Midwest." *Civil War History* 50 (2004): 145–174.

Seed, Patricia. *Ceremonies of Possession in Europe's Conquest of the New World, 1492–1640*. New York: Cambridge University Press, 1995.

SenGupta, Gunja. "Bleeding Kansas: A Review Essay." *Kansas History: A Journal of the Central Plains* 24 (Winter 2001–2002): 318–341.

———. *For God and Mammon: Evangelicals and Entrepreneurs, Masters and Slaves in Territorial Kansas, 1854–1860*. Athens: University of Georgia Press, 1996.

Sheridan, Richard B. *Freedom's Crucible: The Underground Railroad in Lawrence and Douglas County, Kansas*. Lawrence: University Press of Kansas, 1998.

Shoemaker, Nancy, ed. *Negotiators of Change: Historical Perspectives on Native American Women*. New York: Routledge, 1995.

Sklar, Kathryn Kish. *Catherine Beecher: A Study in American Domesticity*. New Haven: Yale University Press, 1973.

Slotkin, Richard. *The Fatal Environment: The Myth of the Frontier in the Age of Industrialization, 1800–1890*. New York: HarperCollins, 1985.

———. *Regeneration through Violence: The Mythology of the American Frontier, 1600–1860*. New York: HarperCollins, 1973.

Smith, Henry Nash. *Virgin Land: The American West as Symbol and Myth.* New York: Vintage Books, 1950.

Stampp, Kenneth. *America in 1857: A Nation on the Brink.* New York: Oxford University Press, 1990.

Stauffer, John. *The Black Hearts of Men: Radical Abolitionists and the Transformation of Race.* Cambridge: Harvard University Press, 2001.

Steinfeld, Robert. *The Invention of Free Labor: The Employment Relation in English and American Law and Culture, 1350–1870.* Chapel Hill: University of North Carolina Press, 1991.

Stevenson, Brenda. *Life in Black and White: Family and Community in the Slave South.* New York: Oxford University Press, 1996.

Stratton, Joanna. *Pioneer Women: Voices from the Kansas Frontier.* New York: Simon and Schuster, 1981.

Takaki, Ronald. *Iron Cages: Race and Culture in Nineteenth-Century America.* New York: Knopf, 1979.

Thorne, Tanis. *The Many Hands of My Relations: French and Indians on the Lower Missouri.* Columbia: University of Missouri Press, 1996.

Toole, K. Ross, ed. *Probing the American West.* Santa Fe: Museum of New Mexico, 1962.

Unrau, William. *The Kansa Indians: A History of the Wind People, 1673–1873.* Norman: University of Oklahoma Press, 1971.

———. *Mixed-Bloods and Tribal Dissolution: Charles Curtis and the Quest for Indian Identity.* Lawrence: University Press of Kansas, 1989.

Usner, Daniel. "An American Indian Gateway: Some Thoughts on the Migration and Settlement of Eastern Indians around Early St. Louis." *Gateway Heritage* 11 (Winter 1990–91): 42–51.

———. *Indians, Settlers and Slaves in a Frontier Exchange Economy.* Chapel Hill: University of North Carolina Press, 1992.

Varon, Elizabeth. *We Mean to Be Counted: White Women and Politics in Antebellum Virginia.* Chapel Hill: University of North Carolina Press, 1998.

Wallace, Anthony. *The Death and Rebirth of the Seneca.* New York: Vintage, 1969.

Washburn, Wilcomb. *The American Indian and the United States: A Documentary History.* New York: Random House, 1973.

Watts, Dale E. "How Bloody Was Bleeding Kansas? Political Killings in Kansas Territory, 1854–1861." *Kansas History: A Journal of the Central Plains* 18 (1995): 116–129.

———. "Plows and Bibles, Rifles and Revolvers: Guns in Kansas Territory." *Kansas History: A Journal of the Central Plains* 21 (1998): 30–45.

Weslager, Clinton. *The Delaware Indians: A History.* New Brunswick: Rutgers University Press, 1972.

West, Elliott. *The Contested Plains: Indians, Goldseekers, and the Rush to Colorado.* Lawrence: University Press of Kansas, 1998.

———. "Reconstructing Race." *Western Historical Quarterly* 34 (2003): 7–26.

White, Deborah Gray. *Ar'n't I a Woman: Female Slaves in the Plantation South.* New York: Norton, 1985.

White, Richard. *The Middle Ground: Indians, Empires, and Republics in the Great Lakes Region, 1650–1815.* Cambridge: Cambridge University Press, 1991.

Williams, Walter. *The Spirit and the Flesh: Sexual Diversity in American Indian Culture.* Boston: Beacon Press, 1986.

Wyatt-Brown, Bertram. *The House of Percy: Honor, Melancholy and Imagination in a Southern Family.* New York: Oxford University Press, 1994.

———. *The Shaping of Southern Culture: Honor, Grace and War, 1760s–1880s.* Chapel Hill: University of North Carolina Press, 2001.

———. *Southern Honor: Ethics and Behavior in the Old South.* New York: Oxford University Press, 1982.

Zaeske, Susan. *Signatures of Citizenship: Petitioning, Antislavery and Women's Political Identity.* Chapel Hill: University of North Carolina Press, 2003.

INDEX